Gendered Interventions

Frontispiece: Caricature of a nineteenth-century woman orator
addressing a "promiscuous" audience. From Eduard Fuchs, *Die Frau
in der Karikatur: Sozialgeschichte der Frau*, 1906; reprint 1973.
(Courtesy of Harvard College Library.)

Gendered Interventions

Narrative Discourse in the Victorian Novel

Robyn R. Warhol

Rutgers University Press
New Brunswick and London

Parts of this book have appeared in published articles. Most of Chapter 2 comes from "Toward a Theory of the Engaging Narrator: Earnest Interventions in Gaskell, Stowe, and Eliot," *PMLA* 101 (1986): 811–818; Chapter 5 draws upon "Poetics and Persuasion: *Uncle Tom's Cabin* as a Realist Novel," *Essays in Literature* 13 (1986): 283–298; and passages from "Letters and Novels 'One Woman Wrote to Another': George Eliot's Responses to Elizabeth Gaskell," *Victorian Newsletter* 70 (1986): 8–14 appear in Chapters 3, 5, and 7. A condensed version of Chapter 7 is forthcoming in *Psychohistory Review*.

Library of Congress Cataloging-in-Publication Data

Warhol, Robyn R.
Gendered interventions : narrative discourse in the
Victorian novel / Robyn R. Warhol.
p.   cm.
Bibliography: p.
Includes index.
ISBN 0-8135-1456-8
1. English fiction—19th century—History and criticism.
2. Feminism and literature—Great Britain—History—19th century.
3. Women and literature—Great Britain—History—19th century.
4. Authors and readers—Great Britain—History—19th century.
5. Direct discourse in literature.   6. Point of view (Literature)
7. Sex role in literature.   8. Narration (Rhetoric)   I. Title.
PR878.F45W37   1989
823'.8'0923—dc19   89-30379

British Cataloging-in-Publication information available

Contents

Preface

I WANT TO TALK about something embarrassing: direct address to readers or audiences. In narrative contexts it always poses problems, unless the speaker is making a joke. Groucho Marx or Woody Allen or a character in a Godard film can turn to the camera to "break the frame" with an ironic remark and get a laugh, as can the narrators in novels by W. M. Thackeray, John Fowles, or John Barth. Direct address in narrative begins to embarrass, however, when it is no longer offered in jest—when the speaker who assails "you" is in earnest.

If I may judge by my experience of academic readers—colleagues and students—I can safely guess that you dislike serious direct address in texts. You find it preachy, or cute, or coy. You think of it as a technical error, a lapse of artistry, a cheap effect. It irritates you when you run across it in Victorian novels, and it is irritating you at this very moment, as you read. Why is that?

I contend that our prejudice against earnest (as opposed to ironic) direct address stems from our culture's aversion to feminine gestures. In Victorian novels written by women, earnest direct address evolved as an alternative to public speaking "in person," which was forbidden to respectable females. Realist novels provided opportunities for women to speak through their narrators to "you," in a serious, nonliterary way seldom practiced by male Victorian novelists. Those earnest interventions, those direct appeals to "you," took on a feminine gender in the middle of the nineteenth century. As women's narrators used them to intervene in their fictional texts, women novelists used them to intervene in history. Hence, in the feminine "gendered intervention," history and text converge while a feminine presence is projected, for the moment, into the reading experience.

vii

And that feminine presence inspires embarrassment, even now, when women's literal presence in public is a matter of course.

Recent criticism focusing on the role ideology has played in forming the literary canon has taught us that women's writing has been systematically devalued, and for the most part flatly excluded from the Great Anglo-American Tradition. Most of that criticism concentrates on what narratologists would call the "story" (*histoire*) in men's and women's novels, or, as Seymour Chatman puts it, "the *what* in a narrative that is depicted" (19). Some elements of story that have been receiving attention from ideologically inspired critics include the nature of characters and events represented in fiction, the reiteration of typical scenes and themes, and the "moral" or message transmitted by the text. Until now, no one has scrutinized the "discourse" (*récit*) of mid-nineteenth-century novels, the precise ways in which those stories get told. By focusing on interruptions in the story—which Gérard Genette calls "narrative interventions," thus avoiding the negative connotations of "intrusions"—I propose to examine a less obvious difference between "masculine" and "feminine" Victorian texts. In analyses (not readings) of individual novels, I look at the structure, stance, content, and evident intention of passages addressed to "you," in order to uncover that difference.

I stress that these are analyses, not readings, because interpretation is not the goal of this study. I propose no new way of understanding *what* Victorian novels are trying to communicate. Instead, I am looking at *how* they try, in order to point out that critical prejudice against narrative techniques can be as much affected by issues of gender as can critical assumptions about the forms and contents of fiction.

The three parts of this book are themselves interventions in three ongoing conversations among critics. Part I enters the debate among feminist theorists over the usefulness of androcentric critical models for feminist criticism and offers a model combining feminism with structuralist narratology. Part II addresses criticism of novels written by male and female authors, examining narrative interventions as guides to what kind of novels these are. Following the model proposed in Part I, I analyze novels whose narrators rely upon feminine, masculine, and cross-gendered modes of intervention, looking at their authorial intrusions in the context of the novelists' gendered experience and their implied or expressed novelistic goals. Part III moves the conversation to the realm of history, both social and literary. It describes the historical circumstances under which men and women found themselves making choices among modes of narrative stance in novels and it questions the theoretical and critical tradition that has suppressed or derided earnest direct address to this day.

In that it makes narrative interventions in nineteenth-century novels its central subject, this study does not seek to (re)do what other books on feminist theory or Victorian fiction have done. Because the combination of feminism, narratology, and Victorian studies must necessarily frustrate some critical expectations, even as it raises new ones, I want to outline what the book will not do, before beginning to do what it will.

First, although speaking of "gendered writing" inevitably raises the specter of "difference" in its many contemporary forms, I will not tackle more than a few of its manifestations. My primary concern with gender differences springs neither from deconstruction's model of *différance* nor from the new French feminisms' psychoanalytic theories of essential sexual difference. I am treating gender instead as a social construct, a set of learned behaviors that an individual adopts to express or demonstrate his or her gender identification. Gender, in this social or anthropological sense, includes outward signs of one's sexual identity, such as clothing, gestures, vocal inflection and—I would suggest—narrative strategies. Just as men and women can cross dress to present themselves in the mode associated with another gender, novelists, too, can choose (somewhat less self-consciously, no doubt) to use techniques associated with the other sex. Eve Sedgwick, Teresa de Lauretis, and Nancy Miller, among others, have looked into the ways gender colors the production of *story* in narrative; to complement what they have done, the present study concentrates on gender's influence upon *discourse*.

Though narratology's basic distinction between story and discourse and its precise language for describing textual phenomena are central to this project, I will not be limiting my categories of narrative stance to those already proposed by other narratologists. Among them, only Gerald Prince has elaborated a theory of the "narratee" (augmented by the work of Mary Ann Piwowarczyk) to account for the possible answers to the question, Whom does the narrator address? Prince has described the relation between narrator and narratee that prevails in many canonical texts, from the beginnings of the novel to the modern period. As I intend to show, however, the same relation does not always prevail in British and American novels of the mid-nineteenth century. Like most contemporary narrative theorists, Prince takes it for granted that the narratee is always a fictive, created figure, standing in roughly the same relation to the actual reader as does the narrator to the actual author. In the strictest sense, this assumption is certainly valid: when actual readers vary so obviously, from period to period, or from person to person, the logical impossibility of "the real reader's" presence in any text is obvious. And, to be sure, every text must inscribe a created "reader" within either what Prince calls its "overjustifications" or what Wolfgang Iser has called its "gaps" and "indeterminacies." But analysis of narrative discourse has not yet accounted for texts in which the narrative voice seeks to efface the boundaries between the inscribed reader or narratee and the actual reader who holds the book and reads. At one extreme, a narrator might do this by speaking to Prince's "zero-degree narratee," who possesses only the minimal characteristics necessary to be competent to decode the text. At the other extreme, however, certain realist novels' narrators encourage the actual reader to identify with a narratee liberally endowed with characteristics and frequently addressed as "you."

Like other narratologists, I do not follow the traditional assumption that narrative interventions are, a priori, out of place in realist texts. Under the influence of an Anglo-American formalist theory of the most aesthetically pleasing way to render truth in fiction, critics in the first half of the twentieth century subscribed, for the most part, to certain prejudices about the impressionistic fictional forms best suited to maintaining an "illusion of reality." Modern criticism of realist fiction retains many Jamesian attitudes; following James, modern critics took it for granted that reminders of an author's presence, through narrative interventions and addresses to the reader, must necessarily disturb the illusion and thereby undermine the goals of realism. More recently, postmodern critics have returned to Dr. Johnson's commonsense observation that no one sitting in a London theater watching a play ever "really imagines himself at Alexandria" (329). When we look at the insistently metafictional frame that Thackeray, for instance, places around *Vanity Fair,* we are no longer surprised to realize that such novels are always and inevitably about novels, and that narrative interventions draw attention to this fact.

I am not willing, however, to rest comfortably with what has by now become a critical truism: all texts are self-referential, all writing mirrors itself, all fiction is, first and foremost, about fiction. These assumptions, which serve critics of eighteenth- and twentieth-century novels so well, cannot account for all the conventions of nineteenth-century realism. Every novelist is interested in novels, and all fictional narratives comment, more or less overtly, upon the conventions of fictions that preceded them or the conventions they "take up, cite, parody, refute, or generally transform," as Jonathan Culler puts it (*Pursuit of Signs* 38). But, as political critics (Marxists and, more recently, feminists among them) have long recognized, many of the realist novelists were also interested in the world of lived experience and in the impact their novels might have on it. Writers such as Elizabeth Gaskell, George Eliot, and Harriet Beecher Stowe thought of the novel as a vehicle for exerting influence on readers who would, in turn, work changes in the worlds of politics, society, and personal morality. These women novelists had very specific reasons for choosing the genre of realism. I suggest that their strategic reliance on earnest direct address illuminates their concept of what "realism" is.

When I turn my attention to the writers' idea of realism, expressed both within and outside their texts, I indicate that I do not share some of the essential assumptions of semiotics, even though that field has been so closely allied to narratology in the past. Culler's account of those assumptions helps clarify my reasoning. According to semiotics:

> a text can be read only in relation to other texts, and it is made possible by the codes which animate the discursive space of a culture. The work is a product not of a biographically defined individual about whom information could be accumulated, but of writing itself. To write a poem the author had to take on the character of poet, and it is that semiotic function of poet or writer rather than the biographical function of author which is relevant to discussion of the text. (*Pursuit of Signs* 38)

Within the system of semiotics, this reasoning is perfectly consistent. But it ignores one commonsense fact that the irresistible influence of new historicism may permit us to reconsider: the work literally *is* a "product . . . of a biographically defined individual about whom information could be accumulated." Someone wrote it, someone who inhabited a particular culture at a particular time, someone who made certain choices among all the literary codes and conventions available to him or her within that culture and time. A poetics that tries to account for conventions of discourse in a given period or genre cannot ignore the place of those conventions in history, including the circumstances in which the author produced the text. From this observation we can easily proceed to a renewed interest in authors' manipulation of the relation between their texts and the actual people who read them. Semiotics recognizes that the readers in texts, the readers created by texts, are not "real readers," but it provides no framework for acknowledging the real reader who must, after all, exist for the text to have any function or meaning.

I will not try to propose a comprehensive theory of the relation between textual production and narrative discourse; I focus instead on the example of one genre in one time and language. I have chosen Victorian fiction for its didactic reputation: in depicting the "real world," realist novelists often tried to make genuine changes in that world by inspiring readers to transform their own notions of their moral and social selves, their sense of responsibility to others. Not every Victorian novel conforms to this aim of realist fiction—to change the world by representing it. But a realist novel that does attempt to alter the world it strives to represent requires a special relation between reader and text. For readers to act upon the novels' suggestions, they would have to take the texts seriously and think of the fictions as somehow true. Narrative interventions help to position the reader in relation to the text, at the same time expressing the novelists' own goals, either ironically or explicitly. Concentrating, then, on novels written in England and America during the heyday of the Victorian realist novel, from 1845 to 1865, I examine the role that narrative interventions play in establishing the reader's relation to the narrator and narratee, or—more broadly speaking—to the text.

For formal reasons, I do not analyze any texts whose narrators double as characters in the novel. Although Genette has shown, through his analysis of Proust, that there is no reason why a character-narrator in a modern novel cannot be "omniscient," Victorian novelists followed much stricter conventions than Proust did for limiting the knowledge of characters who narrate. The actual reader of *David Copperfield* or *Jane Eyre* can determine who is speaking and from what vantage point comparatively easily: David speaks or Jane speaks, either from the perspective of what he or she knows at that moment in the story, or from the augmented perspective of what he or she has "learned since," or from a mixture of the two vantage points the character-narrator occupies—narrative past and narrating present. In novels like these that take the form of mock-autobiographies, the narrator's stance imitates that of a "real" autobiographer. But in texts with what used to be called omniscient narrators (or, to use Genette's more precise denominations, heterodiegetic narrators in extradiegetic situations of enunciation), the questions of voice and perspective in realist novels are more problematic. The real reader of *Vanity Fair* who pauses to wonder "Who is speaking?" is continually greeted by Thackeray in his guise as "manager of the performance" or "puppet master," a constant reminder of the fictionality of the text. I am identifying a particular kind of Victorian novel that literary theory has so far overlooked: realist novels with narrators who are not characters, but whose narrative strategy is nevertheless to use interventions that efface the fictionality of the text, rather than reinforce it as Thackeray's do.

I wish I could claim that I am not trying to defend serious narrative interventions in realist fiction, because in accordance with the principles of narratology, my goal is not primarily to evaluate texts or strategies. But I must confess that I like interventions, especially earnest ones, and that they have long been the parts of Victorian novels that most consistently attract my eye. Nevertheless, narrative interventions—whether distancing and ironic or engaging and earnest—have habitually annoyed even the most enthusiastic critics of the novels of the 1850s. The technique of pretending to confide in a "dear reader" is traditionally associated with novels that are, at best, drearily didactic and, at worse, cloyingly sentimental. Even in more recent criticism, which has rehabilitated narrative intrusion as one of the many conventions that combine to form the genre of the novel, the "dear reader" intervention is usually only defensible insofar as it is ironic, as in the novels of Fielding or Sterne.

I do not agree with the many critics, traditionalists and progressivists alike, who take it for granted that earnest direct address is always a sign of bad writing. Originating in the tough-minded, prescriptive stance of New Criticism, the objection to direct address in fiction has made its way into many contemporary critical approaches, even among theorists who no longer cling to "maintaining an illusion" as the first goal of realist prose fiction. We find it in Iser, when he speaks of the "boredom that inevitably arises when everything is laid out cut and dried before us" in texts that are so completely narrated as to leave too few gaps for the imagination to fill in (275); we find it in John Searle, when he observes that fictional texts like

Tolstoy's, containing "serious" statements about the message of the work, are "tiresomely didactic" (332); we find it even in Helene Moglen's recent work on narrative form and the ideology of gender. Performing an illuminating deconstructive reading of Dickens's *Dombey and Son*, Moglen explains a difference she sees between "sentimentality" (where emotion passes "between the author and reader" when a narrator addresses the reader on behalf of inarticulate characters such as dying children or suppressed women) and the more potentially radical mode of "melodrama" (where emotion inheres in the characters themselves, who have the opportunity to speak and act out their situations directly). According to Moglen, melodrama is a more effective mode of critiquing the realities it depicts because it is more memorable. Like Iser's and Searle's, her privileging the more dramatic mode seems to look back to the traditional preference among critics of fiction for "showing" over "telling."

But I do not see any reason why we should continue to assume—with James, Forster, Conrad, Ford, and others—that showing must be better than telling. The preference for showing, or for fiction that presents characters and situations dramatically rather than "narrativizing" them, has undoubtedly been instrumental in shaping the canon of texts that are studied as great works of literature. It partly accounts for the lowly place in the canon occupied by such strongly didactic, unabashedly narrated women's novels as Susanna Rowson's *Charlotte Temple* or Harriet Beecher Stowe's *Uncle Tom's Cabin*. Feminist criticism has gone a long way toward redefining literary canons to include such works, in which the story does not conform to the white-male-centered concerns of the "great American novel" whose mid-nineteenth-century conventions were developed by Cooper, Hawthorne, and Melville, often in reaction against popular female fictional traditions. Critics including Jane Tompkins, Elaine Showalter, and Annette Kolodny have shown how works that depict women's experience and women's perspectives have been neglected, and they have investigated various political and literary reasons for that neglect.

One reason for the devaluing of women writers that has not yet been identified is the role that narrative discourse has played. Nineteenth-century women's writing is closely associated with the sentimental and didactic technique of direct address to the reader that dominates texts like Rowson's and Stowe's. (Tompkins, along with other recent commentators including Ann Douglas, Nina Baym, and Thomas Gossett, takes it for granted that this technique is objectionable on the grounds of its sheer conventionality.) As my analysis of selected novels shows, both male and female writers of the period were capable of intervening in both distancing and engaging ways in their novels. But women novelists seem to have used engaging strategies to stir readers' emotions more frequently and more insistently than their male counterparts. This association between earnest direct address and feminine writing can, I think, help explain much more than the low status that sentimental novels have held in the canon. It may also account for the critical reluctance to see earnest direct address in "great novels" as something other than a stylistic lapse.

My purposes, then, are threefold: 1) to analyze the role that direct address plays in realistic fictional discourse; 2) to investigate the connection between gender and narrative strategies; and 3) to consider the ways a narrative strategy's "gender" influences its reputation among critics and theorists. In pursuing these ends, I combine the formalist approach of narratology with the historical, social, and gender-based questions associated with feminist-contextual criticism.

As I said at the outset, I am more concerned with poetics than with thematic interpretation. My research provides no startling new readings of texts; on the contrary, the narrative strategies I analyze tend to reinforce, rather than subvert, the current readings of what these novels "mean." I emphasize instead how they "work" (or, in the case of the masculine-gendered novels, how they "play"), and I hope this emphasis will illuminate the impact that assumptions about poetics have had upon modern literary history, even in critical texts that do not address poetics explicitly.

I believe that critical assumptions about the appropriateness of conventions to genres are often suppressed in scholarly writing, and I am convinced that these assumptions are frequently based on unrecognized gender-bias. By proposing a partial poetics of narrative discourse (as feminists seldom do) that places conventions of discourse in the context of their production (as narratologists almost never do), I hope to uncover one case—the case of the engaging narrator in realist fiction—that will help reveal the central roles both gender and poetics play (albeit covertly) in the history of literary criticism and theory.

Acknowledgments

MY FIRST THANKS go to the institutions that enabled me to complete this project by providing time, space, word processors, and community. I am especially grateful to everyone connected with the Harvard Mellon Faculty Fellowship program and Harvard's Center for Literary and Cultural Studies for giving me an invaluable year. The University of Vermont, too, deserves thanks for two summer grants supporting my research.

For their careful and intelligent readings of parts or all of the manuscript and for their useful suggestions, I thank Barbara Johnson, James Holstun, Shari Benstock, Robert Caserio, and Celeste Schenck. For conversations that changed my thinking about the project, I thank Susan Suleiman, Janet Riesman, and the members of the "Boston–Providence Victorians" group that Carolyn Williams coordinated at Boston University. And for unflagging, energetic support of the project, I thank Leslie Mitchner at Rutgers University Press.

I have received crucial support, too, from my friends Gretchen Van Slyke, Janet Whatley, and Brian Kent, and from my parents, Warren and Patricia Warhol. I appreciate their bearing with me through five years of often-agonizing book writing.

Blurring the lines among all these categories—institutions, colleagues, friends, family—are the members of my writing group, my own dear readers: Jo Ann Citron, Beth Kowaleski-Wallace, and Helena Michie. I hear their voices responding to mine on every page of this book. I hope they can forgive its flaws as generously as they have contributed to its strengths.

And finally, I thank Philippe Carrard, whose intellectual and emotional energy inspired and sustained this project, and from whom I have learned so much about celebrating difference—in gender and in other matters.

I

Proposing a Model: Feminism and Narratology

1

Introduction:

Why Don't Feminists 'Do'

Narratology?

READER, if you are interested, as I am, in the history of narrators' attitudes toward their readers; if you adopt the models of narratology in your attempt to differentiate among the various strategies authors can use in narrative interventions; and if, in your research into nineteenth-century realist novels, you discover that passages of earnest direct address (like the one you are reading now) occur more frequently and more prominently in novels by women than in novels by men, you will run into an interesting theoretical dilemma. Why is there no "feminist narratology" that could help account for such a difference? Until recently, narratology has not asked questions about gender, and feminist criticism, which by definition always asks the gender question first, has not inquired into narrative discourse. Before embarking on a theory of gendered interventions, then, I want to consider the reasons why these two theoretical approaches have resisted coming together.

NARRATOLOGISTS, FEMINISTS, AND FEMINIST NARRATOLOGY

Narratology, in its original forms, seems to be gender-blind. Gérard Genette, using Proust as the primary example for his "essay in method" and referring to scores of other novelists in passing, mentions only half a dozen women writers in *Narrative Discourse,* and never hints at the possibility of any gender-based differences or patterns among narrative structures. Neither Gerald Prince nor Mieke Bal, in their less specific and more comprehensive presentations of narratology, mentions gender as a factor influencing the models they describe.[1] The oversight is not a sexist one: not only gender, but all variables of context remain outside of classical narratology's realm. As proponents of structuralism, the first practitioners of narratology lifted texts out of their contexts in order to distill from them the essential structures that chararacterize all narrative. If a general theory of narratology were to consider the influence of gender on the production of certain kinds of narrative structures, for instance, it would depart from the basic premises of a study that—in its earliest, strictest forms—purported to operate ahistorically, outside the restrictions imposed by consideration of the period and circumstances in which a text is written. For this reason, we cannot be surprised that a feminist critic such as Bal has shifted the emphasis of her scholarship to semiotics, where she can study recurring textual signs and structures in the context of the cultures that produce them.[2]

Not all critics who apply the tools of narratology have maintained this pure distinction between narrative structures and their contexts. A critic who looks at the ways in which ideology shapes narratives—as Susan Suleiman has in *Authoritarian Fictions* (1982), her study of the French *roman à thèse* during the first half of the twentieth century—returns the text to its place in history. Combining descriptive poetics with interpretive criticism, Suleiman proposes a model for the genre of the ideological novel, then reads individual texts against the model. Proceeding from structuralist methods, she offers various charts and diagrams to illustrate her assumptions. The most useful of these—a map of the "Principal Constituents of the Narrative Text" (157)—most clearly reveals the current intersection between narratology and contextual criticism.

This "schema," as Suleiman calls it, is "based chiefly on the works of A. J. Greimas and Gérard Genette," with slight modifications of their terminology (156): it divides the narrative text's main components into the "Level of Story" and the "Level of Discourse." Under "Discourse" are listed "Narration" (the functions of the narrator, that is, to tell the story, to signal the organization, to address the narratee, to provide "testimonials," and to interpret the story); "Focalization" (Genette's useful term for describing narrative perspective); and "Temporal Organization" (the "order, duration, and frequency" of occurrences in a story). Under "Story" appear the components one would expect: "Characters" (both in terms of what they are and what they do in the story); "Events" (including the sequences of actions); and "Context" (including historical, geographical, cultural, and "local"). I have reproduced the substance of Suleiman's chart to illustrate a point: narratology typically regards context as a component of story, rather than discourse. In other words, context has been a factor in narratological analysis of *what* fiction depicts, but not in discussions of *how* fictions' contents get rendered in language.

Neither Suleiman nor Genette says anything to rule out the possibility of considering narrative *discourse* within its historical or ideological context. To study, as Suleiman does, the narrator's testimonial function (that is, the ways in which the narrator explicitly accounts for what he or she "knows") or, more strikingly, the narrator's interpretive function (especially instances where the uncharacterized or "omniscient" narrator analyzes, interprets, or judges characters, events, or situations within the story) is necessarily to look at the narrator's utterances within a context. This context might be the historical period and setting that a narrative voice shares with the story, as in Dickens's *Hard Times* or Trollope's *The Way We Live Now,* or it might be the context of a narrative voice that places itself in a time different from that of the story, as in Scott's Waverly novels, Cooper's Leatherstocking tales, or—for a much more explicit example—John Fowles's *The French Lieutenant's Woman.* To take the possibilities a step further in the direction Suleiman's book beckons, away from purely formalist consideration of structures, we might look at the narrator's utterances in the context in which they were literally produced, that is, in terms of the categories of the novelist's own experience—historical, social, or even personal. Nothing prohibits us from asking, among other questions about the role of social factors in shaping narrative strategies, what part the writer's gender plays in the kinds of interventions he or she uses in narrative.

Although narratology itself has not addressed gender, and though gender has not yet been a factor in many narratological studies of the level of discourse, structural analysis on the level of story has proven very useful for feminist criticism. Nancy Miller's *The Heroine's Text* (1980), a study of the two basic plots that characterize novels about women's experience written in France and England during the Enlightenment, shows the potential usefulness of narratology to a feminist project. Her study of "feminocentric" novels includes only texts written by men, and her analysis of strategy remains on the level of story, restricting itself to interrogating what happens to the female protagonists of these novels. Miller's approach carries her far into a critique of the culture that produced the novels: as she observes, "The plots of these feminocentric novels are of course neither female in impulse or origin, nor feminist in spirit, . . . despite their titles and their feminine 'I'" (149). The narratological analysis of these plots allows Miller to conclude that the feminocentric novel was written by men in the interest of men: women may be "its predominant signifiers, but they are also its pretext" (150). Narratology has obvious advantages for a project like Miller's, among them the way in which categorical descriptions of plots can lend an evidently objective authority to potentially inflammatory conclusions about male writers and masculine-centered culture.

Despite its sophisticated theoretical apparatus, Miller's book belongs to the "images of woman" movement in feminist criticism, that is, the study of how women are portrayed in texts. This emphasis keeps her analysis focused on the level of story. To date, no feminist critic has taken a detailed look into gender's effect on the level of discourse in fiction, using "discourse" strictly in the sense established by Genette, Chatman, Suleiman, and other narratologists. I think that stepping past the level of story to analyze the level of discourse within a framework of questions about gender can bring narratology to the service of a later moment in feminist criticism.

THEORIES OF GENDER DIFFERENCE IN WRITING

Elaine Showalter has recently summarized the brief but rapidly developing history of feminist literary theory, tracing the roles that questions of gender have played in critical discussions during the past three decades. According to Showalter, criticism of women's writing originally

> took the form of an *androgynist poetics,* denying female literary specificity. The women's movement initiated both a *feminist critique* of male culture and a *Female Aesthetic* celebrating women's culture. By the mid-1970s, academic feminist criticism entered a new phase of *gynocritics,* or the study of women's writing. With the impact of European literary and feminist theory by 1980, *gynesic* or poststructuralist feminist criticism,

6

dealing with "the feminine" in philosophy, language, and psychoanalysis, dominated the field. And in the late 1980s, we are seeing the rise of *gender theory,* the comparative study of sexual difference. ("A Criticism of Our Own," 21)

Questioning Showalter's account of the history of feminist theory on the grounds that it treats the field as a linear series of advances over previous approaches, Jonathan Culler has challenged the implication that each kind of feminist criticism has been superseded by the next. As Culler pointed out during a panel at the 1986 Modern Language Association convention (and, for that matter, as Showalter's essay explicitly acknowledges), the debates among the various schools of feminist thought continue as a conversation that operates synchronically, even if some voices have joined in more recently than others. Still, the appeal of "narrativizing" critical movements diachronically, as Showalter had done, is strong: to tell the story of feminist criticism is to account, if only experimentally, for why and how the field expands as it does. If we consider the position of narratology within Showalter's historical frame, we can more clearly see its potential and its limitations as a prospective aid to feminist literary criticism.

Clearly, narratology originally belonged to the moment in literary history that assumed an "androgynist poetics." If Prince, in the English translation of his "Introduction to the Study of the Narratee," uses more than seventy-nine examples and only two of them are from female-authored works, this is not merely because he is concerned with describing the features of a canon that is traditionally dominated by male writers. The very existence of that canon is predicated on an assumption that Prince naturally shares: regardless of whether any differences exist among the forms and strategies that male and female authors choose to employ in fiction, to ask questions about such differences would be to depart from the structuralist enterprise. As Showalter points out, some women writers (for instance, Joyce Carol Oates and Gail Godwin) continue to embrace an androcentric poetics, understandably wishing not to be "separate but equal" to male writers, but simply to be comparable, on precisely equal terms, to their male counterparts. From their point of view, the gender-blindness of narratology's descriptions of discourse would still be welcome.

But, as Showalter explains, the women's movement brought on the Female Aesthetic, along with the feminist critique of male culture; since that time, feminist criticism has always addressed difference in some form.

The Heroine's Text is an important example of narratology's contributions to the feminist cultural critique. As I have already mentioned, using an androcentric tool like narrative analysis in the service of such a critique gives feminist projects such as Miller's an extra-persuasive edge. It allows the critic to confront the masculine biases of feminocentric novels in terms that the male critical community has already created and, to some extent, adopted.[3] In the meantime, the Female Aesthetic mode of criticism was carrying analysis of women's writing equally deep into the level of story. Inquiries into depictions of women's experience, of female communities, of mother-daughter bonds, and of biological differences between women and men concentrated on questions of plot, imagery, genre, and language in the broadest sense, but resisted the apparently androgynous orientation of narratology. Never addressing discourse per se, feminist aestheticians have not looked at such narrative conventions as "voice," "perspective," "focalization," or "intervention." They have developed instead theories of the preferred styles for women's writing, insisting that women's sentences should be shaped differently from men's.

When feminist aestheticians have tried valiantly to establish grounds for evaluating female styles that would not be bound by masculine critical assumptions, the movement suffers from two problems that are endemic to any aesthetic approach to literature. The first problem is that the theorists who try hardest to determine what a female style would look like can hardly describe what the formal features of such a style would be. The problem goes back to Virginia Woolf's provocative attempt in *A Room of One's Own* to propose a "woman's sentence" whose nature would differ fundamentally from a man's prose. But Woolf, like the aestheticians who take their inspiration from her suggestion, cannot really *say* what kind of sentence it would be. Is femininity in a sentence a function of syntax? Of vocabulary? Of imagery? Of punctuation? Of some combination of these and other elements?

When critics have tried to apply Woolf's idea, they have fallen into the second problem that aesthetic criticism invariably poses: it can become as prescriptive as any previous critical tradition, and continues to marginalize some women writers on the basis of their style. Josephine Donovan, for example, in trying to apply Woolf's notion of a "woman's sentence," pronounces George Eliot's prose "turgid, uncomfortable, and inappropriately suited to her context" (348), while finding the sentences of Jane Austen, Kate Chopin, and Woolf "appropriate" for rendering heroines' inner lives (349, 352). If it was unreasonable for androcentric critics to dismiss from the canon women's writing that strayed too far from implicitly acceptable masculine norms of style, surely it is equally unreasonable to object to some women authors for sounding less stereotypically "female" than others. Like the prescriptive critical traditions it emulates, feminist-aesthetic stylistic analysis adheres more closely to models of what women's writing should be than to inquiries into what it has been.

Moving away from prescriptive theories of women's writing to a more descriptive approach, the next phase of feminist criticism, which Showalter christened "gynocritics," sought to avoid the sexist implications of essential sexual difference implied by the Female Aesthetic. Gynocritics tried to return feminist literary criticism to an arena that could address male colleagues, as well as female scholars and critics. The impetus behind gynocritics was to alter the literary canon to include more works by women; in order to do this, the gynocritic adapts critical approaches from the mainstream tradition and applies them to texts signed by women. In projects such as Sandra Gilbert and Susan Gubar's *The Madwoman in the Attic* or Showalter's *A Literature of Their Own,* this practice has led to the alteration of prevailing masculine models of influence, intertextuality, and conventions of story, resulting eventually in the construction of feminine literary traditions that presumably developed alongside the mainstream masculine canon, in continual response to and conflict with what male writers were doing. Like the Female Aesthetic, gynocritics has often led to the seemingly inevitable conclusion of feminist criticism: Women write differently from men.

Explication of the problems raised by such a conclusion can be traced back to Simone de Beauvoir's basic observation about what constitutes a "second sex." To say that women don't write like men is to place men at a normative center and women in the margins; to say that women write differently from men is to decenter the observation slightly, but this formulation still retains men's writing as the standard against which the difference of women's writing must be defined. To avoid perpetuating traditional, binary assumptions, feminist theory has recently embraced the approach of deconstruction, which offers a helpful strategy for focusing on difference while simultaneously dismantling conventional oppositions. In the hands of a practitioner of gynocritics like Elizabeth Meese, deconstruction becomes a powerful tool for interpreting texts with an eye to gender, even though—as Meese observes in *Crossing the Double-Cross* (1986)—

originators and early proponents of deconstruction tended to ignore women's writing.

For Meese, as for Helene Moglen and others who deconstruct texts with an emphasis on the gendered aspect of difference, deconstruction does not limit its goals to the ultimately purposeless, anti-ideological game playing that Terry Eagleton decries in Anglo-American deconstructive criticism. Eagleton observes that deconstruction

> frees you at a stroke from having to assume a position on important issues, since what you say of such things will be no more than a passing product of the signifier and so in no sense to be taken as "true" or "serious." A further benefit of this stance is that it is mischievously radical in respect of everyone else's opinions, able to unmask the most solemn declarations as mere dishevelled plays of signs, while utterly conservative in every other way. Since it commits you to affirming nothing, it is as injurious as blank ammunition. (145)

As Eagleton acknowledges, however—and as Meese, for one, demonstrates—deconstruction can nevertheless help feminist critics who want to emphasize "how, though historically speaking the conflict between men and women could not have been more real, the ideology of this antagonism involved a metaphysical illusion" (Eagleton 150).[4]

Indirectly addressing the appeal of deconstruction for feminist criticism, Alice Jardine has pointed to the irony of the feminist's position in a poststructuralist age: whatever else it may do, feminist theory proceeds from a *belief* (in the fact that women have been oppressed), but it operates in a world from which *Truth* has disappeared. As Jardine remarks, the result of this dilemma may be for the feminist to experience a "vertigo of reading strategies" from the dizzyingly relative heights of infinite possibilities (31). According to Jardine, feminists experiencing this vertigo can avoid responding with mere silence by paying "a continual attention—historical, ideological, and affective—to the place from which we speak" (31). To combine feminist goals with deconstructive strategies is necessarily to attend to the "situation of enunciation" of the readings the approach will produce. And, too, deconstruction is not the only poststructuralist system which can yield this result: gynesic and Lacanian theories that adapt psychoanalysis also exemplify the ways in which feminists can transform interpretive strategies for their projects' purposes.

Poststructuralist theories, then, have served gynocritics well in the enterprise of interpreting texts "signed by women" as well as texts in which women operate as the signifiers. Deconstruction especially is a useful way for the feminist critic to answer the question, What does this text mean? or, more accurately perhaps, What does this text signify? But to what extent has poststructuralist cirticism combined with feminism to ask, *How* does this text mean? Why has feminist theory avoided a systematic study of the conventions of literary discourse in women's writing, to parallel the models that phallocentric and androcentric criticism have produced? Annette Kolodny has claimed that

> A largely male-dominated academic establishment has, for the last 75 years or so, treated men's writing as though it were the model for *all* writing. In other words, the various theories on the craft of fiction, and the formalist and structuralist models that have been based on this closed tradition but have been offered up as "universals" of fictive form or even (under the influence of the psycholinguists) as emanations of yet deeper structures within human cognitive processes may in fact prove to be less than universal and certainly less than fully human. ("Some Notes" 89)

Kolodny concedes that feminist critics should "use what we can from the past." The directions that feminist criticism has taken since Kolodny offered her manifesto suggest that feminist critics want to avoid merely rectifying the narrowness of the prevailing models, as though that would mean simply tinkering with "the tools and methods already available," as Kolodny has implied. Are "formalist and structuralist models" gender-biased in their essence, as well as their details? Does structural analysis have to be discarded, and replaced with feminist-inspired strategies of reading and interpretation?

Looking at the most recent feminist literary theories from the perspective implicit in such questions, I find it significant that Jardine, for example, concludes her important study, *Gynesis* (1985), by jubilantly describing the exhilaration she felt at having discovered that the differences between the male-written and female-written texts of modernity were not, after all, in their so-called "content," but in their *enunciation:* in their modes of discourse ("sentimental," ironic, scientific, etc.); in their twisting of female obligatory connotations, of inherited genealogies of the feminine; in their haste or refusal to use the pronouns "I" or "we"; in their degree of willingness to gender those pronouns as female. (261)

The differences Jardine names are precisely the material from which structural analysis of texts is made: these are categories that careful attention to patterns of discourse might help to define and describe in detail. Yet nowhere does Jardine attempt such definitions or descriptions: her book, like other contemporary applications of gynesic theory and studies of *écriture féminine,* veers away from participating in so overtly structuralist an enterprise.

WHY FEMINISTS DON'T: POTENTIAL CHALLENGES TO NARRATOLOGY

The fact that feminists in the late 1980s tend not to "do narratology" per se, but prefer to concentrate on deconstruction, psychoanalysis, and semiotics, may be partly attributable to the objection Kolodny raises to merely adapting standard models of criticism that already exist. If feminism's first goal is radical subversion of an existing order, then making minor adjustments in well-established critical systems seems unlikely to promote that goal. Of course, deconstruction, psychoanalysis, and semiotics are all established critical systems today, but each of them—despite Kolodny's misgivings—has revealed its own fundamentally radical potential in feminist hands. And, too, feminists do "use narratology," particularly in semiotics, in the course of pointing to the various signifiers in texts; literary conventions of story and discourse are signs, too.

Perhaps feminists avoid the study of narratology as a system because they share poststructuralist assumptions about the basic conservatism of structuralist approaches. Implicit in the structuralist notion that certain systems will repeat themselves—from text to text, or from culture to culture—is the idea that the way things are is the way they must inevitably be. A feminist proceeding (as Jardine says) from a belief that the way things are is that women are oppressed would necessarily find this idea antipathetic. In addition, narratology, as a system within structuralism, shares that movement's faith in the possibility of scientific, orderly classification of data, in the idea that at one deep level—at least—phenomena can be known, named, and thus distinguished as real. The structuralists themselves recognize the potential challenges to such a faith. As Genette so memorably phrases it,

> This is the paradox of every poetics, and doubtless of every other activity of knowledge as well: always torn between those two unavoidable commonplaces—that there are no objects except particular ones and no science except of the general—but always finding comfort and something like attraction in this other, slightly less widespread truth, that the general is at the heart of the particular, and therefore (contrary to the common preconception) the knowable is at the heart of the mysterious. (*Narrative Discourse* 23)

Because it embraces constructs of truth, structuralism participates in the Western intellectual tradition of binary oppositions that Derrida has sought to deconstruct (sometimes in the name of "woman") and that some theorists would say has always been undermined by that otherness that constitutes gynesis.[5] Orderliness, whether in systems of metaphysics, politics, or literary criticism, has too often implied hegemony and hierarchy for radical critics to operate comfortably within it.

But orderliness has its advantages, too. What I find appealing about the narratology that Genette, Greimas, Prince, Shlomith Rimmon-Kenan, and Bal have elaborated is the way it expedites communication about texts. Narratology provides a precise language for describing the features of texts within a genre and delineating the differences between any given text and others of its kind. It can do what feminist aesthetic criticism, for example, cannot do: describe exactly what the conventions of fictional discourse are and how they operate. Narratology has given us names for literary conventions that formalist terminology made very difficult to discuss. (For example, consider the complications of describing the narrative techniques of Henry James or Jane Austen without the concept of "focalization"; consider the absurdity of referring to "Fielding" in *Tom Jones* as a "third-person narrator" when his "I" is so omnipresent.) What makes narratology so useful is that it can take gender studies a step further into a tangible, arguable position on particular texts: instead of simply talking in generalities about "women's styles," it can genuinely point to the features that constitute those styles in narrative.

In addition to the descriptive power conferred by its terminology, narratology has another important advantage over the traditional formalist methods that contemporary feminists eschew: it seeks to describe texts, not to evaluate them, in terms of their formal features. In spite of the justifiable anxieties about the Western intellectual tradition that poststructuralist theories have made explicit, order does not have to involve hierarchy. Certainly, the critic who selects texts for narratological study necessarily privileges those texts: this fact of scholarly life is practically as explicit, though, in such projects as Genette's or Suleiman's as it is in the work of a critic such as Stanley Fish.[6] Any narratological system that presents itself as comprehensive while being based on a privileged selection of texts will necessarily contain gaps that studies of other, unconsidered texts could fill. But, as most narratologists would probably agree, if a particular text does not "work" within a narrative model, the limitation is in the model, not the text. After all, narratology acknowledges that no text can be entirely described by any model. The specificity of every text resists duplication in any description of how it works: the only really comprehensive account of all the structures that operate in a text is the text itself.[7] The continuing study of narratology has sought only to test and expand the models, in the interest of making them more comprehensive. As a branch of descriptive poetics, narratology does not set out to exclude narrative texts of any kind from the parameters of its inquiry.

Narratology's desire to be comprehensive, rather than exclusive, is what makes it especially suitable to feminist criticism. And the flexibility of its models is narratology's answer to any objection that might be raised about the method's being too orderly or too systematic to be (as Kolodny might put it) "fully human." By testing the models of discourse (not story) against women's texts, we can sketch in some of the gaps in models that are based almost exclusively on men's writing; by placing the narratological analysis of those texts in a historical context that takes into account the circumstances in which they were produced, we can use narratology as a bridge to cross over from gynocritics into what Showalter calls "gender theory, the comparative study of sexual difference." ("A Criticism of Our Own" 21).

GENDER THEORY AND TEXTUAL STRATEGIES

When it takes the form of studying gynesis, gender theory can emphasize essential differences between the sexes—between their psychlogical natures, or between their operation as subjects or signifiers in history and philosophy. Gender theory can also be useful in the study of culturally determined differences between the sexes, or differences between the biological and cultural signs of gender. The subjects of gender theory may be the distinctions between male and female, masculine and feminine, or even male and masculine, female and feminine.

Since this last application of gender theory may seem paradoxical in the abstract, I will borrow an illustration from Susan Brownmiller: female humans grow hair in their armpits, but American culture insists that it is not feminine to leave that hair unshaven. As social critics such as Brownmiller have emphasized, cultural constructs of gender differences are often based entirely on convention, rather than on biological realities. (The fantasy of the hairless "feminine" body, for instance, can be traced back through the idealized portrayal of nudes in Victorian painting to the smooth surfaces of Greek sculpture.[8]) Whether such conventional conceptions of gender are grounded in politics (does the desire to deny that women's bodies grow hair inhere in a wish to emphasize the biological differences between the sexes in order to perpetuate patriarchy?) or psychology (does the fantasy of the hairless female body betray a repressed cultural inclination for pedophilia?) or metaphysics (does the idealization of smooth feminine bodies, in denying part of the physical reality of femaleness, participate in an attempt to separate women from material nature, and to align them with the "spirit"?) is grounds for interesting speculation. Narratology traditionally has not trafficked in such speculations, for we need not inquire into the causes of cultural concepts of gender to study their effects. Unlike gynesic or psychoanaltyic theory, narratology alone would not be helpful in determining the original causes of differences that might occur among the structures in men's and women's texts. What narratology can do is to help describe such differences when they occur, which would be the first step in developing a poetics of gendered discourse. The second step would be to augment narratology with history, by placing those differences in context: that is, to consider their relation to the culture's concept of gender differences at the time the text in question was written.

Cultural signs of gender—unlike biologically determined sex characteristics—develop more or less arbitrarily within societies, and are subject both to general change and individual choice. Masculine and feminine norms for dress, hair length, or use of jewelry and makeup change fairly rapidly, as any comparison of Western fashions over the past thirty years will show. One of the hallmarks of twentieth-century fashion has been that cross dressing no longer signifies the kind of radical rejection of gender roles that it would have a century ago. While it is still strictly feminine to wear a skirt and nylon stockings, a woman who dons a pair of khaki chinos and an Oxford-cloth, button-down shirt from Brooks Brothers is no longer treading the dangerous ground that George Sand risked when she put on a man's-style suit. Nor is the man who wears an earring necessarily making a statement about his sexual orientation or his gender identity. Opportunities for ambiguously displaying one's gender identification are much more widely available today than they were in the 1950s, let along the 1850s.

That cultural norms for outward signs of gender distinctions were stricter in nineteenth-century England and America than they are today is perhaps too obvious to point out, at least insofar as they concern clothing, personality traits, and social roles. What may be less obvious is that writing could take on the same kinds of gender differentiation in a culture where gender lines were as distinctly drawn as they were in the mid-Victorian Anglo-American world. Feminist linguists have investigated differences among twentieth-century men's and women's oral and written language, and even in the relatively androgynous era of the Women's Movement, they have discerned differences ranging from sentence length, to use of parallelism, to vocabulary choice.[9] (Of course, linguistic analysis often finds differences, as Mary Hiatt's did, that subvert received assumptions about what masculine or feminine writing should be like.)

Analysis of narrative discourse, too, sometimes approaches the boundaries of a theory that would distinguish modern women's writing from men's. Susan Sniader Lanser's analysis of the ways in which ideology shapes narrative point of view sets up a contrast between the techniques in a woman's text ("The Story of an Hour" by Kate Chopin) and a man's ("The Killers," from Ernest Hemingway's *Men Without Women*). Lanser's application of her formulation of point of view certainly points out differences between the woman's text and the man's, but it stops short of distinguishing on that basis between women's *texts* and men's. Her more recent work "Toward a Feminist Narratology" takes bolder steps in the direction of uncovering gendered differences in discourse. [10]

As Lanser has observed, strategies of narrative perspective change over time, varying according to literary period and according to the ideology that informs each text. At any given historical moment, certain techniques may be associated with male writing, while others are associated with female texts. Feminist critics often assume that women writers—like all female activists, and, for that matter, like the principle of gynesis itself— have always strained against convention, subverting the expected or traditional literary codes. I would suggest—along with most practitioners of gynocritics, I suppose—that women's writing in the nineteenth century had codes and conventions of its own. Comparison of narrative techniques at the middle of the century in realist novels written by men and women shows that certain narrative strategies dominate texts according to the writer's gender. The difference, described in the next chapter, between what I call the "distancing" strategies that dominate novels signed by men and the "engaging" strategies that dominate novels signed by women in the mid-nineteenth century is an example of one such instance of gendered writing.

The "tests" for my models of distancing and engaging interventions in Part II should show, however, that this study departs from gynocritics and moves toward gender theory in that I would not claim that engaging strategies are specific to women's texts, nor that distancing strategies occur exclusively in men's. Every realist novel of the nineteenth century contains some ironic narrative interventions that seek to distance the actual reader from the fiction, by addressing a narratee with whom the reader should be reluctant to identify or by drawing attention to the fictionality of the text; similarly, every realist novel of the period contains some passages of earnest interventions that attempt to engage the actual reader, to encourage him or her to take the narrative commentary seriously and to take the novel's story to heart. The difference between the novels written from 1845 to 1865 by the women writers in this study (Elizabeth Gaskell, George Eliot, and Harriet Beecher Stowe) and those written by the men (William Makepeace Thackeray, Charles Kingsley, Charles Dickens, and Anthony Trollope) is that engaging interventions dominate the women's texts and distancing interventions dominate the men's. When I say they dominate I mean that instances of one kind of strategy occur more frequently and in more rhetorically prominent positions than do instances of the other type of intervention. Although no novel is perfectly consistent in its strategies, the texts in this study use techniques of intervention that color the overall rhetorical effect of the novels and that are, for the most part, consistent with their author's stated theories of how the texts should operate. As I show in Part III, there are historical reasons why women and men in the mid-nineteenth century would use the discourse of realist fiction to differing ends. Whereas men had ample opportunity to exert serious, didactic influence over others, women had few forums in which they could publicly "say something"; the realist novel provided one of the few socially acceptable and effectual outlets for their reforming impulses.[11]

This is not to say that men's novels of the period are not earnestly didactic; they often are. Nor is it to claim that women's realist novels are never ironic or metafictional. My analysis of novels that don't fit the model of feminine-gendered engaging interventions and masculine-gendered distancing interventions shows how novelists could, if only momentarily, "cross dress," usually for specific rhetorical purposes. Up to now, reader-centered critical theory that focuses on gender has asked the question that Judith Fetterley so effectively raises in *The Resisting Reader* (1978): What happens if the reader of a text whose narratee is implicitly male happens to be a woman? Jonathan Culler, making the almost chivalrous gesture of treating this subject first (before deconstruction proper) in his *On Deconstruction* (1982), summarizes the work of several feminist theorists to extend that question a step further toward gender theory. Speaking as a male critic and following the examples of Showalter, Peggy Kamuf, Shoshana Felman, and Gayatri Spivak, he transposes the question into: What happens if the reader is *reading as* a woman?[12]

Gynocritics has been asking the corollary of Fetterley's question: What happens to a text when the writer is a woman? In analyzing the strategies in nineteenth-century texts, I want to follow the direction that Culler's approach implies. My question for the novels I study is: What happens to a text when the writer is *writing as* a woman? Although the question is not at all a strictly biographical one (since male writers borrowed feminine-gendered techniques, and vice versa), I consult authors' personal circumstances and historical contexts, as well as textual signs of the kinds of interventions they use, in considering the "situation of enunciation" that their texts reproduce. In this respect, what I am doing is not, strictly speaking, semiotics, which would inquire into textual codes exclusively as products of their textuality. I am trying instead to extend narratology's usefulness to a more literally historical analysis of literature.

Feminist theory takes it for granted that everything a woman does, she does "as a woman"; gender distinctions, whether biologically or culturally imposed, color our experience so deeply as to take part in our every move. Many feminist critics have lamented the "immasculation" of such canonical writers as George Eliot, who seems so often to adopt a man's writing to suit her man's pseudonym. A phenomenon that is even closer to home is the immasculation of female scholars and critics who are trained to read as men (in the sense that Fetterley and Kolodny have described) and, of course, to write as men. When I was a graduate student in the late 1970s, I took a seminar called "Authorial Voice in Verse and Prose." Gender's relation to written "voice" was one of the professor's interests, and he asked us one day to submit unsigned samples of our writing, specifying that the samples should represent what we considered to be our characteristic styles. Reading through the dozen or so samples, he felt he could determine the gender of only two or three writers. He was absolutely sure he could identify the gender of the person who wrote my sample. The ironic tone, the scrupulously correct punctuation, the parallel sentences, and the logical structure of my paragraphs convinced him the writer was male. I confess that I was proud to have fooled him: still in the grip of an androcentric attitude toward literature and scholarship, I was glad to be able to "pass." But I realize today that when I choose to write an academic "man's prose" in order to address a mainstream critical audience, I am imitating the gestures of George Eliot and Harriet Beecher Stowe (who sometimes borrowed masculine-gendered strategies in their fiction) and of Dickens and Trollope (who also sometimes borrowed feminine-gendered writing to suit their novelistic ends). Gender in writing strategies arises, I believe, from the writer's making a series of rhetorical choices, whether or not those choices are consciously intentional.

Doubtless, the texts in this study contain material for other distinctions that could be drawn on the basis of gender.[13] Narratological analysis on the level of story, for instance, might reveal gendered differences between treatments of relationships among characters, shapes of plot, or influence of ideology. I restrict my attention, however, to an examination of gendered interventions. I look at those moments in realist novels where (as Eliot put it in *Adam Bede*) "the Story Pauses a Little" while the narrator explicates, evaluates, or comments upon the materials of the text. The interventions that I see as being most clearly gendered are those in which the narrator establishes his or her attitude toward the reader, toward the characters, and toward the act of narration itself. My analysis of texts focuses upon the degree to which the narrators present themselves as distancing or engaging, and the ways that they play the two kinds of strategy off against each other in individual novels. Elizabeth Gaskell's *Mary Barton* has the definitively feminine-gendered engaging narrator; Charles Kingsley's *Yeast* and William Makepeace Thackeray's *Vanity Fair* exemplify two extremes of the masculine, distancing approach. To reveal the interplay among strategies in texts by novelists who "cross dress," I look at George Eliot's *Adam Bede* and Harriet Beecher Stowe's *Uncle Tom's Cabin,* both earnest, realistic novels whose narrators sometimes make moves to distance the actual reader from the fictional world, as well as Charles Dickens's *Bleak House* and Anthony Trollope's *Can You Forgive Her?* two more self-consciously metaliterary novels that nevertheless rely, in certain rhetorical moments of crisis, on engaging techniques.

SOME REMARKS ON METHODOLOGY: DOING NARRATOLOGY TODAY

Pointing to narrators and declaring them distancing or engaging tends to look like a critical reversion to a period of theoretical innocence when we could accept binary oppositions without blinking. Indeed, the poststructuralist problematization of the subject raises many questions that a narratological study simply cannot address: Is it really possible for the scholar to stand outside a text, conducting critical operations on it that are unaffected by the operations the text conducts on the scholar herself? Can anything in a literary text transcend its textuality—is it possible for the fictive "you," the narratee, to have any relation to an "actual reader"? Does an individual "reading subject" even exist, independent of the text? Can a critic ever propose oppositional labels for textual phenomena without distorting the text through the lens of ideological bias? Does the very act of finding binary categories in a text imply the imposition of a hierarchy? How can hierarchy be justifiable in literary study? Such questions could paralyze any narratologist who was to take them as central to all studies of literature.

The theory of distancing and engaging narrative strategies cannot refute the philosophical arguments that motivate such questions. But it can, I believe, provide one example for the reasons why these are not the only questions at the heart of every critical inquiry. Granted, if I claim to find differences among the rhetorical strategies in texts, what I am reporting are the results of one person's subjective/selective reading, as are the products of all literary criticism. But finding a textual difference and trying to account for it raises questions that interpretive reading strategies such as deconstruction or psychoanalysis do not often address. What, specifically, does the difference look like? Where is it to be found?—that is, in which texts? in what parts of those texts? How did it get there? A narratological approach that draws on contextual criticism can seek answers to these questions that refer more specifically to texts and to literary history than other approaches have so far allowed.

This is not to say that a narratological study must aspire to a "scientific" stance, as though untouched by poststructuralist inquiries. Like most specific applications of narratology, the theory of engaging and distancing strategies does not prescribe hard-and-fast categories into which narrators must discretely fit. On the contrary, the ground between the most extremely distancing narrator (perhaps Fielding's in *Tom Jones*) and the most engaging one (probably Gaskell's in *Mary Barton*) is not an empty space, but rather a spectrum of techniques. Like Seymour Chatman and Susan Sniader Lanser, I see the terms I am proposing as the extremities of a continuum that includes countless combinations of distancing and engaging strategies. In fact, the combinations occur within the oeuvre of each nineteenth-century novelist, within any single novel, and even in some instances within a single passage from one novel. I have constructed models to describe the features of the two extremes, and following the examples of the classical structuralists (for instance, Roland Barthes, Claude Lévi-Strauss, and Fernand Braudel) I play off individual examples against those models in my analysis of specific cases. The purpose is not so much to learn which novels fit the models and which do not, as it is to recognize the models' limitations as well as their power to describe the functioning of individual texts. Inevitably, I look at those texts through a subjective lens, but the focus it provides reveals, I believe, genuine differences.

And those differences signify more than the authors' gender. As I illustrate throughout the descriptions of the two models in the next chapter, distancing techniques generally characterize metafiction and engaging techniques occur in realism. Initially, I was surprised to realize (and almost reluctant to admit) that the mid-nineteenth-century metafictional novels relying on distancing strategies are most often written by men, and the engaging, realist novels by women. It is already a critical commonplace to think of the story in nineteenth-century women's fiction as typically belonging to the genre of realism, with its emphasis on domestic settings, financial concerns, and psychological detail, but the reasons for women novelists to wish to exploit realist discourse are less obvious.

"Realism" signifies various literary matters: depending on the context in which the term is used, it is the dominant mode of Victorian fiction, a philosophical stance, a critical construct, or a genre of fiction that seeks to be representational by employing strategies of verisimilitude. Those strategies may be functions (narratologically speaking) of story or of discourse. The story in each of the seven novels in this study conforms to the generally current definition of what realist fiction would contain. The move away from realism and into metafiction that I see in distancing novels is mainly located in the discourse of some of the novels. No nineteenth-century novel in the canon is as explicitly metafictional in its discourse as Sterne's and Diderot's were in the eighteenth, or John Barth's and Italo Calvino's are in the twentieth century. Still, some Victorian novelists seem to have taken more delight in playing at the boundaries of the fictional illusion than others; not coincidentally, the more playful novelists of the period are the men.

If we were to think of metafiction as the more advanced form of novel because of its resurgence in the postmodern period, we could easily assume that the nineteenth-century female novelists' adherence to earnest, serious realism betrays a naive literary conservatism on the women's part. But self-conscious self-reference in fiction that is explicitly "about" fiction, and that draws attention to its own structures of artifice, is as venerable a tradition as the English novel itself. No twentieth-century narrator could pay more attention to the fiction's frame than Fielding, with his elaborate arrangement of *Tom Jones* into "Books," each containing a prefatory essay that discusses the protocol for writing and reading the comic-epic-poem-in-prose. Part of what made the form "epic" in the first place was the distance Fielding's narrative establishes between the narrator, the narratee, and the fictional material. Metafiction is nothing new, and even if it were, one could hardly defend privileging more "modern" fictional techniques over traditional ones: it makes more sense simply to examine literary forms within their own historical contexts. The women novelists of the mid-nineteenth century in England and America strove for a heightened realism in their novels, not because of a straitened imagination or a conventionally limited vocabulary of techniques, but rather (as I argue in chapter 7) because the novel was their one public opportunity to exert some political or moral influence on the "real world."

Discriminating among male and female writers is, at best, a risky business for any critic who seeks to base a theory on textual evidence, rather than arguing from essentialist principles of gender difference. Selecting and analyzing a corpus of works becomes a problem for the literary historian interested in narratology, through difficulties that do not arise for theorists of essential difference. Proponents of "*écriture féminine*" like Monique Wittig or Hélène Cîxous are not troubled by any necessity to find examples of women's writing that illustrate their theories—they simply generate original texts that exemplify what they are talking about. Supporting arguments about gendered differences in literary history is simultaneously simpler and more problematic than what the new French feminists do: simpler, in that discussing differences within a historical context obviates the necessity of making universal claims about essential differences between the sexes; more problematic, in that the potential samples for analysis exist in daunting numbers and at prohibitive length.

In choosing texts for analysis, I face only obliquely the problem of whether my theory of gendered differences in writing strategy is "generalizable": my conclusions about engaging and distancing uses of direct address, and their relation to gender in writing, are strictly limited—as is my corpus—to novels written in England and America at mid-century. Some colleagues, more statistically inclined than I, have suggested that I might strengthen this study's claims by using a computer to scan hundreds of novels looking for the word *you* outside of quotation marks (and therefore occurring in interventions, rather than dialogue), or by randomly sampling pages from dozens of texts and reading for instances of intervention a computer could not recognize. Such an approach might determine that a phenonemon existed, but it could not begin to account for how direct address functions in individual texts, how distancing and engaging strategies strain and play off against each other within a novel, or how they got there in the first place. I have therefore limited myself to the number of novels I could analyze without a computer's assistance, and have chosen a sample that represents the range of possibilities I perceive.

The questions that motivate this project are not How do women write? or How do men write? but rather, What are the conventions of narrative discourse in nineteenth-century realist fiction? In what respects do realist novels, seen through the lens of narratology, depart from conventional critical notions about their techniques? Why has the engaging narrator been omitted from the formalist, narratological, and phenomenological models of fiction? Can it be a coincidence that the few canonized novels relying on engaging strategies (that is, Gaskell's, Eliot's, and—more recently included in the canon—Stowe's) are written by women?

To this last question, my answer is obviously no. I focus here on male- and female-written novels that are concerned with some kind of political, moral, or social reform. Having didactic goals in common, the novels might be assumed to share techniques as well: the fact that their strategies diverge is evidence of a gendered difference reflecting the relative positions of mid-nineteenth-century men and women in public life. My ultimate goal is not only to point to this gendered difference in writing strategies but also to expose the gender bias in literary theories that have overlooked the engaging narrator as a convention central to realist fiction. As I "do narratology" toward that end, my question to feminists is: Why don't we?

2

A Model of Gendered Intervention:

Engaging and Distancing Narrative

Strategies

Uncle Tom's Cabin is a very bad novel, having in its self-righteous, virtuous sentimentality, much in common with *Little Women*. Sentimentality, the ostentatious parading of excessive and spurious emotion, is the mark of dishonesty, the inability to feel . . . and it is always, therefore, the signal of secret and violent inhumanity, the mark of cruelty. (Baldwin 578–579)

BEHOLD A READER (James Baldwin, to be precise) who is not even remotely engaged, who is more than distanced—is revolted, disgusted. As Baldwin's powerfully argued essay on Stowe's novel reveals, the social circumstances, political convictions, and aesthetic standards of individual readers can combine to construct insurmountable walls of resistance to narrators' tactics. Accustomed as she doubtless was to attacks from proslavery Southerners, Stowe would probably have been appalled to know that any black reader in any era would virulently refuse to identify with the sympathetic narratee her novel usually assumes.

THE NARRATEE AND THE ACTUAL READER

Discrepancies such as this between narrators' moves and audiences' responses warrant mention here: strategies are rhetorical features of texts, choices of technique indicating novelists' apparent hopes about the emotional power their stories might wield. Strategies can misfire; they guarantee nothing. A reader's response cannot be enforced, predicted, or even proven. And, in the context of poststructuralist criticism, trying to determine a text's effect on a reading subject (trying, for instance, to ascertain the impact of interventions on the "illusion of reality") seems as futile as discussing an author's intention. Baldwin's expressed aversion to the "sentimentality" of *Uncle Tom* is itself rhetorically shaped for the purposes of his essay. In order to make his point, he may have constructed an image of secret inhumanity and masked cruelty more striking than what he actually experienced while he was reading—or, for that matter, he may have toned down his real feelings about the novel. Even in a case where a reader seems so candid in reporting his reaction to a text, it is difficult to make claims about the actual effect of narrative strategies. The participial forms of the terms *distancing* and *engaging* are not meant to imply an action that a text or a narrator could take upon a reader, but rather to identify the rhetorical moves these strategies represent. To understand their function in novels is to arrive at a new recognition of the narrative structures that constitute realism.

Studying narrative structures, such as interventions and addresses to the reader, is clearly not the same activity as studying "reader response," though in many ways the two approaches have converged in the critical imagination. Perhaps because the English translation of Prince's "Introduction to the Study of the Narratee" first appeared in Jane Tompkins's anthology, *Reader-Response Criticism,* theorists tend to identify the study of the narratee in fiction with the study of actual reading audiences or the reading process. An example of the conflation of the two areas of study is Mieke Bal's brief bibliographic section on "the Audience and the Reader," where she lists Prince's work on the narratee alongside that of Iser and Umberto Eco, which "discusses the reader's activity in building a fictional world while decoding a text" (*Narratology* 152). Although we should be grateful for having Prince's essay in so widely available a source as Tompkins's anthology, we should also be careful—as is Tompkins herself in her introduction[1]—to distinguish between Prince's typology of the kinds of narratees that can occur in texts and the inquiries into the process, reception, and epistemology of reading that characterize the selections from Fish, Iser, Georges Poulet, Norman Holland, and the other reader-centered theorists represented in the anthology. The study of the narratee, like studies of narrators, restricts its attention to the text, without reference to what happens when an actual person reads it.

Still, the temptation to conflate the two kinds of inquiry is strong: the narratee is, after all, a figure of a reader, or as Prince puts it, "someone whom the narrator addresses" ("Introduction" 7). It stands to reason that the degree to which an actual reader can or cannot identify with the figure being addressed affects that reader's reaction to the fiction. If I pick up a novel that assumes a narratee who has attitudes, opinions, and experiences that resemble my own, I am likely to read that novel with particular absorption. My response to the text would necessarily be affected by the attitude the novelist adopts toward the narratee I recognize as a mirror of myself. If the narrator needles, annoys, or offends me, my feeling about the literary work will be very different from what it would be if the narrator were to encourage, validate, and flatter me. Both kinds of reading, and all the range of attitudes between them, yield pleasures of their own. A detailed account of those pleasures would be, by definition, subjective, individualized, and perhaps too personal to be generally interesting (unless, indeed, it were written by someone like Roland Barthes).[2]

In terms of the actual response of real readers, a systematic study of the relations between individual members of a reading audience and narratees in given texts would be difficult or even impossible to accomplish. Too much depends on variables: not only would readers' responses to being addressed through particular narratees vary according to their own subjectivity, it would also change with their moods, their relative degree of concentration or distraction, the number of times they have read the text in question, and so forth. This is not to suggest that studies of reader-response cannot or should not be done; it is only to point out that the kind of study that Holland or David Bleich conducts entails questions about psychology and epistemology that do not enter into investigations of such textual strategies as the role of the narratee.

Having acknowledged that descriptions of narratees in texts cannot account for the actual responses of real readers, I do want to dwell on the relationship of narratee to reader, not so much from the perspective of the audience as from the perspective of the text itself. Every choice that an author makes in constructing a fiction can be regarded as a matter of rhetoric, in that each strategy or convention of fiction that a novelist can use will have certain connotations, inherited from its forebears, models, and antitypes among the fictions that preceded it. Depending on how actual readers situate themselves in regard to these conventions, their reactions to the text will be influenced by the text's rhetorical moves. If we cannot determine that actual readers would always (or even usually) respond in a certain way to any narratee, and if we cannot recover the author's original "intention" in creating the narratee, we can base some conclusions on textual analysis. By investigating the narrators' stances toward their narratees, and by comparing and contrasting the various stances of narrators within the genre of realism, we can arrive at a more specific poetics of how that genre operates textually. Without making any grand claims, then, about how actual readers, Victorian or modern, would respond to the narratees in realist novels, let us focus on responses that the novelists evidently *hoped* readers would feel. We can get at this hope, I believe, by inquiring into the relations narrators try to establish between the actual reader and the "you" in the text.

In recently revisiting his original theory of the narratee, Gerald Prince has admitted that his previous work no more than suggests "the possible differences between narratee, addressee, and receiver," which he takes "to be analogous to those between narrator, addresser, and sender" ("Narratee Revisited" 302). He mentions that studying the distinctions among these three entities (that is, the "you" that may be inscribed or encoded in a text, the implied reader suggested by that "you," and the actual reader who receives that "you") might lead to "a better appreciation of the ways particular texts— as well as narrative itself—can function" ("Narratee Revisited" 303). In fact, Prince's work on the narratee has assumed, as a general rule, a necessary distance between the narratee, the addressee, and the receiver of fictional texts.[3] The canonic example, used by both Prince and Genette, is that of the narratee of *Le Père Goriot* (Genette, *Nouveau discours* 9; Prince, "Narratee Revisited" 301). Certainly, as Prince and Genette have observed, when Balzac's narrator speaks to a "you" who sits in a well-padded armchair, holding the book with white hands, this narratee may or may not be a figure with whom the actual reader can identify. "If it should occur that the reader bears an astonishing resemblance to the narratee," Prince writes, "this is an exception and not the rule" ("Introduction" 9).

Prince is certainly correct for most novels in which the narrators and narratees are—to borrow Genette's terms in *Narrative Discourse*—both extradiegetic (that is, where the act of narrating occurs outside the fiction) and heterodiegetic (that is, where neither narrator nor narratee functions as a character).[4] The more specifically a heterodiegetic narrator characterizes the narratee, the less likely will be a resemblance between this addressee and the actual receiver of the text. A narrator who provides so much information about the narratee that the addressee becomes, as Prince says, "as clearly defined as any character" necessarily places a distance between the actual reader and the inscribed "you" in the text ("Introduction" 18). Such a narrator I call distancing. But not every narrator who intervenes to address a narratee does so to set the actual reader apart from the "you" in the text. Another kind, which I call engaging, strives to close the gaps between the narratee, the addressee, and the receiver. Using narrative interventions that are almost always spoken in earnest, such a narrator addresses a "you" that is evidently intended to evoke recognition and identification in the person who holds the book and reads, even if the "you" in the text resembles that person only slightly or not at all.[5]

To be sure, narrative structures are always complex: novelists who typically employ distancing narrative interventions sometimes use direct address to engage their readers, and even the most consistently engaging narrators sometimes intervene in their texts in distancing ways. And, too, the critic cannot claim to distinguish authorial intent in textual manifestations. We can only read through the "tone" of authorial intrusions—and place our interpretations of what the intrusions say alongside extratextual assertions of intent—to find the signs of what writers wish their texts would do. But certain women novelists in mid-nineteenth-century England and America—particularly Gaskell, Stowe, and Eliot—seem to have been experimenting with engaging narrative as a strategy integral to their idea of realist fiction. Writing to inspire belief in the situations their novels describe—and admittedly hoping to move actual readers to sympathy for real-life slaves, workers, or ordinary middle-class people—these novelists used engaging narrators to encourage actual readers to identify with the "you" in the texts.[6] An examination of the ways their works diverge from the conventions of distancing narrative intervention would not only help complete Prince's typology of the narratee but also contribute to a more comprehensive understanding of the conventions of realist narrative.[7]

I should pause to emphasize that when I refer to "the reader" I mean the *actual* reader. While this is a somewhat unorthodox thing to do in a work of literary theory, in some respects it follows the lead that other narratologists have taken. Like Genette (*Narrative Discourse* 260) and Suleiman ("Of Readers and Narratees" 91), I do not try to analyze the implied reader, the virtual reader, the ideal reader, or even (as I have mentioned) individual readers. The first three are figures created between the lines of novels, and as such, are unusually difficult to pin down: they are the products of literary interpretation of texts, and not textual features themselves. Just like individual readers, they are too variable and indefinable to categorize in a narratological study. When a created reader is inscribed within a text, I refer to that figure, with Prince, as a narratee. When I want to point to the relation between those fictive figures and the receiver of the text, the person—whoever it might be—who actually holds the book and reads, I call this latter entity "the reader." The actual reader, is, after all, an essential link in the chain of communication a text represents; without a receiver to process the text, the text lies inert, silent. The reader to whom I refer is not, like the narratee, a feature of the text or even (except in the strictest poststructuralist sense) a product of language. The reader is an unpredictable, infinitely variable person who is physically present in the act of reading—a person realist novelists often confessed to trying to visualize as they wrote.

Embracing Suleiman's proposal of "a moratorium on the implied reader, with more attention paid to narratees and actual readers, and to the possible relationships between them," then, I concentrate here on the relation in engaging narrative between the narratee and the actual reader ("Of Readers and Narratees" 92). I examine the differences in strategy and effect between distancing and engaging narrative interventions, providing specific examples of distancing narrative from works that are commonly mentioned in studies of the narratee (for example, *Tom Jones* and *Vanity Fair*) and juxtaposing them with examples of engaging strategies from Gaskell's, Stowe's, and Eliot's early novels. The two modes of intervention constitute the gendered difference that I see in mid-nineteenth-century fiction; as the examples here and in Part II indicate, the differences inhere in these male and female novelists' apparent ideas about the purposes and functions of realist fiction.

DIRECT ADDRESS: THE ENGAGING AND
DISTANCING MODES

Generally speaking, a distancing narrator discourages the actual reader from identifying with the narratee, while an engaging narrator encourages that identification. Sketching out the similarity between the narrator-addresser-sender relationship and the narratee-addressee-receiver relationship, Prince has used a simple example that can help describe the significantly different rhetorical effects of distancing and engaging addresses to narratees. Prince writes, "Just as in 'I ate a hamburger for lunch,' the character-I is the one who ate and the narrator-I the one telling about the eating, in 'You ate a hamburger for lunch,' the character-you is the one who ate and the narratee-you the one told about the eating." Prince uses the example to show that "the difference between intra- and extradiegetic narratee is no more fundamental than the one between intra- and extra-diegetic narrator" ("Narratee Revisited" 301). This can be true in only a limited sense, however, as we must realize if we consider the rhetorical effect these utterances would have on an actual interlocutor or an actual reader. Depending on (1) the accuracy of the statement about "you" and (2) the speaker's stance toward "you" in making the assertion, the relation between the narratee and the receiver of the statement could be either distanced or engaged.

Consider the effect the two statements about lunch might have in a real-world conversation. If I tell you that I ate a hamburger for lunch, you may or may not believe me, according to your sense of my reliability (you may not know me well enough to know whether I am characteristically truthful, or you may know that I habitually lie about my calorie intake) and according to anything you know about my lunch beyond my assertion (maybe you sat across the lunch table from me and watched me eat that hamburger, or maybe you watched me eat quiche instead). But you can never be certain whether my report of my own experience is true: possibly I did not lie about what I ate for lunch, even if I customarily do; possibly I slipped away after I had the quiche and secretly ate a hamburger as a second lunch. You may believe my statement or not, but you can never be as certain of its truth as you can be about my statement "You ate a hamburger for lunch." You know—if you are not impossibly absentminded—whether you ate a hamburger, just as you know, while you are reading *Père Goriot,* whether your hands are white and your armchair is comfortable.

The example shows that in fact there is a difference between the narrator-addresser-sender relationship and the narratee-addressee-receiver relationship, a difference that must occur to the actual reader in reading the text. The reader may or may not be interested in how closely the narrative "I" resembles the actual author; readers can only speculate about such a resemblance, which—even if it exists—would have no bearing on the rhetorical effect of the text. But one can know whether the narrative "you" resembles oneself, and surely the way one experiences the fiction is affected by how personally one can take its addresses to "you."

Keeping this in mind, we can pursue the example for its distancing and engaging potentialities. The effect of my assertion "You ate a hamburger" will depend on your interpretation of my rhetorical intent. Since you know whether you ate a hamburger, you may assume that my assertion is not intended to convey information to you. If you know I saw you having quiche for lunch and I say "You ate a hamburger," my utterance will be ironic. I might expect you to respond with laughter, annoyance, or perplexity, but in any case—since you would be unable to identify your experience with my assertion—you would separate your actual self from the "you" in my statement. My remark would then be distancing.

The distancing narrator may evoke laughter, or even annoyance, from an actual reader who cannot identify with the narratee. The task of the engaging narrator, in contrast, is to evoke sympathy and identification from an actual reader who is unknown to the author and therefore infinitely variable and unpredictable. The engaging narrator is in the position I would be in if, to win your trust and support, I had to approach you, a stranger, and tell you what you had for lunch. I could try to win you over through what I say or through the way I say it, through the substance of my assertion or through my attitude in asserting it. I could make a guess about what you ate, based on my idea of what most people eat; engaging narrators often do base assertions about "you" on such general assumptions. Chances are, though, that my guess would be inaccurate, in which case I could only hope to win you with the appealing attitude I try to take in addressing you. In realist novels—engaging narrators functioning as their authors' surrogates in earnestly trying to foster sympathy for real-world sufferers—work to engage "you" through the substance and, failing that, the stance of their narrative interventions and addresses to "you."

While the distinction between engaging and distancing stances may seem inconsequential on the purely textual level, the significance of the difference asserts itself in novels that aim to inspire personal, social, or political change. When the narrator of *Uncle Tom's Cabin* speaks to "you, generous, noble-minded men and women of the South—you, whose virtue and magnanimity and purity of character, are the greater for the severer trial it has encountered" (622), the speaker can have no certain knowledge of the virtue and magnanimity of actual Southern readers, nor of the Southern affiliations of any individual actual reader. Operating in a context where her information about the "real you" may be faulty, the narrator tries to win "you" with the ingratiating rhetoric of her engaging appeal. And if she can thus draw you in, she could possibly change your mind; if she does change your mind and you happen to be a Southern slave owner, she might change the world.

INTERVENTION STRATEGIES: THE ENDS OF THE SPECTRUM

In Gaskell's *Mary Barton* (1848), Stowe's *Uncle Tom's Cabin* (1851–1852), and Eliot's *Adam Bede* (1859), earnest, engaging strategies of intervention are strikingly present in passages of the novels addressed to "you." Typically, these novelists' engaging narrators differ from distancing narrators—such as Fielding's in *Tom Jones* (1749), Thackeray's in *Vanity Fair* (1846–1847), Trollope's in *Barchester Towers* (1849), Hawthorne's in *The House of Seven Gables* (1851) or Eliot's in her first novel, *Scenes of Clerical Life* (1857)—in their explicit attitudes toward the narratees, toward the characters, and toward the very act of narration. The differences occur in five forms:

1. *The names by which the narratee is addressed.* Whereas a distancing narrator may specify a name or title for an extradiegetic narratee (for example, "Miss Bullock," "Miss Smith," or "Jones, who reads this book at his Club," in *Vanity Fair*, "Your Majesty . . . my lords and gentlemen" in Dickens's *Bleak House* [1852–1853]; "Madam" or "Mrs. Farthingale" in Eliot's *Scenes*), an engaging narrator will usually either avoid naming the narratee or use names that refer to large classes of potential actual readers. In

Mary Barton, the most straightforward example of the first engaging approach, the narrator never calls the narratee anything but "you." In *Uncle Tom's Cabin,* the most extreme example of the second approach, the narrator will, Walt Whitman-like, specify narratees in a group ("mothers of America") or include large numbers of more specifically defined groups in passages of direct address ("Farmers of Massachusetts, of New Hampshire, of Vermont, of Connecticut, who read this book by the blaze of your winter-evening fire,—strong-hearted, generous sailors and ship-owners of Maine . . . Brave and generous men of New York, farmers of rich and joyous Ohio, and ye of the wide prairie states" [623]). Even such exhaustive lists exclude more readers than they can include. Straining against the limitations such specific names must enforce on actual readers' ability to answer appeals to the narratees, Stowe's narrator intersperses her novel with remarks directed simply to "Reader" or "you," designations that can signify any actual reader.

2. *The frequency of direct address to the narratee.* A distancing narrator, such as Fielding's, often refers to "the Reader" or "my reader" as a third party, someone not present (as it were) at the narrative conversation. Actual readers perusing the novel are no more likely to take such third-person references personally than they would take remarks that refer to characters in the novel. "He" and "she," whether the pronouns stand for Tom Jones and Sophia Western or for "my readers," have referents within the text—they do not shift as does the referent of "you." Whether an actual reader answers to remarks directed to "my reader(s)" will depend on how much the portrait of those readers actually resembles him or her: the actual reader gets to choose whether to take such narrative interventions to heart. An engaging narrator avoids giving the actual reader a choice in the matter, and, very much like an evangelical preacher, more frequently speaks to "you."[8] In *Mary Barton,* for instance, the narratee is addressed as "you" in at least twenty-two passages, included in the narrative "we" in at least five passages, and seldom, if ever, referred to in the third person.

3. *The degree of irony present in references to the narratee.* Irony is, of course, always multivalent, and never definitively determinable. If verbal irony may be defined as a presumably self-conscious disjunction between what a speaker says and what he or she appears to mean, then two particularly ironic conventions characterize the distancing narrator's attitude toward the narratee. Both kinds of irony occur in passages of direct address to

the narratee that are distinctly not engaging in their approach. The first of these is a distancing narrator's pretense that "you" are present on the scene of the fiction; the second is a distancing narrator's habit of inscribing flawed "readers" from whom actual readers should want to differentiate themselves. In both kinds of ironic intervention, the effect is distancing in that the strategy encourages the actual reader *not* to identify with the narratee being addressed.

The sarcastic pretense that "you" are present on the fictional scene is one way that a distancing narrator discourages the actual reader from identifying with the textual narratee. These are passages in which narrators play the game of "endangering the Reader's Neck" (as Fielding calls it) by pretending to locate the reader at the side of the characters or the narrator himself. A nineteenth-century example of this narrative jest would be Hawthorne's heterodiegetic narrator's intervention in chapter 28 of *The House of Seven Gables,* the scene which describes the room where the dead Judge Pyncheon sits alone: "You must hold your own breath, to satisfy yourself whether he breathes at all. It is quite inaudible. You hear the ticking of his watch; his breath you do not hear." In the climax of the scene, the voice places the narratee even more clearly on the narrator's diegetic level, by including the narratee in a collective "we": "Would that we were not an attendant spirit, here!"[9]

Genette's term for this technique is *metalepsis,* or the practice of crossing diegetic levels to imply that figures inside and outside the fiction exist on the same plane (*Narrative Discourse* 236). To illustrate the term: in this example, the extradiegetic narrator (who is inside the novel, but not inside the "diegesis," or story, because he does not participate as a character) places himself in the same room, and therefore on the same plane of "reality," with the extradiegetic narratee (the person to whom the story is being told, who—like the narrator—does not exist within the story) and the character (the judge, the only one of the three figures involved in this scene who, properly speaking, belongs in the diegesis). The effect of metalepsis in distancing narrative is usually to affirm the fictionality of the story: when Hawthorne's narrator pretends, for instance, that "you" are present with him in the room with the dead judge, the fictionality of the scene becomes obvious. *You,* the actual reader, are not a ghostly presence in the Pyncheons' house. You are a person holding a copy of *The House of Seven Gables,* reading it.

Describing the use of metalepsis in Cortázar, Sterne, Diderot, Proust, and Balzac, Genette has pointed to its metafictional potential: its effect, he writes, "is either comical (when, as in Sterne or Diderot, it is presented in a joking tone) or fantastic" (*Narrative Discourse* 235). Genette's account of the metaleptic effect describes very well the goal of the distancing intervention: "The most troubling thing about metalepsis indeed lies in this unacceptable and insistent hypothesis, that the extradiegetic is perhaps always diegetic, and that the narrator and his narratees—you and I—perhaps belong to some narrative" (236).

Stowe, Gaskell, and (especially) Eliot can also use metalepsis that pretends to place the reader on the scene of the fiction. A notable example would be the narrator's introductory description of the rectory in *Adam Bede*. The narratee is invited into the Irwines' dining room. "We will enter very softly," the narrator tells "you," "and stand still in the open doorway, without awakening [the dogs]" (98). But in *Adam Bede* the overall dominance of engaging interventions tends to transform the intended effect of a passage like this one. Instead of experiencing a comical or fantastic awareness of the activity of reading, the actual reader should indulge in a momentary exercise of imagination. Readers are encouraged to feel that perhaps they *could* be in Hayslope; perhaps the world they are reading about *is* as real as their own. The invitation to "enter very softly" both beckons the reader into the fictional world and emphasizes the fact that he or she is not really part of it; the implication is, though, that if the reader will participate in re-creating a real world predicated on the lessons of sympathy that reading the novel imparts, perhaps the real world, as well as the actual reader, will be transformed. Indeed, the engaging narrator's frequent appeals to the reader's imagination, her earnest requests to the reader to draw upon personal memories to fill in gaps in the narrative, prompt the actual reader to participate in creating the fictional world itself, just as he or she should actively alter the real world after finishing the reading.

In the second type of ironic address to the reader, the distancing narrator humorously inscribes the addressee as a potentially "bad reader," thus discouraging the receiver of the text from identifying with the person addressed. Balzac's address to the complacent, pleasure-seeking narratee of *Le Père Goriot* is an example of this ironic mode. So is Fielding's amusing directive on how to read *Tom Jones,* typical of Fielding in its self-conscious awareness of the distance the narrator encourages between the narratee, the implied reader, and the actual reader:

> Reader, it is impossible we should know what Sort of Person thou wilt be: For perhaps, thou may'st be as learned in Human Nature as *Shakespear* himself was, and, perhaps, thou may'st be no wiser than some of his Editors. Now lest this latter should be the Case, we think proper, before we go any farther together, to give thee a few wholesome Admonitions. . . . We warn thee not too hastily to condemn any of the Incidents in this our History, as impertinent and foreign to our main Design. . . . For a little Reptile of a Critic to presume to find Fault with any of its Parts, without knowing the Manner in which the Whole is connected . . . is a most presumptuous Absurdity. (398)

Here, the narratee is not entirely foolish: Fielding's "Reader" is at least presumably capable of appreciating the contrast between the wisdom of Shakespeare and that of "some of his Editors"; the narratee is also patient and cooperative enough to attend to the "wholesome Admonitions" on how to read this book. But the same narratee has the potential to read badly, or "too hastily to condemn" the novel's parts before apprehending the whole. The "little Reptile of a Critic" is not a narratee, in that the narrator refers to him indirectly, rather than speaking to him. Still, the logic of the paragraph implies that if the narratee were to succumb to the inclination to "condemn," he or she would be imitating the reptilian critic's activity. The implied reader is someone who gets the joke and can chuckle at the expense of the hapless narratee. The actual reader, then, should hesitate to identify with the narratee, in order to avoid becoming laughably ridiculous. Similarly distancing is Thackeray's ironic reference to "some carping reader" who is incapable of enjoying the sentimental passages in *Vanity Fair* (147). As much as the actual reader might be amused and entertained by these interventions, he or she is to be discouraged from identifying with any "carping" "little Reptile of a Critic."

Engaging narrators, in contrast, usually assume that their narratees (not to mention their actual readers) are in perfect sympathy with them. When Gaskell's narrator in *Mary Barton* assures the narratee, "Your heart would have ached to have seen the man, however hardly you might have judged his crime" (422), or when Eliot's in *Adam Bede* interrupts a love scene to remark, "That is a simple scene, reader. But it is almost certain that you, too, have been in love" (537), the narrators' earnestly confidential attitudes toward "you" encourage actual readers to see themselves reflected in that pronoun.

As these two examples show, an engaging narrator sometimes does imply imperfection in the narratee's ability to comprehend, or sympathize with, the contents of the text, even while expressing confidence that the narratee will rise to the challenge. These implications of the narratee's fallibility often come through narrative interventions that Prince calls

> *surjustifications* . . . situated at the level of meta-language, meta-commentary, or meta-narration. . . . Over-justifications always provide us with interesting details about the narratee's personality, even though they often do so in an indirect way; in overcoming the narratee's defenses, in prevailing over his prejudices, in allaying his apprehensions, they reveal them. ("Introduction" 15)

Although engaging narrators tend to inscribe their narratees through overjustifying their own assertions, they usually do so in the spirit of sympathetically and earnestly attempting to convert the narratees to their own points of view. This mode of address encourages actual readers to identify with the narratees, unlike the sarcasm of distancing narrators, which attempts through irony to embarrass readers out of such identification.

The engaging narrators' overjustifications portray their narratees less as potentially bad readers than as potentially limited sympathizers. The narrators defend their characters' rights to the actual readers' sympathy by explicitly demonstrating those rights to the narratees. One of the most notorious passages of such overjustification occurs in *Uncle Tom's Cabin,* interrupting the scene of Eliza's barefoot escape over the frozen river. Anticipating an incredulous response, the narrator encourages the narratee to put herself in Eliza's place: "If it were *your* Harry, mother, or your Willie, that were going to be torn from you by a brutal trader, tomorrow morning—if you had seen the man, and heard that the papers were signed and delivered, and you had only from twelve o'clock till morning to make good your escape,—how fast could *you* walk?" (105). The passage provides specific information about the narratee: she is certainly female, and is perhaps, by the narrator's standards, overly judgmental. But the narrator's stance, implicit in her faith that the narratee can be persuaded to sympathize if actual readers will pause to recognize similarities between Eliza's experiences and their own, is what makes the passage engaging.[10] The actual reader, required to draw upon memory and sympathetic imagination to fill in the emotional details of the story, is engaged in collaborating on the creation of the fictional world.

4. *The narrator's stance toward the characters.* A distancing narrator may seem to delight in reminding the narratee that the characters are fictional, entirely under the writer's control. Some of the most extreme examples would be the references in *Vanity Fair* to the characters as puppets that come out of a box and the famous passage in *Barchester Towers* where Trollope's narrator reassures "the reader" that he would never let his Elinor Bold marry the likes of Mr. Slope, thus predicting the outcome of the plot and reminding the narratee that the fiction is an arbitrary creation, a game. An engaging narrator avoids reminders of the characters' fictionality, insisting instead that the characters are "real." The difference between the distancing and engaging attitudes toward characters thus parallels the difference between metafiction and realism. In moves that parallel their attitudes toward their narratees, both distancing and engaging narrators use metalepsis in establishing their relation to their characters, but whereas distancing narrators use it to subvert realism, engaging narrators use it to reinforce the veracity of their stories.

A distancing narrator does indeed use metalepsis for the humorous effect that Genette describes. Perhaps the best example of the disconcerting effect of distancing metalepsis is the shifting presentation of the characters in *Vanity Fair*. At the beginning and the very end of the novel they are puppets; often they are fictional figures under the author's explicit control; then quite suddenly, near the end of the story, they are people the narrator met in Pumpernickel before he had heard all the details of their biographies. Their changeable status contributes to the novel's humor, as well as to the narratee's awareness that they are creatures of fiction. An engaging narrator, though, uses metalepsis to suggest that the characters are possibly as "real" as the narrator and narratee, who are, in these cases, to be identified with the actual author and actual reader. Stowe's narrator simply claims that her characters—or people exactly resembling them—exist in the real world (for example, that "the personal appearance of Eliza, the character ascribed to her, are sketches drawn from life. . . . The incident of the mother's crossing the Ohio river on the ice is a well-known fact" [*Uncle Tom's Cabin* 618]). Gaskell's and Eliot's narrators occasionally claim personal acquaintance with their characters, even though the narrators never figure as intradiegetic characters themselves.

One of the many overjustifications in *Mary Barton* is an example of metalepsis that places the heterodiegetic narrator and the intradiegetic characters on the same level. The narrator defends her comments about one character's physical appearance by citing a "personal" impression of the fictional woman: "I have called her 'the old woman' . . . because, in truth, her appearance was so much beyond her years . . . she always gave me the idea of age" (385–386). This heterodiegetic "I" is never present in the fictional world, hence never in a position to see the character in the context of the fiction; the implication is, then, that the character must exist within the context of the narrator's own world. Eliot makes a similar implication in one intervention that refers to a conversation between the heterodiegetic narrator and the hero: "But I gathered from Adam Bede, to whom I talked of these matters in his old age" (225). These instances of metalepsis— implying that the characters exist, as the narrators do, outside the world represented in the fiction—produce an effect that differs from the humorous discomfort that Genette had identified as the usual result of the device. Instead of distancing the actual reader from the characters by reminding the narratee that they are fictional, these metalepses are meant to reinforce the reader's serious sense of the characters as, in some way, real.

5. *The narrator's implicit or explicit attitude toward the act of narration.* The distancing narrator, directly or indirectly, often reminds the narratee that the fiction is a game and the characters pawns. Such reminders may be as direct as *Vanity Fair*'s references to the narrator as a stage manager or puppet master, as indirect as the mock-heroic "epic" language in the "battle scenes" of *Tom Jones* or *Joseph Andrews,* or as comparatively subtle as the type names that Fielding, Thackeray, Dickens, and Trollope assign to minor characters. In each of these examples, the distancing strategy pushes a text that in many other respects conforms to the conventions of verisimilitude in realist fiction over into the realm of metafiction. This playing with the text's fictionality goes hand-in-hand with the irony that characterizes the distancing approach.

Henry James heads the critical tradition that has correctly assessed this whole spectrum of self-conscious artifice as a means of destroying the illusion of reality and reminding the reader that the text is, after all, only a fiction.[11] Objecting to Trollope's penchant for such names as Dr. Pessimist Anticant, Mr. Neversay Die, and Mr. Stickatit, his frequent authorial hints about the probable outcome of the plot, and his narrative reminders that the novelist "could direct the course of events according to his pleasure," James called Trollope's "pernicious trick" of narrative intervention "suicidal." James's summary of Trollope's strategy describes the distancing narrator's attitude perfectly: "There are certain precautions in the way of producing that illusion dear to the intending novelist which Trollope not only habitually scorned to take, but really, as we may say, asking pardon for the heat of the thing, delighted wantonly to violate" (115–18).

James does not distinguish between distancing and engaging narrators, since all narrative interventions must, at some level, interfere with the illusion of reality, if in fact such an illusion could ever exist in the mind of a reader sophisticated enough to process these texts. Like any intervening narrator, the engaging narrator also intrudes into the fiction with reminders that the novel is "only a story." The difference is that engaging narrators imply it is "only a *true* story," one that represents personal and social realities virtually, if not literally. In this respect, engaging narrators differ from distancing narrators in that their purposes are seldom playful: they intrude to remind their narratees—who, in their texts, should stand for the actual readers—that the fictions reflect real-world conditions for which the readers should take active responsibility after putting aside the book. Whether the situation depicted is that of American slaves, or the working-class poor in Manchester, or middle-class rural folk in England, the engaging narrator explicitly draws on the actual reader's memory and emotion, through direct address to the narratee, to foster a commitment to improving the extradiegetic situation the fiction depicts. Engaging narrators seldom play with metafiction; rather, they earnestly assert the veracity of their stories as they attempt to inspire the readers' sympathetic action.

Uncle Tom's Cabin is full of direct, sermonlike exhortation to the narratee, demanding sympathy for the slaves and even action on their behalf. The passage mentioned above, addressed to "mothers of America," specifically directs the narratees to transfer their emotional response from the characters to the actual slaves:

41

you who have learned, by the cradles of your own children, to love and feel for all mankind,—by the sacred love you bear your child . . . —I beseech you, pity the mother who had all your affections, and not one legal right to protect, guide, or educate, the child of her bosom! By the sick hour of your child; by those dying eyes, which you can never forget; by those last cries, that wrung your heart when you could neither help nor save . . . —I beseech you, pity those mothers that are constantly made childless by the American slave-trade! And say, mothers of America, is this a thing to be defended, sympathized with, passed over in silence? (623–624)

Here, the narrator's strategy is simply to arouse the egocentric feelings of any actual readers who can identify with the narratees, then to ask the readers to project those feelings into compassion for actual slaves. If the narratees can feel for the characters, then the actual readers the narratees represent should be able to feel for the actual persons—or classes of persons—the characters are supposed to represent.

Gaskell's narrator in *Mary Barton* pursues a similar strategy, asking the narratee to see through a character's eyes and including "you" in her implicit criticism of the character's egocentricity. In this scene, John Barton walks down a Manchester street, absorbed in his own sorrows:

He wondered if any in all the hurrying crowd, had come from such a house of mourning. But he could not, you cannot, read the lot of those who daily pass you by in the street. How do you know the wild romances of their lives; the trials, the temptations they are even now enduring, resisting, sinking under . . . Errands of mercy—errands of sin—did you ever think where all the thousands of people you daily meet are bound? (101–102)

Like many other narrative interventions in *Mary Barton,* the passage demonstrates the way direct address to the narratee can "realize" the fictional situation for the actual reader, that is, transform a fictive event (like John Barton's self-absorbed walk through the city) into a genuine confrontation between "you" and the figures represented in the fiction. Gaskell's strategy for inspiring actual readers to learn more actively to sympathize with people they do not know is to cajole readers into imaginatively aligning themselves with the characters inside the fiction. Having placed themselves in that position, readers should realize how closely the fictional world resembles their own. If readers can look at strangers on real urban streets and imagine biographies for them, just as Gaskell has imagined the histories of her characters, those strangers will take on identities and fates that matter: readers will become responsible for feeling and expressing compassion for them. Even though the strategy occurs in a narrative intervention, it has the odd effect of placing the narrator in the background for the moment: deflecting attention from herself, she facilitates an imaginative moment of connection between the narratee and the characters on her Manchester street, a moment that is supposed to inspire a similar sense of community between actual readers and the people they will encounter when they have put down the book and walked out into their own worlds.

In *Adam Bede,* Eliot's narrator also asks readers to recognize affinities between their own experiences and those depicted in the novel. Her engaging strategies apply the philosophy that Eliot summarized in her earlier novel: "Sympathy is but a living again through our own past in a new form" (*Scenes* 358). The *Adam Bede* narrator's attitude toward the purpose of narration plays such a crucial role in the novel that it is the subject of an entire chapter, "In Which the Story Pauses a Little." This enormous intervention, interrupting the narrative after it has been unfolding for sixteen chapters, is an extraordinary instance of overjustification, defending at length the narrator's refusal to idealize the portraits of the novel's characters. The chapter opens with a classically distancing quotation from "one of my lady readers," a prejudiced narratee with whom few would be eager to identify. The self-referential nature of the entire chapter, drawing attention to the fictional framing of Adam's story, pulls the narrative in a distancing direction that recurs in crucial passages throughout *Adam Bede*. Eliot's strategies are not purely, unconflictedly engaging: the very presence of a chapter on how the novel was written is, in itself, a profoundly distancing move. And yet the tone of this chapter is so earnest, so confiding, that it could hardly be more different from the metafictional gestures in *Vanity Fair* or *Tom Jones*. One way Eliot achieves this tone is by relying, after that opening paragraph, upon engaging direct address to an unnamed, uncharacterized "you." Every engaging address to "you" simultaneously reminds the narratee (and the actual reader) that the story is only a fiction and encourages the reader to apply to nonfictional, real life the feelings that the fiction may have inspired. In this respect, engaging strategies both undermine and underline the realism of texts by stressing the position they occupy in relation to the world they are meant to represent.

In a certain sense, the distancing narrator's stance also emphasizes a "real" aspect of novel reading: in constantly coming forward to confront the narratee, the distancing narrator draws attention to the reality of the novel's textuality, dismissing implications that the story is in any literal sense "true." The actual reader stands clearly and distinctly outside the text; the narrator, narratees, and characters are within. Through engaging narrative interventions, however, novelists can place actual readers in a more ambiguous position vis-à-vis the text. When an actual reader responds to the engaging narrator's call to identify with a narratee, the reader is drawn into the story while at the same time recognizing that it is most certainly a story. The lines between fiction and the world of lived experience blur; the interventions imply that the fiction's referentiality may extend beyond the covers of the book. For the purposes of didactic realism, engaging interventions can both raise readers' questions about the connections between the real and fictional worlds and gesture toward answering them.

II

Testing the Model: Interventions in Texts

3

Engaging Strategies, Earnestness, and Realism:

Mary Barton

In 1848, *intervention* would have had no connotations of anything as rarified as narrative theory. In the language Elizabeth Gaskell spoke, the term referred to one of two controversial alternatives for facing the economic transitions affecting the British working class. Confronting the rapidly widening gap that the industrial revolution was establishing between "masters" and "men," mid-nineteenth-century political theorists debated the advisability of a laissez-faire system that would allow the free market to expand uncontrolled, taking its victims where it would, versus the policy of "interventionism." As Joseph Kestner has pointed out (8), the question of whether the state ought to intervene in economic matters that were adversely affecting the lives of the working poor preoccupied several women who were writing protest novels at the time, among them Harriet Martineau and Charlotte Tonna.

Kestner argues that the rise of the "novel with a purpose" reflects women novelists' attempts to intervene in the process of political decision making. As he puts it, "writing social fiction allowed women, although not enfranchised, to participate in the legislative process" (13). Kestner is concerned (as was Robert A. Colby before him) with the "story" in these novels-with-a-purpose: the idea of narrative intervention enters his discussion no more than it would, perhaps, have entered Gaskell's own description of her novelistic goals and techniques, had she ever attempted such a description.[1] Gaskell did favor the notion that the state should intervene in the establishment of economic stability for the working class, but—as a look at the preface to *Mary Barton* will reveal—her interests lay not so much with the details or results of legislation, as with the conviction that the poor would benefit from recognizing any sympathetic gesture that the middle and ruling classes could extend to them. Gaskell's narrative interventions, then, are related to her adherence to interventionism. Both would function primarily, from her perspective, as signals to the working poor, signs that would indicate a middle-class interest in their plight. The writing of *Mary Barton* therefore embodies two kinds of "gendered interventions": a woman's means of participating in public policy formation was to write a novel, and Gaskell's means of attempting to ensure that her first novel would serve its purpose was to employ earnest, engaging narrative techniques among the realist conventions she adopted.

That a social-problem novel should be realistic to be effective has been taken for granted by commentators on the genre from Louis Cazamian to Kestner, who have tended to emphasize novelists' reliance on documentary fact as the primary indicator of the verisimilitude of these texts.[2] On this scale of realism, *Mary Barton* has often ranked rather low, because of the plot's notorious shift from depiction of the everyday lives of Manchester factory workers to a sensationalist (some have called it Gothic) tale of seduction, murder, and happy-ending romance escapism.[3] To look at this novel in terms of plot is not to see it as entirely or consistently realistic, for despite a conscientious depiction of the circumstances surrounding the rise and fall of the Chartist movement, and a careful representation of the sights and sounds of life in Manchester, the story of *Mary Barton* (and I use "story" here in the narratological sense, to include the characterization and scenic setting as well as the events in the fiction) diverges in many respects from verisimilitude.[4] Gaskell's narrative discourse, however, reveals a concern with the "real" that establishes a pattern for engaging narrative in nineteenth-century novels.

Throughout *Mary Barton,* the consistently engaging narrative interventions reveal Gaskell's attempt to collapse the intra- and the extra-diegetic, to bring together the worlds within and outside the fiction, as though both existed on the same plane of reality. Gaskell's is the definitively engaging narrator, in that she frequently signals a precise identification of her narrative "I" with the actual author and her narrative "you" with the actual reader. The conflation of the real and the textual occurs in three different phases of *Mary Barton*'s writing: first, in Gaskell's decision to write a social-problem novel as a means of reconciling herself to loss and suffering in her own life; second, in her declared intention to stir real readers' sympathy for the poor, thus potentially improving the morale of actual working-class people; and finally, in her narrator's reliance on engaging interventions. In each of these respects, Gaskell's first novel represents an attempt to establish a connecting route between the real and fictive worlds, a bridge of sympathy which her strategies encourage the actual reader to cross in responding to the fiction and carrying that response over into extra-diegetic life.

The circumstances in which Gaskell decided to write her first novel are very familiar to Gaskell scholars, and have provided introductory material for many critical essays on *Mary Barton*. By the summer of 1846, Elizabeth Gaskell had written some stories for her own and her children's amusement and for her clergyman-husband's use in teaching courses for working people in Manchester. She had given no thought to publishing her stories: her energies were absorbed by her roles as mother and minister's wife. But in August of that year, her fourth child and only son, Willie, died of scarlet fever when he was only ten months old. Her husband suggested that she should try writing a novel, "to turn her thoughts from the subject of her grief" (Gerin 74).[5] Elizabeth Gaskell's preface to *Mary Barton*, written for the first, 1848 edition, assures her audience that she wrote the novel out of her personal need for distraction, as well as her interest in the working people of Manchester, and not—as her contemporaries presumably might have suspected—to exploit the topicality of the social upheavals then occurring in Europe.[6]

Despite being shielded by anonymity on the novel's title page, Gaskell shrinks from directly mentioning her son's death in the preface, which begins: "Three years ago I became anxious (from circumstances that need not be more fully alluded to) to employ myself in writing a work of fiction." She goes on to explain that she had originally thought of diverting herself by writing a historical romance:

> Living in Manchester, but with a deep relish and fond admira-
> tion for the country, my first thought was to find a frame-work
> for my story in some rural scene; and I had already made a lit-
> tle progress in a tale, the period of which was more than a cen-
> tury ago, and the place on the borders of Yorkshire, when I

bethought me how deep might be the romance in the lives of some of those who elbowed me daily in the busy streets of the town in which I resided. I had always felt a deep sympathy with the care-worn men. (37)

Imaginative escape to remote times and to places reminiscent of her happy childhood in the countryside could not answer her need for consolation. Struck by the unhappiness of the working people whose prevailing melancholy corresponded at this time so closely to her own, she determined to write of the "romance" in their lives, but nonetheless, in choosing a subject and setting so vividly present to her everyday existence, Gaskell was following an impulse toward realism.[7]

What Gaskell imagined to be the possible romance in the lives of the urban poor turns out to include, as critics have noted, elements of plot and imagery that are as far from being realistic as her historical romance might have been, particularly the melodramatic framework of coincidence, murder, and intrigue over which the story of *Mary Barton* is stretched. But the romance also includes portrayals of working people's emotions about more common occurrences, such as the loss of children. One of John Barton's primary motives for murdering Harry Carson, the mill owner's son, is his own long-festering anguish from having watched his infant son die of scarlet fever, unaided by any of the food or medicine that a tiny portion of the mill owners' profits could have supplied. By giving John Barton a basis for sorrow that was very similar to her own (and one that was common even among middle-class families, in that age of high infant mortality), and by making Barton's situation still more miserable than hers because of his poverty, Gaskell gave herself and her middle-class readers personal ground for sympathy with the character. Building on her imagination's version of their common loss, Gaskell expands her sympathy for John Barton to encompass the whole realm of the working man's frustration over misery that he is helpless to abate.

Writing a novel could not restore her son or abolish scarlet fever: that part of Gaskell's sorrow, like Barton's, was indelible. But she apparently believed that her novel could "intervene" in the unhappy lives of the poor, not so much by changing the circumstances causing their grief, as by inspiring her "more happy and fortunate" readers to feel and to express sympathy with the workers. The preface makes explicit her belief that such sympathy could lighten the emotional load that was pressing the lower classes into desperation and violence. Claiming to know "nothing of Political Economy," Gaskell emphasizes that she wished to work changes not on a political, but on a personal scale. Many critics, dismissing this prefatory confession as irrelevant to the text proper, have gone to great lengths to explicate the political ideology that the novel seems to endorse; as Elaine Jordan has shown, however, the political stance of *Mary Barton* is notably confused and confusing. If we take the preface seriously, we can see that Gaskell's hopes for social "intervention" had very little to do with details of public policy. As Gaskell puts it, she had become

> anxious . . . to give some utterance to the agony which, from time to time, convulses this dumb people; the agony of suffering without the sympathy of the happy, or of erroneously believing that such is the case. If it be an error, that the woes . . . pass unregarded by all but the sufferers, it is at any rate an error so bitter in its consequences to all parties, that whatever public effort can do in the way of legislation, or private effort in the way of merciful deeds, or helpless love in the way of widow's mites, should be done, and that speedily, to disabuse the work-people of so miserable a misapprehension. (37–38)

Interestingly, she does not urge legislation, merciful deeds, and widow's mites on the grounds that such actions could improve the physical living conditions of the working poor. Her primary concern is that the middle and upper classes should make these gestures as signals of sympathy to the working class. The reasoning of the preface implies that this novel's function should be to move middle- or upper-class readers to perform philanthropic actions demonstrating compassion, regardless of the effect of these actions on the daily lives of the poor. Keeping this in mind, we can see that a critical analysis of the novel's political content, such as Jordan's, although it demonstrates the interplay of competing ideologies and literary genres in the text, does not necessarily reveal a fundamental contradiction to the declared goal of the novel. The introduction of confusion, romance, and Gothicism can be seen as part of *Mary Barton's* machinery for stirring actual readers' emotions to the point where sympathy for the characters might spill over the border between the actual and imagined worlds—as did Gaskell's own.

PATTERNS FOR SYMPATHETIC RESPONSE

The redeeming power of sympathy is, accordingly, a dominant theme in *Mary Barton,* in both the novel's realistic and its melodramatic sections. The novel does indeed fall into these two distinct parts, although (as Jordan has argued) elements of Gothicism surface in the first part, foreshadowing the sensationalist mode of the second. The first seventeen chapters recount the family histories, daily joys and disappointments, and ordinary loves and deaths among the Barton family and their neighbors, the Wilsons and the Leghs. This part of the narrative includes some political debate among the working-class characters, as John Barton turns the pain resulting from the losses of son, wife, and job into union activism and feelings of re-crimination against the masters. John's disappointments culminate in Parliament's refusal to support the Chartist demands, which he, with high hopes, had helped carry to London. The details of the book's first half lead plausibly enough to John Barton's final desperation. The climax comes when Harry Carson, the son of Barton's employer, refuses to listen seriously to the requests of a delegation of his father's workers. Young Carson further offends the delegation by drawing caricatures of their haggard faces on a bit of paper which he tosses carelessly into the fire as he leaves the room. The unhappy men retrieve the paper and denounce the cartoonist. Speaking to the other members of the delegation, John Barton reviles the masters, who cannot comprehend that the men need more wages, not for luxury, but simply for the essentials of life. He particularly condemns the extravagant and jolly Harry Carson: "Now I only know that I would give the last drop o' my blood to avenge us on yon chap, who had so little feeling in him as to make game on earnest, suffering men!" (239). With this, the delegation decides to assassinate young Carson, and the novel begins its eleven-chapter journey into melodrama. True to Gaskell's stated thematic purpose, what finally drives Barton over the edge of desperation is young Carson's indifference to the men's suffering; after Harry's murder, sympathy and forgiveness become the final saving grace both for Barton and for Harry's stricken father.

Mary Barton reinforces its theme with the narrative "redundancy" that Susan Suleiman has identified as a characteristic of the *roman à thèse:* the story repeatedly depicts the power of sympathy dramatically, while the narrative discourse contains many assertions that underline the relevance of sympathy to the novel's point. Gaskell constructs the story so as to provide numerous models for the behavior she hopes to inspire in readers; the admirable poor people in this novel all practice sympathy and forgiveness. In the opening scenes, Mary Barton's pregnant mother has recently lost her sister Esther to what the Bartons assume must be a life of prostitution. This blow, which later leads to Mrs. Barton's death during a miscarriage, depresses Mary's mother a great deal, but does not prevent her from entertaining family friends at a tea party. When Alice Wilson, a very old, well-meaning, but absentminded woman, proposes a toast "to absent friends," Mrs. Barton "put down her food, and could not hide the fast dropping tears. Alice could have bitten her tongue out" (53). This blunder breaks up the party, and prompts "the self-reproaching Alice" to apologize to Mrs. Barton, who surprises and delights her by embracing, forgiving, and blessing her, promptly and openly. "Many and many a time, as Alice reviewed that evening in her after life, did she bless Mary Barton for these kind and thoughtful words" (54). A simple instance of compassion suspended and renewed among friends, the scene illustrates the healing power that sympathy and forgiveness can wield in the fictional world Gaskell depicts, even when they can make no material difference in the unhappy situation.

As the action becomes more involved with the dramatic repercussions of Harry Carson's murder, the instances of sympathy and forgiveness take on more significant thematic resonances. Just as Harry Carson's lack of sympathy for the working men inspires their plot to kill him, John Barton's depleted store of sympathy for the masters enables him to carry out the deed. While Mary travels to Jem's trial in Liverpool and remains in the port city in a catatonic state after the trial, John Barton wastes away in guilt at home in Manchester. After Mary and Jem return, her father calls them and Harry Carson's father together and confesses to the crime, asking Carson to forgive him. Not until he witnesses Carson's anguish at this moment does Barton look past his own guilty misery and sense of loss to see the effects of his act. He cries out to Carson,

> "My hairs are gray with suffering, and yours with years—"
> "And have I had no suffering?" asked Mr. Carson, as if appealing for sympathy, even to the murderer of his child.
> And the murderer of his child answered to the appeal, and groaned in spirit over the anguish he had caused. (434)

53

The point of the episode is to demonstrate Gaskell's earnest conviction that compassion can break down class barriers and the desire for revenge: "The eyes of John Barton grew dim with tears. Rich and poor, masters and men, were then brothers in the deep suffering of the heart; for was not this the very anguish he had felt for little Tom. . . . The mourner before him was no longer the employer . . . no longer the enemy, the oppressor, but a very poor, and desolate old man" (435). The spectacle of Barton's compassionate penitence at first appears to have no impact on the "desolate old man," who initially resists the appeal. But after witnessing a minor incident of trespass and forgiveness among two children on the street and after reviewing the Gospel account of Christ's plea that "they know not what they do," Carson joins Barton in sympathy and forgiveness. In a scene that is exuberantly melodramatic—which renders it no less consistent with or necessary to the novel's project—John Barton dies in the arms of his murder victim's father. Victimizer and victim come full circle, breaking the perpetuation of the cycle, each by recognizing his affinity with the other (an affinity that the novelist makes obvious even in the orthography of their names) and by acknowledging his own responsibility for the pain in the life of the other.

The novel's movement from realistic situations of distress into sensationalist excess finds a parallel in Gaskell's own emotional activity in writing the book. She could identify with the suffering of John Barton and his wife over the loss of their son, but she elaborates upon that pain, giving John heartrending memories about the circumstances of the boy's death: not only had little Tom, like Willie Gaskell, contracted scarlet fever, but he had become ill at a time when his father was laid off from work. Tantalized by the doctor's suggestions that luxurious foods and comfortable living might save the boy, John had lurked around a food shop contemplating a robbery, only to see his former master's wife come out of the store laden with extravagant purchases for a party. The narrator explains that John would have considered stealing food "no sin," a conclusion she implicitly endorses through the "ethic of care" that Carol Gilligan has identified at the core of feminine morality. Having no opportunity, however, John had returned home "to see his only boy a corpse" (61). In imagining this excruciating experience for John Barton, Gaskell was adding many layers of frustration, helplessness, envy, and revenge to the loss that she herself had felt so keenly.

The entire novel follows a similar train of amplification, moving from the simple moments of hurt among friends, to the more profound but still familiar pain of losing children, mothers, wives, and jobs, to the sudden, sweeping blow of Harry Carson's murder and all its sensational consequences for the young heroine. The opportunities for the characters to sympathize with one another—and for the willing reader to join them—become almost grotesque in their number and scale. If this is the "romance in the lives of some of those who elbowed [Gaskell] daily" in Manchester, it is not all that far from the outlandish story she might have set a century earlier and hundreds of miles away from that city.

Still, as the preface and many of the narrative interventions make clear, Gaskell took the difference between historical romance and social-problem novel seriously. If the plot exaggerates the characters' claims on the sympathies of the narratee, it does so for an explicitly rendered purpose. As the narrator remarks near the end of the tale:

> There are stages in the contemplation and endurance of great sorrow, which endow men with the same earnestness and clearness of thought that in some of old took the form of Prophecy. To those who have large capability of loving and suffering . . . there comes a time in their woe, when they are lifted out of the contemplation of their individual case into a searching inquiry into the nature of their calamity, and the remedy (if remedy there be) which may prevent its recurrence to others as well as to themselves. (459)

"If remedy there be": again, we are urged to recognize that Gaskell's novel endorses no particular political solution for the "calamity." The context of this thesis-statement within the text is Mr. Carson's gradual conversion to compassionate awareness of what John Barton has lived through; like Carson's spiritual transformation, the remark constitutes a gesture toward significance that would extend beyond the text. To inspire actual readers to that state of "earnestness and clearness of thought" where "they are lifted out of the contemplation of their individual" woes, to move readers to emulate her activity in identifying John Barton's suffering with her own—and her characters' activity in recognizing one another's unhappiness as a kindred link among them—Gaskell employs numerous engaging narrative interventions. Her narrator circumvents the difficulty of rendering a melodramatic plot realistic by encouraging the narratee to acknowledge the affinities between the story and the literally real. The first of her rhetorical moves in this direction is the narrator's consistent identification of her "I" with the actual author; the corollary move is her implication that "you," the narratee, stands for each actual reader.

THE ENGAGING NARRATIVE "I"

An essential characteristic of Gaskell's engaging narrator, then, is her candid and consistent depiction of herself holding a pen, creating the book. Through repeated references to her act of writing, she makes herself a concrete presence in the book; she is the narratee's friend and correspondent, who can be depended upon for generous interpretations of the characters' motives and of the narratee's own motives as well. She speaks directly, innocent of any self-consciousness about the danger of breaking into the illusion of reality her scenes might create. For instance, when Alice asks Mary's friend Margaret to sing "The Owdham Weaver," Gaskell's narrator shifts from her depiction of the scene in Alice's room to an acknowledgment of her own narrative responsibility to fill in the gaps in the narratees' information:

> With a faint smile, as if amused at Alice's choice of a song, Margaret began.
> Do you know "The Oldham Weaver"? Not unless you are Lancashire born and bred, for it is a complete Lancashire ditty. I will copy it for you. (71)

The narrator proceeds to do exactly what she proposes, and then comments on the tone of the old "ditty." Fearing that "to read it, it may, perhaps seem humorous," she assures her narratee that "to those who have seen the distress it describes, it is a powerfully pathetic song" (73). As a transition back to the narrative, she declares that Margaret has witnessed such distress, and continues with a description of Margaret's rendition of the ballad. An intervention like this, one of the many overjustifications that Gaskell's narrator employs, serves two strategic functions: it suggests a narratee with whom the vast majority of the actual readership (every reader who is not "Lancashire born and bred") can identify, and it depicts the narrator as a person *writing,* a person identified with, if not identical to, the author.

On other occasions the narrator similarly pictures herself at her writing desk. Explaining the interest that amateur botany holds for some Manchester workmen, she mentions a biography that describes their scientific enthusiasms: "If you will refer to the preface to Sir J. E. Smith's Life (I have it not by me, or I would copy you the exact passage), you will find that he names a little circumstance corroborative of what I have said" (76). *Mary Barton,* like all novels, is full of implicit intertextuality, especially in its allusions to other literary texts and traditions.[8] However, a specific reference to another text, the biography of Sir. J. E. Smith, in the form of a citation lends an unusual element of the real to this fiction. Because Smith's biography actually exists, and because Gaskell's narrator acknowledges that she could copy the passage for the convenience of the narratee, the intervention places both the narrator and the biography on a plane of existence where the narratee exists, too. The plane where the biography exists is the actual world; thus, by implication, the narrator and narratee exist there as well, in the forms of the author and the reader. In frequent comments on her way of telling the story, Gaskell reinforces the same implication. For example, she draws attention to her role as the source of the narratee's information when she confesses to having omitted pertinent information from her narrative, saying, "I must go back a little to explain the motives which caused Esther to seek an interview with her niece" (288). The identification between narrator and author is thus reinforced.

This narrator who manifests no desire to screen herself from the reader's attention could simply have been a sketchily realized fictional character, such as Mary Smith of *Cranford,* except that she gives herself no fictive name or circumstances; on the contrary, she places herself specifically in the author's particular situation. Describing the miserable, lonely night in Manchester that Mary Barton endures after realizing that her father has murdered Harry Carson, Gaskell comments on how little sympathy the "outward scene" of the city seems to manifest for Mary's "internal trouble":

> All was so still, so motionless, so hard! Very different to this lovely night in the country *in which I am now writing,* where the distant horizon is soft and undulating in the moonlight, and the nearer trees sway gently . . . and the rustling air makes music among their branches, as if speaking soothingly to the weary ones, who lie awake in heaviness of heart. The sights and sounds of such a night lull pain and grief to rest. (303, emphasis added)

The romantic argument on the surface of this intervention—that nature's beauties, unavailable to Mary in the city, can soothe internal pain in those who have access to them—does not contribute much to the narratee's understanding of Mary's state of mind, unless the actual reader happens to have experienced the soothing power the passage describes. What the intervention does, though, is create for the narratee a vivid picture of the author herself, seated comfortably in the country somewhere, gazing out a window and feeling a strong sense of contrast between Mary's circumstances and her own. Detailing the "sights and sounds of such a night," the narrator implies that her own "pain and grief" can be consoled by them. Whether or not the picture is biographically accurate (that is, whether or not Elizabeth Gaskell really wrote these lines in the circumstances she depicts), the intervention draws the narratee's attention to the figure of an author who, like the actual reader, lives in much more comfortable circumstances than the unfortunate characters do.

A later passage hints at the source of this narrator's unnamed grief, in an unusually personal intrusion. The paragraph describes Mary's fears that Jem's mother, who has fallen asleep after learning that she must testify against her adored son at his murder trial, may be driven mad "in the horrors of her dreams"(327). The disjointed prose mirrors Mary's own mental distress, but the long parenthetical interruption speaks with an "I" that cannot be Mary's.

> What if in dreams (that land into which no sympathy nor love can penetrate with another, either to shake its bliss or its agony,—that land whose scenes are unspeakable terrors, are hidden mysteries, are priceless treasures to one alone,—that land *where alone I may see, while I yet tarry here, the sweet looks of my dead child*)—what if, in the horrors of her dreams, her brain should go still more astray? (327, emphasis added)

Mary Barton has no child, alive or dead: the "I" is the narrator (who in this instance exactly resembles Gaskell herself) recalling dream visions of her own dead baby. The very personal pronoun here serves a double function in the passage. Not only can it be read as the narrator's specific reference to herself, but it also resembles the "I" of a lyric poem or a folk song: a persona with whom most readers or listeners can sympathize and identify in a general way. In this second sense the narrator's use of the pronoun "I" parallels her use of "one" in the preceding description of dreams as "priceless treasures to one alone." In shifting from that third-person observation to the personally voiced "I," however, the narrator once again prompts the narratee to attend to the presence of an author.

In addition to these personal reminders of Gaskell's presence behind the pen, her engaging narrator often refers to her own opinions and impressions, giving the reader a strong sense of the personality that narrates the novel.[9] The narrator openly displays her sympathy with the working people, her opinions about their plight, and her personal experience with them, citing these as her authority for writing the book. She is sometimes very definite in her assertions. She is positive, for example, that the poor have reasons to be dissatisifed, and that they deserve better. In one intervention that interrupts the story, she introduces a long catalogue of miserable conditions with an impassioned testimony that she has heard it all first-hand: "And when I hear, as I have heard, of the sufferings and privations of the poor . . .—can I wonder that many of them, in such times of misery and destitution, spoke and acted with ferocious precipitation?" (126–127). One goal of the novel is to ensure that, having read it, actual readers will also "have heard of the sufferings and privations of the poor."

Trying to circumvent possible objections that the picture she presents is unrealistically distorted, the narrator is particularly anxious to demonstrate her own distance from the conclusions her characters draw about their condition. While emphasizing her awareness that impoverished people have a limited understanding of economic conditions, she insists that the poor merit sympathy nevertheless. After describing John Barton's feeling that "he alone" must suffer from bad times, she interpolates a comment: "I know that this is not really the case; and I know what is the truth in such matters: but what I wish to impress is what the workman feels and thinks. True, that with child-like improvidence, good times will often dissipate his grumbling, and make him forget all prudence and foresight" (60). This aside, like the narrator's depiction of her own serenely comfortable surroundings, functions to establish the narrator and narratee as middle-class observers who regard the working man as an unfortunately inferior "other." Understandably, the passage has been cited as evidence of the narrator's self-satisifed condescension to the class she writes about: David Smith observes, on the strength of this passage, that Gaskell "can never escape the patronizing tone of the Health Visitor" (103). The rhetoric of the passage does

59

condescend to its object (the working man), but functions to solidify the link between the speaking subject (the narrator's "I") and the intended receiver of the text. The "I know . . . and I know" construction works in two ways: in second-guessing the narratee's objection to Barton's feeling, it sketches out the narratee's middle-class assumptions and demonstrates the narrator's familiarity with those assumptions; at the same time, the construction of the intervention establishes the narrator's authority as an even-handed, open-minded figure who speaks on behalf of the working class without belonging to it. The strategy enables her to follow up this intervention with confident assertions such as: "The vices of the poor sometimes astound us *here;* but when the secrets of all hearts shall be made known, their virtues will astound us in far greater degree. Of this I am certain" (96).

Whereas the content of such interventions places a barrier of difference between the middle-class narrator and narratee and the working-class characters, Gaskell's narrative stance simultaneously operates to overcome that barrier by insisting that characters, narrator, and narratee all populate the same world, the "real world" of nineteenth-century England. The engaging narrator takes advantage of her confident, assertive side by commenting about the characters as if she were discussing real people. In one such scene, where Mary decides not to speak to Jem in jail about establishing his legitimate alibi, Gaskell brings Mary's thoughts around to the realization that she would not be permitted to see Jem, even if she tried to. Then Gaskell skips again from Mary's thoughts to assess the heroine's feelings: "and even if she could have gone to him, I believe she would not" (312). To bring in this hypothetical possibility, to state a belief about what a character would or would not do, and to personalize that belief by saying "I," is certainly to employ metalepsis in the extradiegetic narrator's stance toward a fictional character. During the same scene, the narrator yokes Mary with herself in their common fear of subpoenas, suggesting that author and character inhabit the same reality: "Many people have a dread of those mysterious pieces of parchment. I am one. Mary was another" (313). The narrator, who has consistently linked herself with the real-world Elizabeth Gaskell, here transports Mary Barton to that same real-world plane of "many people."

Although the narrative "I" is definite in her opinions about some issues, her assertions more often falter, as she expresses doubts about her grasp of the facts that she must narrate and insecurity about her ability to transmit those facts accurately to the narratee. This hesitant attitude is more characteristic of Gaskell's engaging narrator than is her more confident side and serves rhetorically to reinforce the implication that the real world and the fictional may be identical. The doubts the narrator so frequently and candidly expresses are her own acknowledgment that her vision is subjective, her judgment fallible, and her talent limited. By emphasizing her subjectivity, the narrator also implies that she is reporting events that are "true," and therefore open to subjective interpretation.

Gaskell's insistence that she doesn't have all the "facts" suggests that facts exist, even though she claims they are out of her grasp. For instance, of a workman's day off, she writes, "I do not know whether it was on a holiday granted by the masters, or a holiday seized in the right of nature and her beautiful spring time by the workmen" (40). Similarly, she claims not to know all the facts about Mary's friendship with Margaret: "I do not know what points of resemblance (or dissimilitude, for the one joins people as often as the other) attracted the two girls to each other" (79–80). She sometimes "confesses" to not knowing the exact physical occurrences of a scene, as when she describes a collision among pedestrians: "I don't know how it was, but in some awkward way he knocked the poor little girl down upon the hard pavement" (437). At other times, she sets limits to her ability to read characters' thoughts. She summarizes the feelings of Mr. Carson during the night before Jem's trial, emphasizing that "until he had obtained vengeance," Mr. Carson could not rest. But then she pulls herself up, in a parenthetical aside: "I don't know that he exactly used the term vengeance in his thoughts; he spoke of justice, and probably thought of his desired end as such" (381).

Strictly, such disclaimers are nonsense, or even lies. (P. N. Furbank, arguing from the bizarre premise that the "truth" about characters' motives is not only determinable, but provable against a narrator's assertions, has dubbed Gaskell "the poet of mendacity" for her reliance on this kind of narrative prevarication.[10]) Of course the narrator could supply these facts if the author chose for her to, by inventing them along with the rest of the story. And the disclaimers are not, by any means, completely consistent: when she does choose to, the extradiegetic narrator is perfectly capable of reading characters' thoughts. But because the author does not choose to invent every detail—and because the narrator draws the narratee's attention to this choice—the narrative has the air of being one fallible observer's account of actual events.

Her expressed doubts about the facts of the story would seem to separate the voice of the narrator from that of the author, or the entity responsible for creating the "givens" of the story as well as for rendering it in discourse. This is offset, though, by other engaging remarks, which establish the narrator's doubts about her ability to achieve accuracy in the novel. These particular disclaimers of omniscience refer more directly than other interventions to Gaskell herself, because they describe the limitations of her knowledge on extra-fictional matters and reflect her own expressed lack of confidence in herself as an all-knowing novelist. In these interventions, the narrator is quick to acknowledge her own confusion, as when she makes a generalization about "the Jews, or Mohammedans (I forget which)" (132), or when she describes Mary's discovery of her father's "bullets or shot (I don't know which you would call them)" (300). When she could attribute the lack of knowledge to a character, the narrator still takes the responsibility for slight gaps in the narrative, as in the scene in Liverpool in which Mary listens, bewildered, to sailors' speech that she cannot understand. Mary hears "slang, which to [her] was almost inaudible, and quite unintelligible, and which I am too much of a land-lubber to repeat correctly" (352). A self-effacing narrator could have omitted any extended mention of the slang, since the scene is focalized through Mary's perspective and the speech does not enter her consciousness. But the narrator specifically reminds us of her own presence, in order to ally herself with Mary in her ignorance and fear of the sea and to intensify the narratee's awareness of reading a text that has been created by a fallible (that is, human and therefore possibly real) person.

Added to these confessions of limited knowledge, the narrator's self-deprecating comments on her ability to tell the story intensify her subjective pose. On the first page of the novel she chooses to deprecate her own descriptive abilities, conveying the "charming" effect, rather than the exact appearance, of a stile that figures in the opening scene. The narrator gives some details of sight and sound in this rural setting, but interrupts with a passage addressed directly to the narratee; "You cannot wonder, then, that these fields are popular places of resort at every holiday time; and you would not wonder, if you could see, or I properly describe, the charm of one particular stile, that it should be, on such occasions, a crowded halting-place" (39). Gaskell's confession of her inability to describe the stile's appearance serves as both a compliment to the reader's power of imagination and a slight to her narrator's power of description. Gaskell usually appeals directly to "you" in passages that serve this double function, as when she instructs the narratee to "picture to yourself (for I cannot tell you)" Mary's tumultuous thoughts (329); similarly, she avoids attempting a potentially unsuccessful description of Mr. Carson's strong feelings, asking "how shall I tell you the vehemence of passion which possessed the mind of poor Mr. Carson?" (396). The cumulative effect of such expressions of doubt is to underline the implication that the characters' feelings and the story's events are real, and therefore that confident narrative assertions about them would necessarily be oversimplified, subjectively biased, or otherwise flawed.

Although, as I have mentioned, Gaskell's narrator treats the characters as though they were real people, she seldom goes so far as to claim personal acquaintance with them, and is vague about the sources of her definite information. Nevertheless, two comments—both occurring in the courtroom scene, a setting that evokes questions about "evidence"—suggest that the engaging narrator places herself within the characters' world. The metaleptic effect of these comments is more emphatic than it would be if the narrator were to place herself more consistently (for instance, as a fellow character) in the world of the fiction. When Jem's mother enters the witness-box, the narrator digresses into a brief explanation of her epithets for Mrs. Wilson: "I have often called her 'the old woman', and 'an old woman', because, in truth, her appearance was so much beyond her years, which might not be many above fifty. But partly owing to her accident in early life, . . . partly owing to her anxious temper, partly to her sorrows, and partly to her limping gait, she always gave me the idea of age" (385–386). Anxious to demonstrate her firsthand knowledge of Mrs. Wilson, the engaging narrator defends her term, "the old woman," on the grounds that the "real" Jane Wilson gave her the impression of being old. At the same time, the narrator does not place herself at the scene, as her disclaimer of being present at the trial indicates: "I was not there myself; but one who was, told me" (389). The stance of the engaging narrator is a tenuous mixture of knowing and doubting, of inhabiting the fictional world and of remaining invisible. This narrator offers no answers for the technical questions that were later to be tackled by the narrators of impressionist fiction, questions such as How do I know what I claim to know? and Why should my reader believe me? In this sense, Gaskell's narrative technique could have had a highly distancing effect, inspiring actual readers to turn such questions against the persuasive intentions of this sometimes confident, sometimes dubious narrator.

ENGAGING STRATEGIES AND "YOU"

The effect of all these narrative interventions could have been to prompt the actual reader to recognize a distance between the real world and the fictional one, or to intensify the actual reader's sense of the story as fictive. But the narrator manipulates her direct address to the narratee in order to subvert that distancing effect. In her stance toward the reader, the narrator places "you" on the same plane of reality that she herself occupies, a plane which, she seems to suggest, could place "you" within the world of the fiction—hypothetically, at least. The narrator never challenges the narratee to admit to having been present at any of the story's events, but by using subjunctive phrases to describe the reader's probable reactions, she suggests that "your" presence *could* have been possible. For instance, the narrator posits the reader's hypothetical presence at Mary's unhappy vigil after her refusal of Jem's proposal: "She could not have told at first (if you had asked her, and she could have commanded voice enough to answer)" (176). The narrator's parenthetical remark encourages the reader to imagine himself or herself at Mary's side, in a position to question or comfort her. The narrator similarly places the reader at the scene of John Barton's confession: "Your heart would have ached to have seen the man, however hardly you might have judged his crime" (422). Again the appeal aims at the narratee's imaginative sympathy: the narrator asks the actual reader to forget for the moment that he or she is reading. Significantly, she does not even address the narratee as "reader," but uses only "you." The narrative strategy here encourages actual readers to picture themselves in the scenes that the narrator's descriptions have evoked in their minds.

And this engaging narrator quite often speaks to "you." She frequently refers very openly to information she has previously related that the actual reader could have forgotten: such phrases as "the shelf I told you about" (66), "you remember the reward?" (273), "as you know" (363), or "the facts were as well know to most of the audience as they are to you" (384) all reinforce the narratee's sense of the story's being conveyed through the medium of narrative. Rather than merely stating facts or descriptions, the narrator often asks the narratee to participate in the creation of scenes, asking, "Can you fancy the bustle. . . . can you fancy the delight?" (67), or "Do you not perceive?" (80). She calls upon the narratee's mental images of common objects, as when she refers to "that sort of striped horsecloth you must have seen a thousand times" (300). In addition to these appeals for imaginative participation in the narrative, she often reminds "you" that she speaks directly to "you." The novel is sprinkled with such phrases as "you may be sure" (443), "If you think this account of mine confused" (413), and "I must tell you; I must put into words the dreadful secret" (299). If the actual reader were to take these pronouns seriously and personally, he or she would experience an intensified sense that the novel is a personal act of communication between Elizabth Gaskell and "you."

Of course, Gaskell's narrator sometimes uses "you" in the conventional sense that actually means "one." An example of this usage occurs in an aside that is not necessarily directed to the individual, actual reader. A character says, "Well-a-well," and the narrator amplifies, "(in a soothing tone, such as you use to irritated children)" (376). Not everyone speaks to irritated children in a soothing tone; not every actual reader could identify with this "you" as he or she could with the receiver of a remark such as "I must tell you." Though this infrequent usage of "you" to mean "one" is less personal than other uses of that pronoun in the novel's interventions, it is also more informal than the more polite "one" would have been. The casual tone converts even Gaskell's truisms into partly personal remarks. Consider, for instance, how different the effect of this exhortation would have been, had the narrator substituted "one" for "you": "It is a great truth, that you cannot extinguish violence, by violence. You may put it down for a time, but while you are crowing over your imaginary success, see if it does not return with seven devils worse than its former self!" (232). Gaskell evidently wants each reader to consider his or her personal responsibility to the people represented by the characters in the novel, as her narrator's use of "you" in order to personalize general observations bears witness.

When Gaskell's narrator uses the word "we," then, she is including the author herself and the actual reader in that plural pronoun, often implicitly linking author and reader with the novel's characters.[11] Her use of "we" underlines how much the narratee and the actual reader have in common with the speaker, as well as with those of whom she speaks. Describing the anxiety that preoccupies all the travellers en route to the Assizes in Liverpool, the narrator remarks that their emotional state says "little or nothing" about them in particular, "for we are all of us in the same predicament through life. Each with a fear and a hope from childhood to death" (343). Gaskell's strategy is similar when she writes that "you and I, and almost everyone, I think, may send up our individual cry of self-reproach" (328). Such generalizations embrace Mary Barton, as well as the narratee and the actual reader, reminding the receivers of the text that Mary and her kind inhabit a common plane of humanity with the narrator and themselves.

At times, Gaskell's narrator implicitly excludes the poor from her "we," subtly indicating that her intended audience is comfortable and well-fed, without her having to address them specifically as such. Of Mr. Carson's servants, who fail to offer a hungry workman any of their plentiful food, she says, "they were like the rest of us, and not feeling hunger themselves, forgot it was possible another might" (106). The scene and its commentaries are reminders of the purpose of reading a social-problem novel: so that a complacent bourgeoisie does not forget that working people might experience physical strain which the middle classes have no occasion to share, as well as feeling emotional strains with which they could identify. Gaskell's tone in such passages is consistent with the sympathetic, confidential attitude she has established in her relations with the narratee. Capitalizing on the strong links her engaging direct address has attempted to establish between the narratee and herself, she again uses the pronoun "we" as she confronts the reader with the central moral question of the first, more realistic portion of the novel: "The people rise up to life; they irritate us, they terrify us, and we become their enemies. Then, in the sorrowful moment of our triumphant power, their eyes gaze on us with a mute reproach. Why have we made them what they are; a powerful monster, yet without the inner means for peace and happiness?" (220). The reproach she levels at herself and at us is far from being "mute," but the passage certainly draws the narratee's attention to the narrator's sad, steady gaze as she awaits the actual reader's looked-for response: emotional commitment to improve the lot of the poor, to give them that "inner means for peace and happiness" by expressing (and not only by experiencing) compassion for them.

For the arousal of the actual reader's sympathy is the declared aim of the book. Although the tension of the melodramatic trial plot may be effectively riveting, that part of the novel tends to deflect the particular kind of active empathy that Gaskell wanted most explicitly to evoke. The narratee may be presumed to hold his or her breath throughout the trial scene, to pity the catatonic Mary, and to rejoice with the triumphant Jem, but these characters' problems, strongly within the tradition of Gothic romance, end with the narrative. They flee the Old World, leaving behind Jem's tainted reputation, the reminders of John Barton's crime, and the place Carlyle called "sooty Manchester." Jem's merit enables their emigration to Canada, where he takes a respectable foreman's job and becomes a solid member of the very middle class to whom the novel is addressed. The end of the story runs counter to the urgent message with which the novel began: within the world of the fiction, all of the main characters are either dead or comfortably settled even though the actual reader did nothing more (and possibly less) than experience sympathy for them; the reader need take no further action in order to be able to experience the gratification of seeing the characters' suffering end at last. This is, of course, the limitation of all rhetoric as a means of intervention in real-world problems: because a novel is only a text, it cannot exert any material power over the actual reader. On the level of story, though, *Mary Barton* makes it manifestly clear that sympathetic intervention in unhappy circumstances can improve the emotional state of a sufferer, for the story's closure follows from the individual acts of sympathy and forgiveness that accumulate throughout the plot. On the level of discourse, too, the engaging narrator's own interventions attempt to wake the reader up to the necessity of transferring his or her sympathy from the characters to their counterparts in the real world.

Perhaps the definitive example of an engaging narrative intervention in *Mary Barton* is a passage among those first realistic chapters, where the narrator insists that the actual reader should project some compassionate imagination upon his or her understanding of the lives of the poor, both in the novel and in the world. The passage echoes Gaskell's declaration in her preface that she "bethought me how deep might be the romance" in the lives of people she met on the street; here, she asks readers to place themselves in that same position and to consider what some specific possibilities for that romance might be:

> But [Barton] could not, you cannot, read the lot of those who daily pass you by in the street. How do you know the wild romances of their lives; the trials, the temptations they are even now enduring, resisting, sinking under? You may be elbowed one instant by the girl desperate in her abandonment, laughing in mad merriment with her outward gesture, while her soul is longing for the rest of the dead, and bringing itself to think of the cold-flowing river as the only mercy of God remaining to her here. You may pass the criminal, meditating crimes at which you will to-morrow shudder with horror as you read them. You may push against one, humble and unnoticed, the last upon earth, who in Heaven will for ever be in the immediate light of God's countenance. Errands of mercy—errands of sin—did you ever think where all the thousands of people you daily meet are bound? (101–102)

The "wild romances" to which the narrator refers here represent little more than the condition of being human in a nineteenth-century urban environment. The open-endedness of the possibilities she predicts for the narratee ("you *may* be elbowed," "you *may* pass," "you *may* push") resists closure in a distinctively engaging way: these are not assertions of experiences that actual readers must have had in order to identify with the "you" being addressed, but are only suggestions for what could conceivably occur to anyone in Gaskell's intended audience. The intervention sketches out a model for ways in which the actual reader could imaginatively project life-histories onto the strangers he or she does encounter. Although such projections would bring the actual reader no closer to knowing the realities of the strangers' lives, it would at least place the strangers in the same category as the novel's characters: they are to be seen as real people, with feelings and lives that could command the actual reader's sympathetic attention. The use of "you" in this passage—in addition to the examples of the types "you" may encounter in the real (as well as the fictional) world—demonstrates the engaging narrator's attempt to extend what Elizabeth Meese calls (in another context) "the play of the signifier beyond the text." [12]

GASKELL AND HER READERS: ABANDONING
INTERVENTION

To skip from *Mary Barton* to Gaskell's late novels is to see engaging narrative strategies disappear from her work. Her later fictions rely on other, more conventionally established strategies for creating verisimilitude and the most sympathetic of Gaskell's critics have traditionally seen this shift in technique as a sign of her improving her novelistic art.[13] Edgar Wright, for instance, makes a case for "reassessing" Gaskell as a serious novelist whose techniques developed in their sophistication over the course of her career; according to him, "the most important development is probably in the gradual shift away from use of authorial commentary" (18). Gaskell never articulated any theories of literary art, nor did she write or speak directly about her practicing narrative interventions, so we can only speculate about whether she considered the reduction in direct address an improvement over her early techniques. However, if we look at narrative discourse not as the product of "artistic intention" or "mastery of technique," but rather as the result of an author's choices about the relations she hopes to establish between her text and her actual readers, we can trace Gaskell's abandonment of engaging interventions to a loss of faith in their efficacy. It came about through a loss of faith in her readers.

Gaskell's shift in assumptions about her readers can be glimpsed in a letter she wrote to her friend Charles Eliot Norton in 1858, ten years after *Mary Barton* was published. In 1853 she had published *Cranford,* with its minimally characterized, first-person narrator, and *Ruth,* which employs a consistently engaging, extradiegetic narrator resembling *Mary Barton*'s. After *Ruth,* she had written *North and South,* which is entirely devoid of direct address to a narratee, for serialization in Dickens's *Household Words* in 1854–1855. Her *Life of Charlotte Brontë* had appeared in 1857. As far as Gaskell was concerned, the biography was strictly true, and she let the "facts" speak for themselves: the *Life,* too, contains no remarks directed to "you." In her letter to Norton, Gaskell speaks of a painful awareness that was preventing her from thinking too concretely about her readers as she wrote:

> I *can* not (it is not *will* not) write at all if I ever think of my readers, and what impression I am making on them. "If they don't like me, they must lump me," to use a Lancashire proverb.

It is from no despising my readers. I am sure I don't do that, but
if I ever let the thought or consciousness of them come between
me and my subject I *could* not write at all. (*Letters* 503)

"From no despising" her readers, perhaps, but rather from having learned
to suspect their lack of sympathy, she had come to refrain from continuing
the overt conversation between narrator and narratee in her later work.

This attitude could be connected with the vehemence of the criticism
of *Ruth,* a sympathetic fictional account of a highly idealized unwed
mother. Enraged readers (or a public that pretended to have read it) burnt
the book, denouncing Gaskell as an improper woman because of her choice
of heroine. The attack was similar to that which Harriet Beecher Stowe had
just suffered for *Uncle Tom's Cabin,* but Gaskell had less resilience than the
American author, and the letters of praise that she finally received for *Ruth*
did little to reassure her. As Winifred Gerin writes of Gaskell, "She was far
too sensitive to people's opinion, to blame or praise, not to be deeply
bruised by the public nature of [*Ruth's*] condemnation; she was crushed by
the news of Bell's Library withdrawing it from circulation, and by the
personal tone of such reviews as the *Literary Gazette* which deplored her 'loss
of reputation'" (139).

Though Gaskell insisted that in spite of the painful criticism, she
"would do every jot of it over again tomorrow," (Gerin 139), the experience
appears to have left its mark on her narrative technique. When she was new
to writing novels and hadn't yet tested her audience's responsiveness, both
to her narrative interventions and to her implicit endorsement of "interventionism," she had been able to try to establish an open, personal, earnest
communion among author, narrator, characters, and reader. *Mary Barton*
had drawn a sympathetic public response, on the whole, but *Mary Barton* is
half romance, and never trespasses beyond the bounds of Victorian "moral"
propriety in its treatment of the heroine. Ironically, Gaskell could employ
her engaging narrator in realist fiction only as long as she could maintain for
herself a fictive idea of what her audience would be like. The reading public
had betrayed her engaging narrator's faith that actual readers would live up
to her narratees' generous capacity for imaginative compassion. Perhaps,
after that disappointment, Gaskell felt the need to shield herself from the
thought of the disapproving or hard-hearted actual reader, and thus chose
to stop making direct narrative appeals to a sympathy she could no longer

be sure would respond. Gaskell's answer was simply to stop intervening in her narratives, apparently because she was convinced that intervention of this kind would not work.

There was, of course, another strategic option available to the novelist who assumed failings on the part of narratees and actual readers: the distancing narrator, who sets up flawed narratees to tease and taunt them, to shame actual readers out of identifying with them. Distancing strategies, which tended to undermine the rhetorical goals of realism, may have been too metafictional to be useful to Gaskell. Furthermore, in the 1840s the distancing narrator was a strategy associated with male-written texts, as a close look at the interventions in Thackeray's *Vanity Fair* and Kingsley's *Yeast* will show.

4

Distancing Strategies, Irony, and Metafiction:

Yeast and *Vanity Fair*

CHARLES KINGSLEY'S name is probably not among the first to come to mind in a discussion about nineteenth-century novelists and metafiction. This Anglican minister—whose demeanor while delivering lectures in history to Cambridge undergraduates was "grave as a church and earnest as an owl" (Huxley 113),[1] whose commitment to Christian Socialism and radical principles of reform was serious enough to impede his preferment to a bishopric (Huxley 28), and whose first two novels reflected his outrage at the inequities of the English class system—seems, at first glance, to be unlikely company for Thackeray in an arrangement of mid-century novelists. Kingsley has long held the reputation of an eminently earnest Victorian novelist.

Indeed, George Eliot, who claimed that her "dominant feeling toward [Kingsley's] work in general is that of high admiration" (*Essays* 132), objected to the novelist's "perpetual hortative tendency." As she put it in a review of one of Kingsley's later novels, "He can never trust to the impression the scene itself will make on you, but true to his cloth, must always 'improve the occasion'" (*Essays* 126). Eliot confessed that she would have liked Kingsley's novels better had he avoided his often illogical "hobbyhorse" (128) and had he not made of each character "a text to preach from" (129). What Eliot's review calls Kingsley's "parsonic habit" (129) in narration characterizes the image of Kingsley as novelist that survives in criticism today.

THE "MASCULINE CHRISTIAN" AND INTERVENTION

For all his personal and parsonic earnestness, though, Kingsley also stands as an emblem of the "muscular" or "masculine" Christian of his era. The traditionally heroic ideals he propounded in his later historical romances, the militaristic patriotism he evinced in his writings on the Crimean War, the outspoken stand he repeatedly took against the dangers of celibacy (which he feared would spread with Catholicism and Tractarianism), his devotion to outdoor sport (especially shooting and fishing) and to the gentlemanly hobby of naturalistic study, his habit of grasping a scythe or pick and pitching in to work alongside his parishioners—all point to his public self-portrayal as a strongly masculine clergyman. His narrative techniques in his first "novel of protest," *Yeast* (1848), are gendered masculine, too. In the narrator's ironic stance and in the novel's frequent excursions out of realistic conventions into highly literary self-consciousness, *Yeast* provides a revealing contrast to *Mary Barton*.[2]

In their origins, *Yeast* and *Mary Barton* (which was published during the same year that *Yeast* was being serialized in *Fraser's Magazine*) have much in common. Both are their authors' first novels. Both address contemporary class inequities, and both depict tragic consequences for upper-middle-class families who neglect their "duty" to the impoverished classes. Both make some reference to Chartism (though *Alton Locke,* Kingsley's second and last novel of protest, more closely resembles *Mary Barton* on this count). Both (unlike *Alton Locke*) have extradiegetic narrators. And both authors took their inspiration from firsthand observation of the living conditions of the poor. Kingsley the clergyman—like Gaskell the clergyman's wife—had become familiar with cottagers living in conditions squalid enough to satisfy the reforming zeal of a Dorothea Brooke; although direct financial intervention in their troubles was beyond his very limited means, he was to argue for reforms ranging from Chartism to public sanitation throughout his career.

Yeast dramatizes Kingsley's concern for various causes by tracing a luxury-loving dilettante's progress as he falls in love, begins to recognize the "condition of the poor," comes to know an admirable gamekeeper, loses his own fortune, and finds Christian faith. The hero's beloved fiancée dies, from a fever contracted while visiting impoverished tenants on her family's land, but the hero escapes England for a paradise even more remote than

Jem Wilson and Mary Barton's retreat in Canada: accompanied by his faithful gamekeeper friend, he follows a "prophet" to a fictional utopia. The story resembles *May Barton* in its depiction of wretched conditions, its rendition of political and religious debates among characters, its attention to relations among the classes, and its resorting to subplots of romantic love, as well as in its conclusion.

Yeast has commanded less attention than *Mary Barton* from readers and critics alike. Not a best-seller in its own day, it has enjoyed no revival of the sort that the gynocritical revolution has brought about for Gaskell's novels. What little criticism of *Yeast* there is has focused mainly on the novel's content as an indicator of its author's political or religious positions.[3] Probably no one would venture to argue that *Yeast* is a carefully crafted novel; indeed, the circumstances under which Kingsley wrote it militated against painstaking craftsmanship. He composed the final chapters, as his most recent biographer says, "under great strain," simultaneously writing, running his parish at Eversley without a curate, commuting to London on the train once a week to lecture young women on Early English Literature at Queen's College, and maintaining an overwhelming correspondence with strangers seeking his spiritual and practical advice. Worse, the editors at *Fraser's* requested Kingsley to speed up the ending during the novel's serialization because so many readers found the work objectionable. Finishing the novel brought Kingsley to a state of collapse that was to last a year, during which he could neither write, read, nor talk without exhausting himself (Chitty 112–118). Critics seeking examples of aesthetic perfection in form or style have dismissed *Yeast* as an obviously flawed piece of work. But looking at it from a descriptive, rather than an evaluative, position reveals a social-problem novel that treats issues very similar to those in *Mary Barton* while establishing a relation between text and reader that is quite different. For Charles Kingsley was a minister, while Elizabeth Gaskell was (only) a minister's wife; whereas she was writing as a woman, he was emphatically writing as a man.

Writing, as Kingsley did, for serialization in a magazine, the editor and audience of which were unenthusiastic about the work, probably contributed to the establishment of a different kind of author-reader relationship from the one that dominates Gaskell's first novel. Whereas Gaskell's narrator expresses a confidence in her narratee's sympathy which she was not to lose until later in her novelistic career, Kingsley was producing install-ments with the knowledge that not only the public but even his most respected colleagues disliked what he was writing.[4] The tone the narrator takes toward "my dear readers" is understandably exasperated by the time he gets to the epilogue, which collapses the novel's denouement in a re-markably discursive account of the flaws the narrator expects readers to find in the novel (364). Even more salient in the context of this study, though, is the stance Kingsley's narrator takes in the early installments of *Yeast,* before he could predict readers' responses with such glum certainty. Like Gaskell's narrator, Kingsley's frequently intervenes, and his interventions (like hers) often address narratees directly. But unlike the narrator of *Mary Barton,* the narrator of *Yeast* is seldom, if ever, "engaging."

To sketch out the difference: Gaskell's engaging narrator never names her narratee anything other than "you"; Kingsley's distancing narrator addresses groups such as "fair ladies" (72) or narrows down his designation of "you" to "reader" (19, 42, 96, 147). Gaskell's engaging narrator always speaks directly to "you," never referring to"the reader" in the third person; Kingsley's distancing narrator speaks *about* "my reader(s)" (18, 20, 40, 41, 173, 269) more often than he speaks *to* "you, reader." The most signifi-cant difference, however, is the contrast between the two narrators' atti-tudes toward readers, characters, and the act of writing a novel. Whereas Gaskell's engaging strategy leads her to treat readers and characters as though they were equally real while insisting upon the veracity of what she writes, Kingsley's distancing approach draws the narratee's attention re-peatedly to the fictionality of the characters and the literary nature of the text. Kingsley's intentions may have been as solemn as Gaskell's, and his commitment to political reform even more earnest than hers: nevertheless, his novel-with-a-purpose presents itself as being a text that is explicitly "about" its own textuality.

YEAST ON *YEAST*: PROTEST FICTION AS METALITERATURE

This self-conscious literariness surfaces most often in *Yeast* in two kinds of narrative interventions: explicit comments about the conventions of writing fiction, and ironic claims (sometimes separated by brackets from the narrative proper) about the author's procedure in composing this novel. The narrative tone is set with an example of the first type. *Yeast* opens with a curiously metaliterary paragraph that firmly establishes the narrator's function as the framer of the story: "As this my story will probably run counter to more than one fashion of the day, literary and other, it is prudent to bow to those fashions wherever I honestly can; and therefore to begin with a scrap of description" (1). The ensuing description runs briefly through a country landscape, a few local personages, and the hero, Lancelot Smith, but soon stops short for another comment on current writing conventions:

> But what is a description, without a sketch of the weather?—In these Pantheist days especially, when a hero or heroine's moral state must entirely depend on the barometer, and authors talk as if Christians were cabbages, and a man's soul as well as his lungs might be saved by sea-breezes and sunshine . . . we must have a weather-description. (2)

Ironically (and perhaps, at this point, predictably), the narrator postpones the weather description for two and a half pages more, embarking first on a satirical transcript of a weather-diary Lancelot kept in his youth and then giving a brief history of the hero's tastes in reading. After a couple of mock-formal apostrophes ("Draw, draw the veil and weep, guardian angel!" [4]; "O fathers! fathers! and you, clergymen, who monopolize education!" [5]), the narrator pulls himself up once again: "But where is my description of the weather all this time?" (5).

Nor do these Shandean shenanigans end with the novel's opening pages. Later in the first chapter, the narrator still hesitates to commit himself to a description ("Up, into the labyrinthine bosom of the hills,—but who can describe them? Is not all nature indescribable?" [14]). And, throughout the novel, the narrator subscribes to the literary convention that challenges the power of language to transmit visual images. After a detailed, two-page delineation of one of Lancelot's sketches, the narrator remarks, "Descriptions of drawings are clumsy things at best; the reader must fill up the sketch for himself by the eye of faith" (175).

In light of so much narrative game playing, one might well wonder: Faith in what? Evidently, the narrator is not referring to anything like faith in the fiction's veracity. These last two interventions resemble Gaskell's narrative observation on the setting of *Mary Barton*'s opening scene, which would move readers "if you could see or I properly describe" it. Both narrators draw attention to their responsibility for rendering the setting in language, but nowhere does Gaskell draw comparisons between her own activity and that of other literary voices, as Kingsley so pointedly does in his novel's very first paragraph. While Gaskell's engaging narrator asks the narratee to draw mental comparisons between the contents of her text and the extra-novelistic world, Kingsley's narrator openly invites comparisons between his text and other texts. This strategy of underlining the novel's status as one among many literary constructs, one that presents itself as resisting prevailing fashions in literature just as it challenges bourgeois fashions in politics, establishes a distancing narrative stance that implies: This novel, like other texts, is a fictional construction; this is not real.

Kingsley's narrator reinforces this suggestion with the second kind of intervention I have mentioned, asides that remark upon his narrative choices in constructing this story. These are sometimes marked as intrusions by Kingsley's unusual habit of placing them in brackets to set them apart from the progress of the story. Still in the vein of Sterne, the narrator interpolates an ironic observation: "[Here, for the sake of the reader, we omit, or rather postpone, a long dissertation on the famous Erototheogonic chorus of Aristophanes's birds, with illustrations taken from . . . the Vedas and Proclus to Jacob Boëme and Saint Theresa]" (18); the irony is, of course, that the postponed dirty joke never recurs. An even more pointedly metaliterary example occurs in a longish bracketed paragraph in which the narrator exhibits the parallels between his heroine, Argemone Lavington, and a character in a Tennyson poem. Within this aside, Kingsley's narrator pretends to confess; "[I should have honored myself by pleading guilty to stealing much of Argemone's character from *The Princess,* had not the idea been conceived, and fairly worked out, long before the appearance of that noble poem]" (31)

The reference to Tennyson is not the only instance of the narrator's defending himself against presumed charges of plagiarism. In a more serious vein, he places his hero in a squalid scene where Lancelot wanders "from farm to hamlet, and from field to tramper's tent," in hopes of "finding out . . . for himself" the answer to the "Condition-of-the-Poor question" (132). "Hopeless and bewildered" by the accounts he has read in "blue books, red books, sanitary reports, mine reports, factory reports," Lancelot decides to look into the matter personally. The narrator remarks,

> What he saw, of course I must not say; for if I did the reviewers would declare, as usual, one and all, that I copied out of the *Morning Chronicle;* and the fact that these pages, ninety-nine hundredths of them at least, were written two years before the *Morning Chronicle* began its invaluable investigations would be contemptuously put aside as at once impossible and arrogant. I shall therefore only say, that he saw what every one else has seen.
> (132–133)

Never mind that the claim of having written 99 percent of "these pages" over two years ago contradicts Kingsley's biographer's account of the novelist's frantically composing the installments at the last minute to meet deadlines: no narrator can be held accountable for failing to speak the author's literal truth. Consider the rhetorical strategy of this passage, though. As in the evocation of Tennyson, the narrator does not defend his portrayal on the basis that it is drawn from life; his defense rests instead on the claim that he wrote it (or in the case of Argemone, "conceived" and "worked [it] out") *before* he read other written versions of similar material. Predicting that the novel will be criticized for being derivative, the narrator makes claims for the literary originality of his work without making claims for its authenticity. On the contrary, he closes the scene of Lancelot's investigations with another resort to a literary parallel: "He at last ended by a sulky acquiescence in Sam Weller's memorable dictum: 'Who it is I can't say; but all I can say is, that *somebody* ought to be wopped for this!'" (133). Argemone resembles the "Princess," and Lancelot feels the way Sam Weller feels, because—the narrative stance seems to suggest—these figures are creatures of fiction.

Yeast's rhetorical insistence on its own fictional status is logically inconsistent with the intended function of a novel of protest: if the characters are, as the narrator calls them, "my puppets" (367), then the world they inhabit must be a puppet stage and the social problems they encounter might be no more real than the characters are. One of the features that renders this novel's narrator most distancing is his refusal either to address or attempt to circumvent this logical dilemma. In fact, it would be fair to say that the narrative discourse of this text is at war with its story.

The distancing narrator of *Yeast* repeatedly places the narratee in the position of acknowledging that the text is a fictive creation. In one late passage that explains the novel's title, the narrator interrupts an account of Lancelot's developing political convictions:

> And here I beg my readers to recollect that I am in no way answerable for the speculations either of Lancelot or any of his acquaintances; and that these papers have been, from beginning to end, as in name so in nature, Yeast—an honest sample of the questions which, good or bad, are fermenting in the minds of the young of this day, and are rapidly leavening the minds of the rising generation. (269)

Kingsley's narrator, like Gaskell's, goes on to disclaim any agreement with the attitudes he is reporting. But here the intervention draws attention to the physical textuality of the novel in the references to "these pages" and to the title. The narrator also emphasizes his self-consciousness about having invented the text: rather than pretending that Lancelot is "real," or that the novel's contents reflect the integrity of someone's actual experience, the narrator transforms the character into a composite figure foreshadowing the controversial subjects of the "new journalism" of the 1970s. He represents "an honest sample" of questions that concern his generation; the narrator's source for the character is not firsthand observation of someone real, but rather a piecing together of prevailing attitudes. To be sure, this is true to some extent for all Victorian novelists' activity in creating characters, because to write novels is inevitably to invent. The difference between a distancing narrator such as Kingsley's and an engaging one such as Gaskell's lies less in the authors' real-life activity as novelists, than in the attitude their narrators take toward the presentation of that activity.

Part of the pointed literariness of Kingsley's narrative stance is his frequent use of apostrophe, a figure which Gaskell's narrator invariably avoids. This 379-page novel contains at least fourteen formal apostrophes. Some of them invoke abstractions in the traditional apostrophic formula: "O Bigotry! Devil, who turnest God's love into man's curse! Are not human hearts hard and blind enough of themselves without thy cursed help?" (332); and "Blest pity! true mother of that graceless scamp, young love" (18). More often the apostrophes are directed to the characters, in a habitual pattern that leads the narrator to raise a question in the character's mind, then answer it in his own voice. The pattern produces interventions closely resembling one another in form: "Certainly, vicar" (224); "True, Argemone" (41); "True, Lancelot" (144); "Not yet, Lancelot" (326); "Peace! Poor Lancelot!" (119). In each of these instances the narrator follows the apostrophe with a paragraph that discusses the characters' limitations, detailing the flaws in the characters' thoughts and perceptions and guiding the narratee through a superior reading of the situation. Doubtless, these are the passages that Eliot saw as transforming Kingsley's characters into "text[s] to preach from." Eliot was using *text* in the sermonic sense of a quotation requiring commentary and preceding exhortation in the preacher's rhetorical routine. But for our purposes, Eliot's objection to the characters' transformation into "texts" takes on different resonances: the apostrophes (with the attendant exegesis) textualize the characters by drawing attention to the fact that they are in, and of, a text. The apostrophes pull the narrative focus back from the characters' consciousnesses, thus underscoring the distance between the characters and the commenting narrator. The commentary that follows the apostrophes injects a perspective on the characters' thoughts that places narrator and narratee in the privileged position of observers who can know what the characters cannot.

Yeast is not devoid of direct address to the narratee. But in a novel that consistently presents itself as a literary text, it is not surprising to find that many of the narrator's direct comments to the narratee refer to the composition of the novel. In this respect, the instances of direct address differ from the engaging strategy of imitating a conversational arrangement where the narrator has information she transmits to an interested narratee. An engaging narrator tells her reader about "facts"; a distancing narrator talks about the fiction. Some of Kingsley's interventions might be taken for engaging addresses to the narratee, in that superficially they resemble such lines in Gaskell's novel as "I must tell you—I must reveal the dreadful secret." Kingsley gives that conversation between narrator and narratee an ironic twist, though, when he interpolates teasing questions: "Lord Michampstead was thinking of cheap bread and sugar. Do you think that I will tell you of what Lancelot was thinking?" (116). The question prompts the narratee to notice the narrator's way of telling the story—of course, the narrator rather gleefully does not "tell you" the hero's thoughts.

Again and again, the narrator disappoints the hopes he attributes to his narratee. In a characteristic example, he withholds information, professes concern for the narratee's desires, and then refuses to deliver what the narratee is supposed to want:

> Whether he was afraid of her—whether he was ashamed of himself or of his crutches, I cannot tell, but I dare say, reader, you are getting tired of all this soul-dissecting. So we will have a bit of action again, for the sake of variety if for nothing better.
>
> Of all the species of lovely scenery which England holds, none, perhaps, is more exquisite than the banks of the chalk-rivers. (42)

As the leisurely descriptiveness of this last sentence implies, the promised "bit of action" is put off for another couple of pages of scene painting, philosophizing, and plot foreshadowing. This narrator—who operates within the great comic tradition of Fielding and Sterne, even when, as in this scene, he eventually focuses his attention on the wretched living conditions of the poor—delights in the game of toying with the expectations of his reader. The air of mutual confidence and presumed ingenuousness that characterizes the engaging narrator is notably absent from *Yeast*'s passages of direct address.

An engaging attitude is by no means absent from all of Kingsley's writing. From time to time, the narrator of *Yeast* embraces the narratee in a brotherly "we": "Do not we all learn love so?" (18); "[Lancelot] meant to keep his promise, as we all do" (154); "What are we all doing from morning to night, but setting up our own fancies as the measure of all heaven and earth?" (121–122). Within a framework of engaging narrative strategies, such questions and observations would contribute to the accumulated sense of similarity between the real and fictional worlds. In the context of this novel's distancing pattern of interventions, however, these appeals to an affinity between narrator, narratee, and characters do little to offset the self-conscious literariness of the text. Furthermore, to compare this narrator's stance toward "you" with the use of direct address in Kingsley's sermons and his political writing is to see that Kingsley could exploit the power of engaging address when he so chose.[5]

KINGSLEY AND THE PRIVILEGE TO SPEAK

Kingsley exploited almost every public forum available to him for the expression of his serious convictions on social, political, and religious matters. He composed and delivered weekly sermons and university lectures, he addressed a public pamphlet to the soldiers fighting the Crimean War, as "Parson Lot" he contributed pro-Chartist essays to *Politics for the People,* and in his own name he wrote on issues such as sweatshop conditions for *Fraser's* and conducted a notorious theological debate with Cardinal Newman for years. It is hardly surprising that in his novel Kingsley evinces so little urgency to say something in a serious way about real-world issues—his opportunities to do so elsewhere were manifold.

Kingsley's own awareness of the privilege he enjoyed in his role as public speaker is revealed in a biographical detail: in private conversation, he suffered all his life from a severe stutter, but in the pulpit or on the podium he almost never stammered unless he tried to improvise. Even then, he had far less difficulty saying something in public than at home, and he attributed his success to his attempts to "remember I was not speaking on my own authority, but God's" (Chitty 68). In situations where he spoke not for God but for himself, speaking was less easy. The first time he spoke at a meeting in London of Chartist sympathizers, listeners were so taken aback by his stammer that they wondered if he might be drunk (Chitty 123). Still, he did speak. As an Anglican minister, an official voice for an institution to which he was devoted, he found himself in a position to speak.

It was a position a woman (even a minister's wife) could not share, a position that allowed Kingsley the leisure to "play" when he turned his attention to writing fiction. In later novels—historical romances, children's stories, retellings of myths, adventure tales—he indulged still more openly in that play than in his social-problem novels. Certainly, as George Eliot's review laments, Kingsley continued to maintain a preacherly stance in the didactic content of his narrators' remarks. But the attitude that novel writing is first and foremost a way to make a contribution to the world of literature—that a novel is, broadly speaking, an aesthetic and entertaining artifact, even if the novel's story fits the category of "fiction with a purpose"—is already incipient in *Yeast*'s pattern of distancing interventions.

PUNCH AND THE PUPPET MASTER: WHO IS
SPEAKING IN *VANITY FAIR?*

Could Kingsley have been thinking of Thackeray when he wrote in *Yeast* of "our most earnest and genial humorist, who is just now proving himself also our most earnest and genial novelist" (20)? The accompanying allusion to a coarse-mannered baronet, who is almost certainly Thackeray's Pitt Crowley, implies that Kingsley did have Thackeray in mind.

To think of Thackeray as a "genial" novelist is to join the ranks of readers and critics who have enjoyed the loquacious humor of *Vanity Fair's* narrator. Unlike Kingsley's, this narrator has recently been a magnet for positive critical attention, as focusing on the narrator has become the typical strategy for defenders of Thackeray's art. As Michael Sundell explained the situation over fifteen years ago:

> Sympathetic, scholarly, and otherwise sensible critics continue to be thrown off balance by outdated attacks on [Thackeray's] cynicism or sentimentality, on his authorial intrusions, and even on his intelligence. Too often they fight again the critical battles which have already been won, conveying the impression that Thackeray still needs to be proven artistically respectable. In defending him, some concentrate excessively on the narrative brilliance of *Vanity Fair,* which only an ideologue or a fool could deny. (514)

Sundell is certainly right to question critics' continued defensiveness about the obviously brilliant narrative manipulations of *Vanity Fair.* And yet, surely not every critic who returns to the debate over how the narrator operates is merely tilting with ideologues and fools. Discussion of the *Vanity Fair* narrator circles around disagreements over the novel's many-layered structure of ironies. With its simultaneous floutings and exploitations of novelistic convention, this "novel without a hero" has long been seen as fundamentally ironic.[6]

What, then, could Kingsley have meant by calling its author an "earnest" novelist? The appellation hardly makes sense unless, indeed, Kingsley's narrator is not speaking in earnest himself. To be earnest is to be determined, eager, zealous, serious, to show deep sincerity or feeling, to treat one's subject matter as vitally important, not trivial or petty. When a novelist creates a narrator who presents himself as "Manager of the Performance" of a puppet play, who implies that he is a "quack" (objecting, as he surveys Vanity Fair, to the "*other* quacks, plague take them!" [33]), and who is depicted in many of the novelist's own illustrations as strongly resembling a Punch puppet himself, the novelist is obviously not "in earnest." And though Kingsley may have genuinely considered Thackeray to be "earnest" as well as "genial," Dickens was the first among many commentators who have "regretted Thackeray's feigning of a 'want of earnestness'" (Olmsted xiii). The narrator's self-presentation in "Before the Curtain," the illustrations, and the frequent narrative interventions in *Vanity Fair* combine to subvert any earnestness this novel might have demonstrated. What could be less vitally important, more trivial and petty, than the activities or observations of puppets?

And yet, constructed as it is on this basic assumption, the novel repeatedly dismantles its own foundations by making the characters' activities matter, by infusing enough life into them to have inspired numerous critical debates of the kind that treat characters as though they were real people. And the narrator, though he may sometimes look like the clownish, silent Punch, has plenty to say, much of it sounding zealous and serious enough. Indeed, many of Thackeray's early, more hostile critics took the narrator's comments to represent Thackeray's own moral standards, which for decades constituted the center of debate over the value of his novels.[7]

Thackeray criticism continually returns to a set of questions which an appreciation for distancing strategies might help resolve. From the beginning, *Vanity Fair*'s interpreters and evaluators considered whether *Vanity Fair* is an example of the kind of moral "history" Thackeray's narrator and his journalistic personae argued novels should be.[8] If *Vanity Fair* is, on the one hand, a work of realistic moral fiction, why does the narrator "repeatedly shatter the illusion by flaunting the inauthenticity of his fictions?" (Segel, "Truth and Authenticity" 55). Or, on the other hand, "If Thackeray's preaching does not lead to moral clarification for the reader, why does he offer his text as a sermon?" (Rawlins 172). What, in brief, is the textually encoded relation between this novel and its audience's real world? In the past two decades, Thackeray's critics have answered each of these questions positively and ingeniously; typically they conclude that *Vanity Fair* is, in the final analysis, a realistic and didactic text that makes its moral points about the world by maintaining a special, intimate relation between the chatty narrator and his readers.[9] Of the recent arguments that seek to demonstrate how *Vanity Fair*'s realism operates, Wolfgang Iser's is doubtless the most sophisticated and influential. I want, therefore, to point to some problems posed by Iser's essay on *Vanity Fair* that it shares with most critical work on Thackeray's narrators. The basic difficulty is this: to use *Vanity Fair* as a model for realistic narrative techniques is to run into logical inconsistencies and to overlook this novel's fundamentally ironic, metafictional nature.

In *Vanity Fair*, Iser comments, "the narrator regulates the distance between reader and events" (106) and "the reader is continually placed at a distance from the characters" (108). Iser's complex argument isolates the "esthetic effect" of this novel in the activity the narrator continually assigns to the "reader," who is supposed to maintain a critical distance from the characters and events, supply personal judgments where the narrator's ironic or contradictory statements leave "empty spaces" (106), and ultimately turn those critical judgments "back upon himself" (119). Choosing *Vanity Fair* as his sole example of the "realistic novel," Iser emphasizes that this text's realism inheres not in its contents but in its effect, which "depends on activating the reader's critical faculties so that he may recognize the social reality of the novel as a confusing array of sham attitudes, and experience the exposure of this sham as the true reality" (112). Iser observes that the novel therefore "remains as 'real' now as it was" in 1848, because "In *Vanity Fair* it is not the slice of life, but the means of observing it that constitute the reality" (119–120).

Iser's choice of *Vanity Fair* as his model for the reader's role in realism is, however, problematic. Of all the canonic English novels of the realist period, *Vanity Fair* is the one that makes the least pretense of presenting a slice of life: as "Before the Curtain" makes clear, the novel is only a slice of a fair—a festive time and place where the participants are absorbed in "playing out" roles donned for the occasion. The "bullies . . . bucks . . . knaves . . . policemen . . . and yokels" are held up for observation alongside the "actors and buffoons." And the Manager of the Performance suggests that this slice of a fair will be doubly enacted, because the characters filling these roles will be played by puppets. Iser does not ignore this metafictional framing of *Vanity Fair*. He acknowledges that the narrator's "reliability is reduced by the fact that he is continually donning new masks: (105) ranging from the Manager, to a novelist, to a character relating a story that he overheard in conversation. Because Iser is trying to account for this text as an example of realism, he is forced into a perplexing conclusion about the effect of this "Protean narrator": "If the narrator is an independent character, clearly separated from the inventor of the story, the tale of the social aspirations of the two girls Becky and Amelia takes on a greater degree of objectivity, and indeed one gains the impression that this social reality is not a mere narration but actually exists" (106). But, as Iser seems rather suddenly to forget, this narrator is usually *not* "an independent character." In order for an actual reader to get the impression that *Vanity Fair*'s social reality "actually exists," he or she would have to overlook, as Iser here does, those parts of the narrative frame that do identify the narrator with "the inventor of the story."

Iser goes to some length to show that his reader's sense of *Vanity Fair* as real arises from the narrator's habit of offering alternative assessments of character's motives and morals, and letting the reader choose or fill in the definitive judgment for "himself" (117–119). His argument for the novel's effect of reality rests, too, on the observation that as the reader begins to realize "for himself the extent to which consideration of personal gain shapes the natural impulses of human conduct, . . . the difference between the reader and the characters in the novel is eliminated" (115–116). The first of these two realistic effects—the personal investment in a story that one has partly helped to create—would be more clearly illustrated, I think, by analysis of an engaging narrator's open-ended questions to a narratee. Thackeray's distancing narrator appears to offer alternatives among which a narratee might choose. But the narrator's irony, which often slides into bitter sarcasm, ususally makes it tolerably clear which judgment a flawed narratee would make and which one a self-respecting actual reader is supposed to want to make. And, as Iser acknowledges, by the end of the novel the "correct" reading becomes explicitly clear (112). The open-endedness is an illusion, just as the narratee who can't tell which option to choose is a fictive figure.

The point in Iser's argument where the conflation of the reader and the narratee poses the biggest problem, though, is the second of those realistic effects, the idea that the reader will "reflect on his own situation" while reading. Iser assumes that the reader will find himself guilty of the ego-centricity and greed for which he has been censuring the characters, and thus will recognize that differences between reader and characters are "eliminated." In this context Iser describes the concept of a narratee without distinguishing it from an implied reader; "Just as the author divides himself up into the narrator of the story and the commentator on the events in the story, the reader is also stylized to a certain degree, being given attributes which he may either accept or reject' (114). This precisely defines the practice of the distancing narrator, who characterizes narratees so completely as to place a necessary distance between them and actual readers. Iser, however, denies this distance; "Whatever happens, [the reader] will be forced to react to those ready-made qualities ascribed to him" (114). True, the narratee might be forced to react: as a function of the text, a narratee is entirely under the author's control. But an actual reader cannot be forced by a text to do anything. The power struggle between the distancing narrator and his narratees may prompt the actual reader to step back even further from the fictional world, to maintain the distance that the novel's metafictional frame has already established.

In *Vanity Fair* that distance dominates the implicit relation between the narratee and the actual reader. The narrator's stance toward the narratee, the characters, and the act of narration fits the distancing model of humorous metalepsis; the narrator moves himself and his narratees inside and outside the diegesis with unpredictably unsettling glee. In addition to the ironies he raises in his addresses to narratees, Thackeray's narrator pushes the metafictional potential of the realist novel to the limit. He does so primarily by making a game of one central, difficult question for realist fiction: Who is speaking?

Who indeed? In "Before the Curtain" the narrator refers to "the Manager of the Performance" in the third person, alternating these references with a more personal "I" (33–34). Yet the Manager takes credit for the ensuing spectacle, and "acknowledge(s) the kindness with which it has been received" (34). Is this "Manager," then, the author? The puppet master? A preacher in motley? Another puppet? A customer at the fair?[10] He implies, as I have mentioned, that he is a "quack" (33); later, the narrator addresses his audience as "brother wearers of motley," adding that his object is "to walk with you through the fair" (229). At the beginning of the sixth chapter he is a "piper," and the accompanying illustration shows a recorder-wielding Punch hypnotizing a small animal with his "mild tune"

(88). As Janice Carlisle has pointed out, Thackeray's line drawings for the original edition depict the narrator sometimes with a clown's face, sometimes as Punch, and even (at the end of Chapter 9, entitled "Family Portraits") as a befuddled-looking caricature of William Makepeace Thackeray with a comic mask and a clown's staff in his lap (Carlisle 36–39). At times the narrator pretends to distinguish himself from his creator. He says that the cover illustration of a "moralist" (a thin and therefore distinctly un-Thackeray-like orator in clown's garb) is "an accurate portrait of your humble servant" (95), but makes no reference beyond the sly chapter title to the cartoon of the novelist in Chapter 9.

As this changeable narrator introduces characters he places them and himself on a stage, asking leave "as a man and a brother . . . occasionally to step down from the platform, and talk about them: if they are good and kindly, to love them and shake them by the hand: if they are silly, to laugh at them confidentially in the reader's sleeve" (117). (Building upon the many layers of irony, this passage placing the narrator and characters on a public stage occurs in a chapter called "Private and Confidential.") But at the end of the novel, the actors shrink down into puppets that the narrator shuts into a box (797). The narrator, like the characters, is a chameleon: existing on many different diegetic levels, adopting the appearances of many different figures, he differentiates himself from any one real person or fictional character. His shifting identity accentuates his fictive status.

So, too, does the brief reference to the narrator's having met the characters at the imaginary town of Pumpernickel. In this scene he places himself for the first time among the principal participants in Vanity Fair, recording the crowd's observations of Amelia, Jos, Dobbin, and their party. This is also one of the few passages where the narrator pretends to claim that his story is true: "It was on this very tour that I, the present writer of a history of which every word is true, had the pleasure to see them first, and to make their acquaintance" (721). Coming as it does so late in the narrative, the assertion is obviously a joke: all the references to puppets, plays, and pipers make the truth of this history highly unlikely. The claim also casts doubt on the narrator's authority for reporting "truly" on the private thoughts of all the characters. The narrator has already made a Shandean witticism about the possibility of proving the novel's truth through examining its temporal structure. Reversing Tristram's perplexities about how much longer it takes to narrate events than to enact them, Thackeray's narrator claims,

> And if you calculate the time for the above dialogue to take place—the time for Briggs and Firkin to fly to the drawing-room—the time for Miss Crawley to be astonished and to drop her volume . . .—and the time for her to come downstairs—you will see how exactly accurate this history is, and how Miss Crawley *must* have appeared at the very instant when Rebecca had assumed the attitude of humility. (188)

An absurdly humorous suggestion, this calculation would only reinforce the sense of this scene's carefully orchestrated resemblance to a meticulously timed stage farce. And the narrator's suggestion raises more questions about the history's truth-status than it can answer: if these actions "really" took this precise amount of time, how does the narrator know?

Sometimes the narrator offers authenticating sources for his information, such as the Peeping-Tom, eavesdropping footman at Lord Steyne's, Tom Eaves. The sources are not always such minor characters; at one point the narrator claims that Dobbin supplied him with a small detail: "The bride was dressed in a brown silk pelisse (as Captain Dobbin has since informed me)" (259). To claim a source for so minor—and, for that matter, so public—a detail, when hundreds of pages' worth of information goes unattributed, is to spoof the very idea that there could be anything true about this history.[11]

When he pretends to be the gatherer and reporter, rather than the creator, of his facts, the narrator draws attention to their fictionality only indirectly. But he is not always so coy about his position. Early on, he admits that he can report Jos's thoughts of Becky because "novelists have the privilege of knowing everything" (62). The narrator even more pointedly asserts the novelist's unique perspective on Rebecca herself: "If, a few pages back, the present writer claimed the privilege of peeping into Miss Amelia Sedley's bedroom, and understanding with the omniscience of the novelist all the gentle pains and passions which were tossing upon that innocent pillow, why should he not declare himself to be Rebecca's confidant too?" (192). Accordingly, he proceeds to reveals Becky's thoughts.

"The omniscience of the novelist" is precisely the issue here: it is a perspective that can only exist in fiction, can never be duplicated in life or even in the writing of history, and is inevitably the source of any hetero-diegetically narrated novel. With this fact in mind, I find it odd that Iser claims "it is not the slice of life" in *Vanity Fair* but "the means of observing it that constitutes the reality." Why try to reconcile Thackeray's jubilant jumble of narrative claims with the label of "reality"?[12] There is nothing literally realistic about the omniscient perspective, despite the fact that it is regarded as a convention of literary realism. But his chameleon narrator's insistence on his own fictive nature and on the powers accompanying his status provides constant reminders that the "means of observing" in this novel is as fictitious as the "slice of life" it observes. Thackeray's fiction points again and again to its own fictionality. The one real aspect of the "means of observing" in such a novel is the fact that actual readers really have to exercise memory and imagination to read it, similar to the reading activity Iser describes. But this is true of all narrative texts, not only of realist novels. Iser seems to reverse the novel's relation to realism when he claims that "*Vanity Fair* aims not at presenting social reality, but at present-ing the way in which such reality can be experienced" (113). The novel's story is full of details representing "social reality": meticulous descriptions of costume and setting, elaborately represented dialogues, and humorous and serious analyses of relations among the classes, to give just a few examples. The mode of experiencing reality that the text presents is the most fictive thing about it.

In another context (that of the novel's ending), Ina Ferris has per-suasively argued that "Thackeray's realist resistance to ending leads finally to a transgression of the logic of realism itself. The uneasy nineteenth-century ending . . . may well be less a gesture of realist fidelity than of anti-realist dissent" (290). *Vanity Fair*'s narrative interventions are, it seems to me, a complex expression of antirealist dissent, a continual reframing and rephrasing of the impossibilities inherent in realist fiction. Despite the fact that Thackeray's *story* draws on so many conventions of the realist novel, sometimes subverting them and sometimes using them straight, the *dis-course* of this novel consistently draws away from realism and into metafic-tion. The ironic distance this inevitably places between the actual reader and the contents of the text is reproduced in the narrator's stance toward his narratees. The narrator repeatedly attempts to startle the actual reader out of slipping into communion with the numerous narratees in the text.

DISTANCING STRATEGIES AND "MY READERS"

The question of "distance"—as Iser's analysis shows—is not easily resolvable for *Vanity Fair*. Commentators have usually taken it for granted that Thackeray's narrator, while placing a distance between himself and his characters, establishes a close relation with his reader. This sense of intimacy is, for example, in the background of Iser's assumptions about the novel; it is also one basis for Robert Polhemus's account of the satirically comic effect of *Vanity Fair*. As Polhemus puts it, Thackeray uses the narrator "to create a psychic distance from experience and characters necessary to satiric comedy and also to establish an intimacy between performer and audience." This intimacy, bringing narrator and reader together, paradoxically serves to distance the reader from the fiction; the closeness of the narrator and reader encourages the reader to view Vanity Fair with an eye as skeptical as the narrator's and (according to Polhemus) to withhold any sympathy "that would distract us for long from the corrupt farce of Vanity Fair as a whole" (152). Some actual readers might disagree with this conclusion about the satire's effect. Anyone who has led a class discussion of *Vanity Fair* knows that despite all the narrator's antics, some readers ("touched," like Becky, "in spite of [themselves]" [366]) cheer for Becky when she flings Johnson's Dictionary back at Miss Pinkerton's Academy, some are moved by Rawdon Crawley's developing affection for his son, and some yearn with Dobbin for his ultimate marriage to Amelia. Still, what's at issue here is the narrator's strategy, not its actual effects. Just as the narrator's irony can fail to obliterate actual readers' sympathies for the characters, his conspiratorial intimacy with his narratee is far from consistent. In fact, the narrator sets up numerous inscribed readers only to knock them down like the puppets that are his characters, leaving the actual reader no solid footing vis à vis the text.

Thackeray's narrative strategies run the gamut of ways to create distance between the actual reader and the narratee. The first of these is his commenting to narratees who are named. A narratee may have a name as specific as "Miss Smith," as the narrator calls the generically envious woman reader who is unimpressed by Amelia's reluctance to rebel against George's faithlessness: "I know Miss Smith has a mean opinion of her. But how many, my dear Madam, are endowed with your prodigious strength of mind?" (292). The flawed narratee—impatient, unsympathetic, and prudish—is sometimes addressed without a proper name, simply as "madam":

> a polite public will no more bear to read an authentic description of vice than a truly refined English or American female will permit the word breeches to be pronounced in her chaste hearing. And yet, madam, both are walking the world before our faces every day, without much shocking us. If you were to blush every time they went by, what complexions you would have! (737–738)

In both examples, the narrator begins with a third-person reference to the figure embodying objectionable attitudes, "Miss Smith" and "a truly refined . . . female." Both references turn, though, to direct address, implicating narratees in the readerly crimes. The strategy is to embarrass actual readers who do share the narratee's feelings of impatience or prudishness out of identifying with these objects of the narrator's scorn. Thackeray's narrator can use this strategy simply and directly, as in his defense of Becky's "setting her cap" at Jos: "I don't think, ladies, we have any right to blame her" (31), or in his sugar-coated but unmistakably bitter attack on yet another unsympathetic lady reader who judges Amelia for her tenderheartedness: "My dear Miss Bullock, I do not think *your* heart would break in this way" (219).

Even more frequently, the narrator names figures of readers whom he does not deign to address. Strictly speaking, these are not really narratees. If the narratee is the figure to whom the narrator is speaking, these are third parties to that transaction, objects under discussion in the narrative conversation. In this respect they resemble characters, but they exist on a diegetic level separate from the world of Becky and Amelia, because they are represented as reading about that world, not participating in it. The most famous of these named readers is probably "JONES, who reads this book at his Club" and "will pronounce [it] to be excessively foolish, trivial, twaddling, and ultra-sentimental." The narrator emphasizes Jones's characterlike status while having some fun with this reader's inappropriate attitude:

> Yes, I can see Jones at this minute (rather flushed with his joint of mutton and half-pint of wine) taking out his pencil and scoring under the words "foolish, twaddling," etc., and adding to them his own remark of "*quite true.*" Well, he is a lofty man of

genius, and admires the great and heroic in life and novels; and
so had better take warning and go elsewhere. (43–44)

Occurring in the novel's first chapter, this remarkably metafictional move
supplies an amusing portrait of a bad reader to instruct us on how not to
read the novel. What's wrong with Jones is not his objection to sentiment;
the narrator obviously disavows any faith in straight-faced, earnest sentimentality. Jones's problem is that in his eagerness to find the "great and
heroic" in the book he does not recognize the distanced position the narrator offers on the "foolish, twaddling" parts. While Jones underlines the
words, the actual reader, standing at a comfortable distance, can laugh.
The narratee's position in the passage is less comfortably clear. Who is the
narratee here? Perhaps the narratee gets the joke at Jones's expense, or
perhaps the narratee is presumed to share Jones's prejudice. In such a
questionable situation, the actual reader might hesitate to identify with the
narratee, since that figure may be inscribed as a poor reader.

Vanity Fair is full of such shifting references to readers who may or
may not represent the narratee. Opening Chapter 12, "Quite a Sentimental
Chapter," with a sketch of another superficial reader, the narrator quotes
her before twitting her: "We don't care a fig for [Amelia], writes some
unknown correspondent with a pretty little handwriting and a pink seal to
her note. 'She is *fade* and insipid,' and adds some more kind remarks in this
strain, which I should never have repeated at all, but that they are in truth
prodigiously complimentary to the young lady whom they concern" (146).
The intervention proceeds to detail "similar remarks by good-natured female friends" that "the beloved reader, in his experience of society" is likely
to have heard. Here, the "beloved reader" is pointedly inscribed as male.
The narratee, then, must either be a man who recognizes the hypocritical
back-biting typical of the kind of woman the narrator has in mind, or a
person, male or female, who doesn't "care a fig for [Amelia]" and therefore
must take the criticism the narrator directs at the "unknown correspondent" and all her "good-natured" sisters. An actual reader who is female has
no choice but to be distanced by this intervention; an actual reader who is
male can form a positive link between himself and the narratee only by
agreeing with the passage's bitter attitude toward female friendships.

And, lest the male reader should get too comfortable in his relation to
the narrator, the sarcasm is turned against him later in this strikingly
unsentimental chapter. Discussing Amelia's "blind devotion" to George,

the narrator remarks, "It is in the nature and instinct of some women. Some are made to scheme, and some to love; and I wish any respected bachelor that reads this may take the sort that best likes him" (153). Like most of the narrator's comments, this one is ironic: if you read the phrase "that best likes him" in the archaic sense of "that he likes best," the wish is a pleasant one. But if you interpret the phrase in its modern sense, that is, "the type that likes him the best," it takes on a sardonic edge. The narrator's wish for his modern bachelor-reader is that he will end up with the sort of woman who finds him most attractive, be she loving or scheming.

If this narrator is intimate with his readers, it is an intimacy characterized by teasing, bantering, and needling that constantly moves in one direction: only the narrator can tease, for the narratee and the actual reader have no opportunity, as it were, to answer in kind. As Roger Wilkenfeld observes,

> Much of the power of *Vanity Fair* resides in Thackeray's tough perception that there is an inevitable separation between the artist who creates and the readers and spectators who look. The artist may provide any number of imaginative access routes to his show but when he chooses to "shut up the box" he does not wait for a signal to act. We who have been metaphorically associated with "yokels" are finally identified as "patrons" but the nominal substitution is no more consoling than the displacement of one engraved fool by another. (318)

Though he does present himself at times as an "engraved fool," the narrator has all the power. The narratee, on the one hand, must submit to sardonic criticism (or, as Iser puts it, is "forced to react to those qualities ascribed to him"). The actual reader, on the other hand, is consistently placed at a distance, outside the combative exchange between narrator, inscribed readers, and narratees.

As often as the narrator refers to "readers" as the objects of his comments, rather than the receivers of what he has to say, he also speaks surprisingly often to "you." Despite all the references to "the astonished reader" (506), "the respected reader" (359), "the beloved reader" (159), "the good-natured reader" (87), "the observant reader" (159), "some carping reader" (147), or "every reader of a sentimental turn" (186), the narrator is not incapable of addressing a reader directly. In the context of the narrator's sarcasms and jokes at his narratees' expense, though, even the most potentially engaging passages of direct address represent distancing moves on the narrator's part. Typically the *Vanity Fair* narrator's addresses to "you" are either sarcastic or accusatory.

We have already seen examples of sarcasm in the narrator's third-person references to his "readers," and the tone carries over into speeches directed at them as well. For instance, his advice to "young ladies" directly reverses his admiration for Amelia's "weakness," so evident elsewhere in the text: "Be shy of loving frankly; never tell all you feel, or (a better way still), feel very little. . . . [N]ever have any feelings which may make you uncomfortable, or make any promises which you cannot at any required moment command and withdraw. This is the way to get on, and be respected, and have a virtuous character in Vanity Fair" (220). The obvious verbal irony of such wise counsel to the narratee casts a shadow over other passages in the novel that might, in a different context, look engaging. When Thackeray's narrator says "You and I, my dear reader" (453) the actual reader might be supposed to wish to identify with this beloved narratee. Yet the narrator has so often used terms of endearment ironically that they take on a permanent taint of sarcasm. The narratee might be happy to have the narrator salute him as "my dear," but the actual reader attentive to textual strategies will be more cautious: he or she must reconsider the tenor of that phrase when the narrator—so unremittingly critical, in story as in discourse, of Becky Sharp—refers to her in her most unloveable moments as "our dear Becky" (593) or "our beloved Rebecca" (557). Considering the pall of sarcasm Thackeray's narrator throws over the adjectives "beloved" and "dear," we should not be surprised that earnest novelists like Gaskell and Stowe seldom, if ever, address a "dear reader": Thackeray ruined the phrase for serious use.

When he is more in earnest, Thackeray's narrator is perhaps even less engaging. He openly criticizes narratees for behavior that has nothing to do with reading novels; on matters extratextual as well as textual, he speaks to narratees who are hopelessly flawed. He accuses the narratee of tormenting little boys by sending them to boarding school: "Who feels injustice; who shrinks before a slight; who has a sense of wrong so acute, and so glowing a gratitude of kindness, as a generous boy? and how many of those gentle souls do you degrade, estrange, torture, for the sake of a little loose arithmetic, and miserable dog-Latin?" (77). Considering the degrading experiences Dobbin undergoes in the setting of a boys' school—not to mention Thackeray's own notoriously unhappy memories of his boarding-school experience—there is no reason to read this passage as pure sarcasm. But the actual reader who is not a sadist will automatically be distanced from the narratee in the passage. If the reader has no connection to any boys, he or she will deflect the question as irrelevant to actual circumstances; if he or she manages boys' educations through another medium than boarding school, the reader can consider the question to be directed to someone else, a narratee who is not the actual reader. And the reader who does send boys to boarding school is unlikely to want to equate that with the decision to "degrade, estrange, torture" them. In any case, the actual reader is actively discouraged from identifying with the narratee.

In less drastic instances, too, the narrator continually badgers the narratee for presumed faults. Usually they are moral or ethical errors that the narratee is imagined to share with the characters (and sometimes with the narrator himself). These failings include the respectable characters' willingness to socialize with Lord Steyne despite his deservedly terrible reputation: "In a word, everybody went to wait upon this great man— everybody who was asked: as you the reader (do not say nay) or I the writer hereof would go if we had an invitation" (553). Or the Crawleys' humoring their unpleasant but wealthy aunt: "You yourself, dear sir, forget to go to sleep after dinner, and find yourself all of a sudden (though you invariably lose) very fond of a rubber" (124). Or Becky Sharp's behavior as she sinks even lower into a life of degradation: "The actions of very vain, heartless, pleasure-seeking people are very often improper (as are many of yours, my friend with the grave face and spotless reputation; but that is merely by the way); and what are those of a woman without faith—or love—or charac-ter?" (738). In each of these examples, the narrator forces the narratee to acknowledge similarities between the erring characters and himself. The relation between narrator and narratee is perfectly summed up in the narrator's dictum: "do not say nay." It would be possible, of course, to read these passages as serious exhortations that are meant to jolt actual readers into awareness of their own culpability in the foibles of Vanity Fair: Iser, Carlisle, and other critics certainly read them this way. But in the context of the novel's pattern of distancing interventions—the metafictional frame, the changing identity of the narrator, the sardonic dismissals of bad readers and the sarcastic comments to "you"—the nature of these accusatory passages seems to shift. Perhaps the narrator is no more in earnest in these little speeches than elsewhere in the text, perhaps the actual reader is no more obliged to identify with these narratees than with "Miss Smith" or "JONES," perhaps the novel's distancing machinery lets the actual reader off the hook. Perhaps the novel is no more than a puppet show depicting a fair—maybe it is all for fun.

WHAT NOVEL WRITING IS FOR: THACKERAY'S GAME

In his characteristically metafictional mood, Thackeray's narrator takes a moment to discuss the kind of novel he is writing and to contrast it with a few of the more popular forms of nineteenth-century fiction. This meditation is introduced by the passage in which the narrator draws attention to his responsibility as entertainer, confessing, "I know that the tune I am piping is a mild one." Playing into the narratee's supposed preference for excitement, he immediately adds, "(although there are some terrific chapters coming presently)" (87). Before embarking on his account of unremarkable occurrences at Vauxhall, the narrator catalogues the choices the novelist has rejected among alternative settings for this story:

> We might have treated this subject in the genteel, or in the romantic, or in the facetious manner. Suppose we had laid the scene in Grosvenor Square. . . . [O]r instead of the supremely genteel, suppose we had resorted to the entirely low, and described what was going on in Mr. Sedley's kitchens. . . . Or if, on the contrary, we had taken a fancy for the terrible, and made the lover of the new *femme de chambre* a professional burglar . . . we should easily have constructed a tale of thrilling interest, through the fiery chapters of which the reader should hurry, panting. (88)

The ellipses in the quotation represent details the narrator supplies for each of these possible kinds of novels, demonstrating, in a sentence or two for every option, his imaginative capacity to operate within all of the genres he suggests. "But," the narrator concludes,

> my readers must hope for no such romance, only a homely story, and must be content with a chapter about Vauxhall, which is so short that it scarce deserves to be called a chapter at all. And yet

it is a chapter, and a very important one too. Are not there little
chapters in everybody's life, that seem to be nothing, and yet
affect all the rest of the history?

Let us then step into the coach with the Russell Square
party, and be off to the gardens. There is barely room between
Jos and Miss Sharp. (88)

At first glance, this intervention appears to be a claim for the realism of
Vanity Fair. It could have been a romance or a sensation-novel, a Silver Fork
or Newgate blockbuster, but it is not; it merely treats the ordinary experiences of unexceptional characters. The argument takes the point a step
further with the comparison of this chapter to those "little chapters in
everybody's life" that turn out to have greater consequences in one's "history" than one might have expected. This fiction is like life, the intervention implies, and what's more, life—divided here into "chapters" as novels
are—is like fiction.

At the same time, though, the passage emphasizes one respect in
which fiction is definitely not like life: the fiction is under the novelist's
arbitrary control and operates at his pleasure. I like the narrative "we" in
this excerpt: it joins the narrator and the novelist into a unified figure who
gets to choose what kind of a story *Vanity Fair* will be, what kinds of details
it will convey, and what kind of denouement it will have. This figure
mounts the stage here to remind the readers that it is, indeed, a stage. The
transition from the intervention back to the action further emphasizes the
fictionality of the narrative, as the narrator invites us to try to squeeze into
the coach between Jos and Becky. We cannot. For all the narrator's pretended claims to the contrary, life and fiction are two separate realms—as
the narrator knows very well and will not allow the actual reader to forget.

When, at the end of the novel, Thackeray's narrator steps back again
from the fiction to say, "Come children, let us shut up the box and the
puppets, for our play is played out" (797), the move is hardly surprising.
The novel has been an entertainment—a moral play, perhaps, but a play
nonetheless. In order to grasp the radical difference between Thackeray's
distancing narrative strategies and Gaskell's engaging approach, one need
only consider how unthinkable it would be for Gaskell's narrator to refer to
John and Mary Barton, Jem Wilson, and Job Legh as "puppets." Even if she
were to use it metaphorically, the image would obliterate her consistent

treatment of her characters as "real," autonomous people. Thackeray's approach, like Kingsley's, is more playful. The distancing narrator represents the male author's access to a metaliterary realm, where novels refer to themselves and to other novels, as much as (or, in these cases, more than) they refer to life. As I argue in Chapter 7, it is no coincidence that the Victorian authors who took access to that playful realm in their texts were male.

What is Thackeray's game? Kingsley is not, after all, the only reader to have considered him "earnest": one camp of twentieth-century critics persists in taking the narrator's preacher pose seriously, treating the exhortative passages as though they were straightforwardly moralistic messages for the edification of "the reader." [13] The self-mockery implied by the preacher's presenting himself in motley, however, should not be overlooked. This narrator is only playing preacher, as he is playing historian, and as his characters are playing out the play. Readings of *Vanity Fair* informed by more recent literary theory have suggested that Thackeray's text expresses profound doubts about the ability of narrative fiction to do more than play: it is, in Ferris's phrase, a pointedly "uneasy narrative" (289). Ferris sees in the *Vanity Fair* narrator an awareness that metaphor inevitably detaches signs from that which they signify (302); Robin Ann Sheets, too, notes that in the world of *Vanity Fair,* words invariably "have their own meaning . . . apart from reality. . . . When words do not correspond to some objective, communally held body of meanings, but become arbitrary and subjective tokens, then literary art ceases to function as a mimetic structuring of extra-literary reality" (430). In a similar vein, Jack Rawlins has shown that Thackeray's narrator mimics a whole range of verbal styles, not only to undercut or parody selected modes of discourse, but also to discredit language and hence "the authorial process" altogether (158, 160). Still, each of these critics views Thackeray through a lens colored by assumptions about the didactic purposes of realist fiction, and each concludes that Thackeray's fiction isn't (as Ferris puts it) "mere linguistic play—far from it" (303). Each finds a message (one could almost say a moral) in Thackeray's text, as though it were still necessary to defend nineteenth-century novels against anyone who doubts their seriousness. [14]

I do doubt that *Vanity Fair* is "serious," and yet I would never mean to imply that it is therefore not good. If we look at this novel's narrative discourse against the backdrop of other novels by Thackeray's contemporaries, we can see that it differs strikingly in its self-presentation and narrative stance from such earnest realist fictions as *Mary Barton*. The difference lies in the novels' relative relations to play: I call the difference one of gender, but not one of quality or value.[15] I argue in Chapter 7 that men's and women's social circumstances played a signifcant role in their choices of narrative stance. Before examining that role, though, I want to inquire into the rhetoric of texts whose authors "cross gender" in writing them. The next two chapters look at women authors who sometimes use distancing strategies and men authors who sometimes employ engaging techniques—not to write "better" novels on any aesthetic or moral grounds, but rather to manipulate the rhetoric of prose fiction to their own ends.

5

Women's Narrators Who Cross Gender:

Uncle Tom's Cabin and *Adam Bede*

ENGAGING narrative strategies, when they work, make actual readers cry. Women novelists who had no personal access to public audiences could use direct address to accost the strangers represented by their narratees, persuade those strangers to identify with the novels' characters, convince them that the suffering depicted in the novels is "real," and goad them into succumbing to that most physical proof of "real" emotional response—tears. Through the first half of the nineteenth century, tears lost the privileged position they had held as the emblems of sensibility and degenerated into a "womanish" activity, a mark of sentimentality.[1] To appreciate the role that emotional response was designed to play in engaging narrative texts, we must entertain the possibility—with Roland Barthes—of rehabilitating tears as a sign. Tears "prove to myself that my grief is not an illusion. . . . [B]y weeping, I give myself an emphatic interlocutor who receives the 'truest' of messages, that of my body, not that of my speech" (427–428). To transmit "the message of the body"—the visceral response that signals the mental movement from identification, to compassion, to pain—is one of the engaging narrator's primary goals. For women writers, evoking tears in an audience was one way to surmount the restrictions upon their public activity. If a reader weeps, the message of the body says that a real event has occurred; it is as though the writer has transcended language to assert her presence and to act directly upon her reader. Making a reader cry was a way for a woman to *do* something.

Making a reader cry was also typically, if not exclusively, something for a woman to do.[2] Men could gain the same kind of access to an audience's emotions in person by delivering speeches or sermons. When George Eliot and Harriet Beecher Stowe set out to make their readers cry, they relied upon a sermonic use of direct address to establish the same link with their readers that revivalist preachers maintained with their listeners. What men accomplished through speech, women could try to accomplish in writing. Direct address, in both oral and written language, is the trope that most vividly asserts the presence of the sender and the receiver of the message. While presence may be—as Derrida reminds us—illusory in either situation, the rhetoric of direct address contributes to that illusion and even, in engaging narrative, constitutes it. The engaging narrator strives to establish her own presence and her reader's, in order to refashion the actual audience's emotional relation to her subject matter.[3]

With their first novels, Eliot and Stowe achieved the response they sought. *Uncle Tom's Cabin* has labored long under its popular and critical reputations for sentimentality, summed up in Hugh Kenner's memorable dismissal of it as "an eleven-Kleenex tract." For Eliot, whose stature as an intellect overshadows her reputation for sentimentality, response was equally important.[4] When she was writing *Scenes of Clerical Life* in 1857, Eliot would read her new pages aloud in the evenings to George Lewes, who, by her own report, "laughed and cried alternately and then rushed to kiss me." Of Lewes's tears and laughter she wrote to a friend, "He is the prime blessing that has made all the rest possible to me—giving a response to everything I have written, a response that I could confide in as a proof that I had not mistaken my work" (*Letters* III 63). The physical manifestations of response were her "proof" that she could use her novel—her "work," in the literal sense of her one available mode of labor—as a means of making something real happen within her audience.[5]

In *Uncle Tom's Cabin* (1851–1852) and in *Adam Bede* (Eliot's first full-length novel, 1859), both Stowe and Eliot exploit earnest direct address as a means of sparking actual readers' emotion through appeals to narratees; both authors insisted, within and outside their fictional texts, that they wanted their novels to be accepted as "real." Paradoxically, though, both novels are distancing as well as engaging in their strategies. At the same time that the texts try to establish a speaker's and auditor's presence, they participate in the inevitable recognition that such presence can always only be a function of language. While the contents of both novels conform to conventions of verisimilitude to suggest their "reality," each of the narrators intervenes in the fiction to insist upon her story's veracity by overtly claiming that it is true. In the most extreme cases—the first chapter of the second volume of *Adam Bede,* "In Which the Story Pauses a Little" and the final chapter of *Uncle Tom,* "Concluding Remarks"—the narrators talk so candidly about the genesis of their stories as to contradict the claims of truth they are ostensibly making. When their narrators find themselves in this self-reflexive mode, the authors are treading the masculine territory of distancing narrative discourse; when they continue to insist upon establishing their own presence and the reader's presence through direct address, the authors are erasing the ironies of narration to inscribe the "truth" of their realist fictions.

STOWE AND THE RHETORIC OF SENSATION

Uncle Tom's Cabin straddles the boundaries of several genres of nineteenth-century fiction. Full of the domestic details appropriate to the realist and sentimental novels of its era, *Uncle Tom* juxtaposes homely scenes with public scandals vivid enough to rival English sensation novels.[6] If fictional accounts of illegal kidnappings, imprisonments, rapes, and murders could "produce a sensation" in the popular British novels of that genre, how much more scandalous must have been *Uncle Tom's* suggestion that in America analogous activities were legal under the system of slavery. The rhetorical challenge that *Uncle Tom* takes on is to convince a white, middle-class public accustomed to thinking of blacks as "other" that the emotional experience of slaves was exactly analogous to their own. As the novel's best-seller status attests, Stowe accurately gauged her audience's willingness to be shocked into sympathy. *Uncle Tom* certainly produced a public sensation—not to mention the private sensations its readers experienced individually.

In its day, *Uncle Tom* prompted scandalized reviewers to question the truth of its story. British and Southern reviewers, especially, expressed doubts about the likelihood that scenes such as Eliza's last-minute escape over the frozen Ohio River or Uncle Tom's final martyrdom at the hands of

Legree's savage slaves could ever really occur.[7] According to their own political agendas, critics labeled *Uncle Tom's* story true or false, its author a prophetess or a liar.

Are the stories told in *Uncle Tom's Cabin* true? This is not a question for postmodern criticism to ask; the stories' being rendered in discourse, and the discourse being that of fiction, already places the novel's signifiers at two removes from its signifieds, and renders the question of its truth-status moot.[8] For Stowe, though, her audience's acceptance of the novel as a "true" representation of slavery was essential. In response to critical attacks, she published *A Key to* Uncle Tom's Cabin(1853), a compilation of newspaper articles, advertisements, bills of sale, and anecdotes about slavery. This accumulation of evidence—much of it, paradoxically enough, invented by Stowe herself— was supposed to prove her novel's authenticity. Of *Uncle Tom* Stowe writes in the *Key:* "This work, more, perhaps, than any other work of fiction that ever was written, has been a collection and arrangement of real incidents,—of actions really performed, of words and expressions really uttered. . . . [T]his is a mosaic of facts" (5). Occurring in a separate text from the novel, and uttered with intense seriousness, the claim inverts the tradition of the framed fiction, or the mock editor's note that ironically introduces *Pamela* or *Robinson Crusoe* as "real" manuscripts. Whereas the (masculine) tradition of the frame only pretends to claim that the story is true, Stowe's (feminine) strategy in the *Key* is to assert literally and earnestly that the story is factual—even though she knows that the novel and the *Key* itself are only loosely true, if they are true at all, based as they are on her own necessarily imperfect recollections and on other persons' reports of the actuality of slavery.[9] The narrator's assertions, even though they are, strictly speaking, inaccurate, are perfectly serious. The speaker of the *Key* justifies her attempt by alluding to the public reception of *Uncle Tom:* "It is *treated* as a reality,—sifted, tried and tested, as a reality; and therefore as a reality it may be proper that it should be defended" (5). For Stowe's contemporary readers, the question of the novel's truth was as important as it was for her: Southern critics cited their states' constitutions to prove that slaves could not legally be abused as they are in *Uncle Tom;* hostile linguists demonstrated that Stowe's renditions of dialects were faulty and geographically misplaced; Southern ladies wrote "anti-*Tom*" novels to refute Stowe's book, picturing the "true" happy situation of slaves in the South.[10]

If the truth-status of *Uncle Tom* was controversial, its emotional impact was never at issue. Stowe's most vehement detractors have agreed that the novel evokes tears: the question has always been whether the novel's sentimental strategies are in themselves objectionable. George F. Holmes, a Southern reviewer who violently derided *Uncle Tom,* saw the sentiment-provoking scene of Eva's death as "a gem shining amid surrounding rubbish" (he canceled out his praise, however, by accusing Stowe of having stolen the scene from Dickens).[11] More recently, critics concerned with the novel's potentially palliative effect upon the activism of individual readers have regarded sentimentalism as a dangerous falsehood. James Baldwin's asserting that "sentimentality, the ostentatious parading of excessive and spurious emotion, is the mark of dishonesty, the inability to feel" (578) returns, in a quirk of history yoking the civil rights activist with the conservative slave owner, to the original proslavery objection to Stowe's work: the accusation of deceit. Baldwin implies that the emotional experience the novel aims to inspire is itself a pretense, and that actual readers of *Uncle Tom* could indulge in a good cry, feel exonerated, and then forget about the issues of oppression and exploitation that the story addresses; the experience of reading sentimental fiction provides a cowardly means for the "sentimentalist" to evade "his aversion to experience, his fear of life, his arid heart."

But Stowe's own understanding of a text's emotional function was entirely different from Baldwin's. His refusal to bend to her text's strategies testifies to the necessity of placing rhetoric in its historical situation before attempting to analyze it, because a message uttered in one period to an intended audience can go completely astray in another context. Increasingly, critics are looking into the content of *Uncle Tom's* message, the political and religious implications of the story's emphasis on feminine domestication of American culture, submission to suffering here as a key to bliss in the hereafter, and reinforcement of Christian family values.[12] Any reader sharing Baldwin's social concerns would find much to object to in all of this.

I am less concerned here, though, with the novel's messages—ostensible or encoded—than with the mode in which the messages get transmitted. As though she could anticipate the political, ethical, and theological objections to her story's content, as though she could predict the intended audience's reluctance to accept *Uncle Tom* as true, Stowe consistently relied on the rhetorical techniques of sermons—strategies she had internalized while listening to her father, brothers, and husband, among others—to bring home her message to her readers. From her point of view, doubt among readers resembles doubt among parishioners. Christianity provides a master-narrative that represents relationships among earthly events and eternal realities; the revivalist preacher who would "awaken" his congregation must inspire them to accept "Divine Truth" on faith. Genuinely hoping to spark a change in the system that condoned slavery, Stowe faced a similar task. Her novel needed to inspire readers to accept, on faith, the truth of her story—even though the story itself, like the "facts" she fabricated to prove it, was invented. Like the preacher, she partly side-stepped the dilemma of how to prove the unprovable by moving away altogether from the message of speech toward the message of the body. Stowe's assertions that the novel is true are, strickly speaking, nonsense: her overriding strategy is not to appeal to sense at all, but rather to sensation.

By trying to provoke an emotional response in her audience, Stowe placed herself squarely in the tradition of the male Calvinist preachers who emulated Jonathan Edwards.[13] Perry Miller has explained how Edwards developed the "rhetoric of sensation" to resolve for himself the dilemma of preaching in language which operated, by Lockean definition, always at one remove from reality. Edwards accepted Locke's theory that words are signs for the things they represent and deduced that "words are of no use any otherwise than as they convey our own ideas to others" (quoted in Miller 177). Edwards was troubled, however, by the implications of abstract speech: to speak in words, to say "God, man, angel," is to evoke the arbitrary signs for those entities, rather than conceiving "the actual ideas." According to Miller, Edwards was torn between appreciating the efficiency of symbolic thought processes and abhorring the system of substitutions as a form of deceit. Edwards was in no position to anticipate—and playfully to accept—the inevitability of what Derrida would call "deferred presence" or "*différance.*" His theology demanded a belief in the existence of "the actual idea," originating in God. In the potential for speaker and listener to take the sign for the actual idea, the false for the true, Edwards saw "the supreme manifestation of original sin." The preacher resolved this conflict by ensuring that the words he must unavoidably use to work upon his congregation would be so pointedly arranged as to inspire the sensations they stood for.

Edwards hoped that the signifier could bring the signified into being within the bodies of his auditors. As he put it, "To have an actual idea of a thought, is to have that thought we have an idea of then in our minds. To have an actual idea of any pleasure or delight, there must be excited a degree of that delight. So to have an idea of any trouble or kind of pain, there must be excited a degree of that pain or trouble" (quoted in Miller 178). Miller observes that Edwards's reasoning on this point was "the most important achievement of his life and the key to his doctrine and practice" (179).

Edwards's rhetorical means of exciting "a degree" of pain or trouble included heavy reliance on direct address, that trope by which he repeatedly pictures "you, sinner" in "the hands of an angry God." Typically, the "application" sections of his discourses shift the sermons' focus from abstract exegesis to personalized accusations. In the final sections of his sermons, audiences would find themselves confronted with catalogues of sins committed by "you": "How *many sorts* of wickedness have you not been guilty of! How manifold have been the abominations of your life! What profaneness and contempt of God has been exercised by you!" (Edwards 671). Lest individual listeners try to shirk the accusations by distancing themselves from this unenviable "you," Edwards supplied details of sins so ordinary that no member of his intended audience could deny having committed them. In order to excite "a degree" of pain, the preacher would work upon the congregation's feelings, enforcing real tears when he could, yet impugning the authenticity of the emotion at the same time:

> Sometimes it may be you weep . . . in your hearing sermons,
> and hope God will take notice of it, and take it for some honour;
> but he sees it to be all hypocrisy. You weep for yourself; you are
> afraid of hell . . . Is it a heinous thing for God to slight you, a
> little, wretched, despicable creature; a worm, a mere nothing,
> and less than nothing; a vile insect that has risen up in contempt
> against the Majesty of heaven and earth? (673)

This worm, this vile insect—observed from an analytical distance—might seem to resemble Fielding's "little Reptile of a critic," the figure with whom the actual receiver of a text would presumably hesitate or even refuse to identify. The context, however, marks the difference in strategies. In Fielding's literary realm, the pretense, the falsehood at the heart of writing fiction is a given part of the game, and the distancing narrator labors under no moral necessity to evoke a genuine experience in his reader. In Edwards's theological realm, the situation is reversed: the preacher's primary goal is to subvert the pretense at the very heart of language by enforcing an emotional experience in the audience, by requiring them to see themselves reflected in that "you."

What Stowe's narrator does in the interventions within *Uncle Tom's Cabin* more closely resembles Edwards's strategy than Fielding's. In the nineteenth-century world, the property of the preacher, the reliance upon earnest, exhortative address, belonged to men (in Chapter 7, I examine some of the reasons why it was impossible for a woman to imitate the preacher's activity directly). Stowe was accustomed to hearing sensationalist preaching from male members of her family. She was awakened to Christianity at age thirteen while listening to one of her father's "frame sermons," a religious exhortation framed by a personal narrative of spiritual experience. The sermon moved Harriet to tears; she later wrote that she was "drawn to listen by a certain pathetic earnestness in his voice" (Gerson 13). That pathetic earnestness, that expressed faith in the link between sensation and genuine experience, and that concern for conveying "truth" despite the "deceitful" nature of fiction and of language itself, combined to create the strategy that Stowe, the woman novelist, borrowed from Edwards through her father and brothers, the male preachers, thus transforming a masculine means of enforcing spiritual presence into a feminine strategy for evoking presence in fiction.

"HOW FAST COULD *YOU* WALK": BUTTONHOLING THE ACTUAL READER

The narrator of *Uncle Tom's Cabin* is unusually explicit about her concern that her novel should be received as a direct representation of reality. In the final chapter, "Concluding Remarks," she explains how her desire to write the novel grew out of her observations of the political and theological debates about whether Northerners should be legally required to return fugitive slaves to Southern owners. From the tenor of these arguments she concluded that "these men and Christians cannot know what slavery is; if they did, such a question could never be open for discussion. And from this arose a desire to exhibit it in a *living dramatic reality*" (622). Though she uses exclamation marks pretty freely, Stowe seldom italicizes for emphasis; evidently, this phrase is particularly important to her conception of the novel.

The power of a "living dramatic reality" repeatedly erupts within the text. Throughout the "Concluding Remarks" and the narrative itself, the narrator frequently employs the conventions appropriate to "realism of presentation," implicitly suggesting the authenticity of her sources. In introducing one of the slave-heroines, for example, the narrator (referring to herself with an authoritatively masculine editorial "we") asserts that "Eliza, such as we have described her, is not a fancy sketch, but taken from remembrance, as we saw her, years ago, in Kentucky" (54). Similarly, the narrator reports of the slaves' horror of being sold down river: "We have ourselves heard this feeling expressed by them" (164). Stowe also adopts the realist convention of "omitting" or "disguising" proper nouns—for instance the name of "——— street" in New Orleans (468)—as if to mask the identities of real people and places. Taking the narrative's truth claims a step further, the "Concluding Remarks" refer often to "the writer's" personal observations of slaves, and quote the novelist's husband, Calvin Stowe, as an authority on slavery, without referring to his relation to the writer (627).

Stowe's narrator manipulates the conventions of verisimilitude in order to realize the problem of slavery for her readers, to let them see "what slavery is" and to encourage them to accept her text as authentic documentation of the situation. As the action of the novel demonstrates every time a character takes a risk to aid a desperate slave, Stowe believed in the power of what the narrator calls "the magic of the real presence of distress— the imploring human eye, the frail, trembling human hand, the despairing appeal of helpless agony" (156). Just as the "magic" of "the real presence" works to stir sympathy among her characters, Stowe evidently intended the verisimilitude, the "living dramatic reality," of her novel to work magic among her readers, to move them to sympathy and action.

Of course, concluding a novel with a chapter about how the fiction came to be written foregrounds the fact that it is not an authentic document, but only a novel. The editorial "we" (the pronoun of male journalists) and the narrator's distancing habit in this final chapter of referring to "the writer," rather than testifying with a personal "I," reinforce the self-reflexiveness suggested by so much intervening commentary: as we have seen, in fiction these are indicators of a preoccupation with literariness.

These distancing elements in Stowe's interventions strain against the continued assertions that the story is real. In an uneasy blending of earnest direct address and distancing ironies, *Uncle Tom's Cabin* presents a turbulent marriage of feminine and masculine modes of fictional discourse.

Stowe uses three basic types of interventions in *Uncle Tom:* (1) passages in the distancing tradition of Fielding's irony, which refer either disparagingly or disarmingly to a third-person "reader" (for example, "our readers" [68, 122, 158], "the reader" [310, 470], "many of my lady readers" [407]; (2) passages that oscillate between the distancing and engaging approaches and are explicitly addressed to specific narratees who are meant to represent large segments of the intended audience, such as "mother" (153–154), "good brother of the Southern states" (156), "sir" (208), "you, generous, noble-minded men and women of the South" (622), "Christian men and women of the North" (624), or "mothers of America" (624); and (3) passages addressed not so much to any fictive narratees created by or within the text, as to the actual reader, under the name of "you."

The first of these categories—third-person references to "the reader"—consists most frequently of straightforward reminders that it is the narrator's duty to keep the narratee informed of the fictional facts; for instance, "it would be injustice to her memory not to give the reader a little idea of [Dinah]" (310), or "we must daguerreotype [Tom] for our readers" (68). Significantly, although these interventions assume the distancing, third-person stance, they subvert the metaliterary implications of that stance by stubbornly insisting upon treating the subject matter as if it were true, speaking of the characters as if they were real people to whose memory the narrator (who is not, after all, a character, but a figure who claims authoritative access to events and information outside the text) must do justice, or whose daguerreotype she would be able to take.

The third-person references to "the reader" serve a rhetorical function very similar to that served by third-person references to "sinners" in a sermon. Even when Stowe's narrator adopts the sarcastic tone that typifies the distancing narrators of Thackeray or Kingsley, she does so to invoke the "real presence" of the distressed characters, as well as "the real presence" of the reader who would sympathize with them. When she refers to "readers" in interventions that bring up presumed failings in her audience's ethics or attitudes, her narrator makes the corrections for those failings perfectly clear. For example, in one passage Stowe twits "any of our refined and Christian readers" who "object to the society into which this scene introduces them" (132), soberly reminding "them" that they belong to a culture that encourages and perpetuates the slave-catchers whom such readers may find disagreeable. The passage aims to spark a feeling of guilt in any actual reader who sees his or her own attitude mirrored in that group of "readers" to which the passage refers.

On some occasions, the narrator inverts this strategy ironically, pretending to disapprove of a "reader's" presumed reaction to an event, but obviously endorsing that reaction. Consider an intervention in a scene describing the exploits of an escaped slave:

> If it had been only a Hungarian youth, now bravely defending in some mountain fastness the retreat of fugitives escaping from Austria into America, this would have been sublime heroism; but as it was a youth of African descent, defending the retreat of fugitives through America into Canada, of course we are too well instructed and patriotic to see any heroism in it; and if any of our readers do, they must do it on their own private responsibility. (299)

The narrator's diction—"bravely defending," "fugitives escaping into America," "sublime heroism"—makes the passage's ironic intent obvious, in a way which seldom occurs among the similarly sarcastic interventions of, for example, *Vanity Fair*. Whereas Thackeray's narrator's opinion on his characters may be difficult to trace through his ironic assertions about them, Stowe's narrator's analogy between the Hungarian hero and the escaped slave can leave very little doubt that she most heartily approves of "any readers" who see the resemblance "on their own private responsibility." And, by implication, any readers who *don't* ought to recognize their own failure, once they have considered the analogy.

The most strikingly engaging of Stowe's rhetorical strategies, and the feature that most closely resembles the rhetoric of sermons, is her narrator's heavy reliance on remarks directly addressed to narratees. Stowe's narrative interventions are structured as direct address nearly twice as often as they are third-person references. The second and third categories of intervention listed above—interventions addressed to a "you" either named or un-named—play an important role in Stowe's attempt to get the actual reader to take the narrative assertions to heart. When naming narratees, Stowe's narrator keeps them in broad categories and avoids limitations that might allow any given actual reader to deflect the remarks being addressed to him or her. Although a few passages of direct address are sarcastically aimed at some presumed flaw in the narratee, the narrator usually attributes amiable motives and compassionate assumptions to the "sir" or "mother" to whom she speaks. Such engaging passages include: "And oh! mother that reads this, has there never been in your house a drawer, or a closet, the opening of which has been to you like the opening again of a little grave? Ah! happy mother that you are, if it has not been so" (153–154). Any mid-nineteenth-century mother, whether or not she had lost a child, would have been sensitive to the appeal.[14] Nor are Stowe's narratees exclusively female: "And if you should ever be under the necessity, sir, of selecting, out of two hundred men, one who was to become your absolute owner and disposer, you would, perhaps, realize, just as Tom did, how few there were that you would feel at all comfortable in being made over to" (476). Although these passages specify the sex of the narratees to whom they are addressed, they imply the existence of impulses which are not necessarily limited to mothers or to gentlemen, and they encourage the actual reader who might be touched by their suggestions to sympathize with the novel's characters who lose their children or their freedom.

Uncle Tom's named narratees are sometimes delineated even more specifically than the "mother" or "sir" in the passages above, but Stowe usually includes a surprisingly large and varied number of groups in her addresses. The aim is apparently to include the largest possible number of actual readers among the figures of readers represented by the narratees. This is most striking in a long passage in "Concluding Remarks," in which the narrator speaks to

> men and women of America . . . [f]armers of Massachusetts, of New Hampshire, of Vermont, of Connecticut, who read this book by the blaze of your winter-evening fire,—strong hearted, generous sailors and ship-owners of Maine,— . . . [b]rave and generous men of New York, farmers of rich and joyous Ohio, and ye of the wide prairie states . . . [a]nd you, mothers of America. (623)

In a late twentieth-century context, this sounds ridiculous: the appeal to "mothers of America" too closely resembles a wartime recruiting poster or television commercial. Stowe's narrator makes the appeal, however, without a trace of irony: the long list of addressees concludes with the main clause of the sentence: "I beseech you . . . I beseech you." The narrator pleads with the narratees—and, by implication, with those readers who can identify with them—to sympathize with the slaves. With the repeated plea, "I beseech you," the distancing references to "the writer" that introduced the "Concluding Remarks" and the masculine editorial "we" that recurs throughout the text have yielded to the personal, engaging, feminine "I," the sign of the woman who would intrude her presence into the text as part of its "living dramatic reality."

Stowe's rhetoric does not end in begging for pity or preaching compassion. The narrator uses interventions of the third type, addressed directly to "you" or "reader," to require the actual reader to recognize parallels between his or her own life and the lives of the fictional slaves. We have already seen examples of this strategy among the addresses to named narratees, for instance, the appeal to the "mother" to remember the pain of losing a child, or the request for "sir" to imagine being put up for sale. At important rhetorical peaks of the novel, the narrator ensures the widest possible response to her appeals by not limiting the regional identity or political biases of her narratees. One of the most famous passages in the novel, Eliza's escape (which I mentioned in Chapter 2) is rendered all the more memorable by a brilliantly wielded example of this strategy. Apparently Stowe was concerned with convincing her audience that the episode was not only plausible, but true, for in "Concluding Remarks" she asserts that "the incident of the mother's crossing the Ohio river on the ice is a well-known fact" (618). But during the scene itself, she exploits the power of engaging direct address to persuade the reader of the scene's authenticity:

> If it were *your* Harry, mother, or your Willie, that were going to
> be torn from you by a brutal trader, tomorrow morning—if you
> had seen the man, and heard that the papers were signed and
> delivered, and you had only from twelve o'clock till morning to
> make good your escape, how fast could *you* walk? (105)

Would a reader need to be a mother, or need to have a son named Harry or Willie, to feel the personal appeal of that italicized *you*? (Probably not—

but still, imagine the impact of this passage on a reader like Elizabeth Gaskell, still mourning the death of her own infant Willie at the time she read *Uncle Tom.*) The narrator requires the reader to exercise his or her imagination in such a way as to draw out the parental feelings that may be active or latent in his or her real life, and, having evoked those real feelings, implores the reader to direct them at the characters. The many passages in the novel addressed to "you," "thou," or "ye," without limiting even the sex of the narratee as this example does, carry as far as possible this strategy of making an appeal to the reader's presumed experience of emotions, in order to render more immediately present the feelings attributed to the characters in the fiction. There are more than twenty-two such passages, (for example, on pages 167, 426, and 383). For any reader willing to take on the imaginative assignments the narrator demands, these interventions should increase the verisimilitude—and therefore, the emotional impact—of the novel.

When it works, this strategy may, indeed, evoke tears: the actual reader who pauses seriously to consider what it would feel like to be in the characters' situations might experience the tightness in the throat, the wetness in the eye, that we conventionally associate with a sentimental response. When the narrator makes you cry, she is taking a prerogative that belongs, in the extratextual nineteenth-century world, to the man in the pulpit. Just as the female author appropriates the male preacher's strategy for enforcing a sense of presence upon an audience, the feminine, engaging narrator wavers between her own territory of discourse and that of the masculine, distancing narrator. For all her earnest insistence that "you" must be persuaded to accept the characters' pain as a present reality, the narrative discourse (as opposed to the overt claims the narrator sometimes makes to the contrary) neither suppresses nor denies that one cannot finally transmit a representation of reality through words. The narrator's distancing moves point to an awareness that written language—even when it manipulates conversational modes of rhetoric to imitate the form of the "message of speech" (to return to Barthes's formulation)—is always and only language. Furthermore, crying over a novel is not the same as taking action against slavery: once the reader's sympathy is aroused, the reader is obliged to act upon the feeling by behaving sympathetically toward real-world slaves.[15] The narrator's engaging moves are her means of circumventing potential roadblocks in her project, to arrive at the "truest of messages," the "message of the body."

SILLY READERS OF LADIES' NOVELS: ELIOT'S NARRATEES

No one disputes that George Eliot was preoccupied with realism when she began writing novels.[16] Her anonymous essays in the *Westminster Review,* her early, pseudonymous correspondence with her publisher, John Blackwood, and her narrators' assertions in the interventions that continually interrupt her first two books repeatedly express her wish to avoid becoming one of those lady novelists who wrote silly novels. Wanting to be a novelist, she had no choice but to become a *woman* novelist; she could signal her unwillingness to be classified among the "lady novelists" by signing her fictions with a man's name and by employing masculine, distancing strategies in her narrative discourse. The silliness she was most concerned to avoid was the lady novelists' lapses of realism: Eliot says at every opportunity that she wants her novels to be *true.* Much like Stowe, she adapted earnest interventions as a means of encouraging a "real" sense of presence in her texts.

Nevertheless, assigning a gender to Eliot's narrators is no straightforward task. The masculine pseudonym coheres with the few hints in *Scenes of Clerical Life* that establish the narrator as a man acquainted with the neighbors whose tales he relates; in *Adam Bede,* however, the narrator betrays no solid clues as to gendered experience.[17] I call the *Adam Bede* narrator "she" partly by default and partly because her engaging strategies dominate the text, marking its discourse as feminine. Still, masculine moves are also present in the novel—expecially in chapter 17—bringing the narrator's gender-identity continually into question.[18] The gender of her narratee provokes questions, as well. The "readers" with whom she argues about the appropriateness of the narrative techniques are often specified as women— "silly ladies," one might call them. And yet the attitudes she attributes to those narratees are identical to the objections that she tries to answer in her letters to her publisher. The letters to Blackwood presume that he wants to transform her into a "lady novelist," even though Blackwood ostensibly believed he was corresponding with a man; the narrative interventions in *Scenes* and *Adam Bede* put Blackwood's supposed objections into the mouths of "lady readers," even though the novelist was drawing upon arguments she was having with a man. Perhaps because the laughing/weeping Lewes—her ideal reader—was entirely sympathetic with her novelistic aims, Eliot projected what she saw as the adversarial position of Blackwood onto the part of her imagined audience that Lewes could not occupy: the ladies.

Eliot implied that lady readers wanted to read "Silly Novels by Lady Novelists," and her *Westminster Review* article by that name specifies her reasons for objecting to that desire. Summing up the lack of "genuine observation" to be found in those novels, Eliot likens them to

> the pictures clever children sometimes draw "out of their own head," where you will see a modern villa on the right, two knights in helmets fighting in the foreground, and a tiger grinning in a jungle on the left, the several objects being brought together because the artist thinks each pretty, and perhaps still more because he remembers seeing them in other pictures. (*Essays* 315)

She decries fiction that imitates other fiction, self-reflexive fiction of a different kind from the metafiction her male contemporaries played with. In hilarious detail, Eliot mocks the results of fiction writing that makes no reference to the extratextual world: ludicrous, improbable plots: awkward, inflated, often unintelligibly abstract language; preposterously overrated heroines, whose creators praise their brilliance while filling their mouths with nonsense; and fantasy visions of religious conversion, social climbing, or historical events. What appalls Eliot about these novels is that their authors know little or nothing about the worlds they are trying to depict. They imitate other art or fantasy, ignoring "reality."

In her attack on "Silly Novels," George Eliot defines the tone that she would presumably wish her own narrators to take, instead of the pedantic, affected, showy style of the "Lady Novelists." She compares narrative tone with social behavior, noting how unpleasant it would be to spend time with any lady who flaunted her learning in the pompous manner of the lady novelists' narrators. Eliot would prefer the company of "a really cultured woman," whose behavior she describes specifically: "In conversation she is the least formidable of women, because she understands you, without wanting to make you aware that you *can't* understand her. She does not give you information, which is the raw material of culture,—she gives you sympathy, which is its subtlest essence" (*Essays* 317). Sympathy, the "subtlest essence" of culture, is what Eliot the reviewer claims to want to see in a woman novelist's narrator. It is also what her own engaging narrators try to elicit from her actual readers. Perhaps because of the imagined battle with Blackwood, the narrator of *Scenes* is not particularly engaging in his stance: he relies upon the distancing motif or positing flawed narratees.[19] His narrative style is gendered masculine, then, as are his sparse autobiographical details.

If Lewes played the role of the ideally sympathetic reader in the novelist's imagination as she wrote, Blackwood also seems to have been present in her mind as the silly reader who cannot grasp the point. If we compare the letters Eliot wrote to Blackwood while she was composing the *Scenes* and *Adam Bede* with the interventions in both novels, we can see that she often directly answered Blackwood's objections (or rather, what she construed those objections to be) while writing her fiction.[20] Her letters to Blackwood show that she was classifying his literary tastes as perfectly aligned with those of the silly readers, and her summaries of his position were not always fair. Still, in the narrative passages of Eliot's first two novels, as in her letters to Blackwood and in the "Silly Novels" essay, she argues consistently for the precedence of the "real" over the "ideal" in fiction.

As Gordon Haight has noted, "Neither George Eliot nor Blackwood was converted" by their correspondence (*George Eliot* 239). Perhaps because Blackwood remained unreconstructed, Eliot persisted in her interventions in *Scenes of Clerical Life* to ask the narratee to consider how much more George Eliot's characters resemble the people in one's own life than they do the figures in other novelists' fictions. Eliot has declared to Blackwood that she could not "step aside from what I *feel* to be *true*" in her fiction (Letters II, 299), and her narrator took up the challenge of making actual readers also feel the fiction to be true, in order to arouse their sympathy.

SYMPATHY: "THE SENSE OF HIS PRESENCE"

For George Eliot, sympathy, the "subtlest essence" of culture, was also the highest moral force operating in the world. In this she departs the company of Stowe and Gaskell, who also preach sympathy, but who see it as the necessary result of Christian faith. Having passed through a fervently evangelical period in her youth, Eliot rejected conventional Christianity in 1842 in a traumatic break with her faith and her father. Influenced by her own painstaking translations of Strauss and Feuerbach, as well as by the events of her life, she gradually replaced her faltering faith in divine love with a humanistic belief in the power of sympathy. George Eliot continued at first to couch her moral writings in terms of a "God," particularly in her anonymous essays for the *Westminster Review.* But these essays contain strong undercurrents of her developing humanism as well. A lengthy article written in 1855 attacks the teachings of the popular evangelist Dr. Cummings. The attack focuses on the harsh, destructive personality attributed to God in Cummings's writings and concludes with a summary of George Eliot's own version of God:

> The idea of God is really moral in its influence—it really cherishes all that is best and loveliest in man—only when God is contemplated as sympathizing with the pure elements of human feeling, as possessing infinitely all those attributes which we recognize to be moral in humanity. In this light, the idea of God and the sense of His presence intensify all noble feeling, and encourage all noble effort, on the same principle that human sympathy is found a source of strength: the brave man feels braver when he knows that another stout heart is beating time with his; the devoted woman who is wearing out her years in patient effort to alleviate suffering or save vice from the last stages of degradation, finds aid in the pressure of a friendly hand which tells her there is one who understands her deeds, and in her place would do the like. The idea of a God who not only sympathizes with all we feel and endure for our fellow-men, but who will pour new life into our too languid love, and give firmness to our vacillating purpose, is an extension and multiplication of the effects produced by human sympathy. (*Essays* 187–188)

According to Eliot, the sympathetic person who senses the presence of an Other—divine or human—capable of sharing in his or her feeling will find supporting strength to intensify that feeling. In *Adam Bede*, Eliot dramatizes the effects of such a presence in two ways: Dinah's sermon evokes the presence of Jesus, bringing "the idea of a God" vividly to life for her auditors; the narrator asserts her own sympathetic presence and that of her actual readers, bringing the fiction "to life." Both the preacher and the narrator depend upon direct address to achieve their effects.

Dinah's sermon occurs early in the novel, functioning as a model for the way in which direct address can instill a sense of presence in an audience. Dinah begins in a low key, with a prayer for inspiration from God and an invocation of her text for the talk: "The spirit of the Lord is upon me, because he hath anointed me to preach the gospel to the poor" (68). Her explication of that text, lasting for six long paragraphs, emphasizes that "Jesus Christ spoke those words," and that the poor are of particular importance to Jesus and to the followers of Wesleyan Methodism. She details Jesus' kindness to the poor, his miracles, and his infinite sympathy, then turns the focus of her talk for a moment on her hearers: "Ah! Wouldn't you love such a man if you saw him—if he was here in this village?" (70). After this brief suggestion that Jesus could manifest a presence in Hayslope, she returns to her doctrine, explaining Christ's status as the son of God and his mission "not to call the righteous, but sinners to repentance."

At this point Dinah's sermon shifts in tone, focusing on her hearers, and convincing the traveling stranger (through whose perspective the scene is focalized) that Dinah has the Methodist's capacity to move an audience, even though her listeners don't fully understand her message. As if openly and spontaneously responding to Jesus' words, Dinah exclaims to her audience: "The *lost!* . . . *Sinners!* . . . Ah, dear friends, does that mean you and me?" (71). The observing stranger notes Dinah's shift in emphasis: "At last it seemed as if, in her yearning desire to reclaim the lost sheep, she could not be satisfied by addressing her hearers as a body. She appealed first to one and then to another, beseeching them with tears to turn to God while there was yet time" (72). The tearful gaze, beseeching tone, and individual appeals, "first to one and then to another," recall the narrator of *Uncle Tom's Cabin,* speaking passionately and personally to specific members of her audience.

Dinah's message, like Stowe's, relies heavily on repetitions of the word "you" to bring a sense of Christ's suffering and of the individual mortal's sins home to each listener. "'All this he bore for you!'" she exclaims of the Passion: "'For you—and you never think of him; for you—and you turn your backs on him; you don't care what he has gone through for you. Yet he is not weary of toiling for you: he has risen from the dead, he is praying for you at the right hand of God'" (74). The effect of her sermon, very much like the discourses in the Edwardsian tradition, is to force Dinah's hearers to feel themselves to be the specific subjects of her list of sins. The heavy, hammering "you . . . you . . . you" of her talk drives a double impression into her listeners: that they are sinners, and that the Jesus of whom she speaks so passionately is real, possibly even physically present among them. As the traveler notices, the individuals in the crowd hardly comprehend Dinah's characterization of themselves as sinners. The narrator asserts that one man resolves to go less often to the tavern and to "[clean] himself more regularly of a Sunday"; another "couldn't help liking to look at [Dinah] and listen to her, though he dreaded every moment that she would fix her eyes on him, and address him in particular" (72–73). The sermon appeals not to their logical sense, but to their sensations.

The auditor who receives the biggest and perhaps the most confused impression from Dinah's sermon is "Chad's Bess," a notorious young woman who, before this day, had always been rather proud than otherwise of her small-scale vanity and frivolity. Like her fellow villagers, Bess only vaguely understands the charges leveled against her. Dinah's doctrine of sin and repentance makes no logical sense to Bess, But Dinah uses the rhetoric of sensation to break through Bess's denseness:

> [Bess] had a terrified sense that God, whom she had always thought of as very far off, was very near to her, and that Jesus was close by looking at her, though she could not see him. For Dinah had that belief in visible manifestations of Jesus, which is common among the Methodists, and she communicated it irresistibly to her hearers; she made them feel that he was among them bodily. (73)

Dinah communicates "that belief in visible manifestations of Jesus" through a rhetoric of sensation that defies sense. She claims literally to see him—"See! . . . where our blessed Lord stands and weeps. . . . He is among us; he is there close to you now; I see his wounded body and his look of love" (74). Her own "sense" of Jesus' presence, transmitted directly through her assertions and indirectly through her address to individual listeners, makes her subject seem so real to them that they respond emotionally, even hysterically. At the climax of her sermon, Dinah turns to Bess, "whose bonny youth and evident vanity had touched her with pity":

"Poor child! Poor child! He is beseeching you, and you don't listen to him. You think of earrings and fine gowns and caps, and you never think of the Saviour who died to save your precious soul. Your cheeks will be shrivelled one day, your hair will be grey, your poor body will be thin and tottering! Then you will begin to feel that your soul is not saved; then you will have to stand before God dressed in your sins, in your evil tempers and vain thoughts. And Jesus, who stands ready to help you now, won't help you then: because you won't have him to be your Saviour, he will be your judge." (74–75)

Poor Bess dissolves into sobs, and thereafter, under Dinah's continued influence, her behavior improves: the narrator establishes that Bess tries to change, not because she has really absorbed the logic of Dinah's argument, but because she has begun—under that barrage of "you's" and "your's"—to think less well of herself than she had. Similar to Jonathan Edwards's jeremiads in its direct application to her audience, Dinah's sermon differs from his in her enormous capacity for sympathy, which contrasts with the historical preacher's accusatory, authoritarian air of self-righteousness that Stowe's narrator so closely imitates.

In her sympathetic mien, Dinah resembles the narrator of *Uncle Tom*. Dinah's specific appeals to particular listeners are more like Stowe's exclamations to "mothers" or "good brothers of the South," than they are like George Eliot's more broadly applicable remarks to "you." But Dinah, according to the narrator, structures her sermon unselfconsciously, never calculating the effect it will have on her audience, though she strives for and believes in that effect. Dinah's technique recalls Eliot's remark about Stowe's narrative personality in *Dred:* "She never makes you feel that she is coldly calculating an effect, but you see that she is all a-glow for the moment with the wild enthusiasm, the unreasoning faith" of her Christian characters (*Essays* 327). The emotive strategy of Dinah's sermon is precisely that of the exhortative passages in Stowe's slavery novels, and the traveler observing Dinah's style makes an inward comment that parallels Eliot's remark on Stowe: "She was not preaching as she heard others preach, but speaking directly from her own emotions, and under the inspiration of her own simple faith" (72). Eliot sets up this Stowe-like figure, opens the emotional life of the book by having her preach a sermon that employs the rhetoric of sensation to make Jesus "real" for her audience, and then endorses both Dinah's motivations and her earnest, engaging preaching style by allowing her to have a positive influence on every life that she touches within the book. Dinah's role in the plot reinforces the suggestion of her power that the sermon establishes. Eliot's narrator, furthermore, seeks to extend that power beyond the realm of the characters to that of the actual reader, relying heavily, as Dinah of course does, on direct, earnest gestures toward "you."

Adam Bede opens with one of the most direct addresses to a reader imaginable:

> With a single drop of ink for a mirror, the Egyptian sorcerer undertakes to reveal to any chance comer far-reaching visions of the past. This is what I undertake to do for you, reader. With this drop of ink at the end of my pen I will show you the roomy workshop of Mr. Jonathan Burge, carpenter and builder in the village of Hayslope, as it appeared on the eighteenth of June, in the year of our Lord 1799. (49)

This, the entire first paragraph of the novel, sets forth the date and location of the first scene as specifically as possible. But even before she mentions these details, the narrator establishes the relationship she is to hold with the reader: with the "drop of ink" at the end of her pen, she will create a world like the illusion that the sorcerer can create. The sorcerer's "visions of the past" are not fabricated from nothing, but are visible in a drop of ink used "for a mirror"; that is, the sorcerer's illusions are reflections of something that is real. Like the magician, this narrator intends to record in ink reflections of a real rural English world, sixty years in the past. The narrator does not call herself a sorcerer or a master of illusion, however; she only draws the parallel between the magician's trick and her own act, writing. Thus introduced to the reader, the narrator often returns, both openly and subtly, to remind the reader that *Adam Bede* is something written, that it is a reflection, as in a mirror, of reality, and not a reality in itself. One could certainly argue that the narrator's recurring presence interferes with the "illusion of reality" within this novel; indeed the opening paragraph is a clear statement from the narrator that she consciously wants the actual reader to keep the illusory aspect of her history in mind.[21] This earnest address—combining the engaging insistence upon "your" presence with the distancing suggestion that the story, though realistic, is not real—

establishes the paradoxical blend of feminine and masculine strategies that run throughout the novel.

In terms of the technical moves of narrative discourse, Eliot's narrator seldom employs the distancing mode. The opening of chapter 17 is addressed to a disgruntled lady reader, that silly, female version of a Blackwood-like critic who would prefer a more idealized portrait of Irwine than the novel offers. The effect is distancing—as W. J. Harvey describes it, "The reader is repelled by having his reactions determined for him; he feels himself, and not the character, to be a puppet manipulated by the author" (*Art of George Eliot* 70). Only once among the other chapters does the narrator refer to the reader in the distancing third person. This occurs near the beginning of the book, in the chapter that follows Dinah's sermon. The narrator reflects that "Methodism" in Dinah's day denoted a faith and a way of life quite different from what Wesleyanism had become by 1859: "It is too possible that to some of my readers Methodism may mean nothing more than low-pitched gables up dingy streets, sleek grocers, sponging preachers, and hypocritical jargon—elements which are regarded as an exhaustive analysis of Methodism in many fashionable quarters" (82). This is distancing in that the actual reader is supposed not to want to identify with those in "fashionable quarters" who are charged with accepting such a reductive version of the history of Methodism, especially after having seen in Dinah's sermon how much more Methodist faith and practice might once have embraced.[22] This reference to "my readers" is clearly not engaging, and for *Adam Bede* it is exceptional.

Each of the many other references to the reader in *Adam Bede* is a direct address, not to the "madam" or "Mrs. Farthingale" who sometimes crops up in *Scenes of Clerical Life,* but simply to "you." As Barbara Hardy has described it, the dominant narrative "tone is personal: it is the tone of voice in which the author tells a story about remembered people. It is also the tone in which she addresses a living reader" (*Novels of George Eliot* 158). The repeated direct addresses inscribe a narratee who attends avidly to the narrator's discourse, sympathizing with the characters and paying scrupulous attention to her assertions. Often the narrator compliments the narratee when repeating a bit of information or explaining an obscure motive, by deferring to the narratee's memory and perspicacity: "you must remember" (145), "you perceive . . . you remember" (170), "you understand" (172), "as you know" (356), "you know Hetty did not" (443), and again, "you perceive" (258) or "you perceive how it was" (573). As if in conversation, the narrator thus graciously concedes that she is perhaps repeating or even belaboring points, while nodding to her listener's capacity for recognizing this, and trusting in her listener's indulgence.

The narrator is more peremptory, though always gently so, when instructing the sympathizing narratee on how to receive what she is saying. Examples of these civil directives are "do not suppose" (118), or "do not reason about it, my philosophical reader" (294). These instructions presume that the actual reader might be inclined to suppose or to philosophize wrongly, were he or she without the benefit of the narrator's admonitions, but their tone implies the narrator's assumption that her "philosophical reader" will tractably follow her advice. Other passages of address reveal the response that the narrator expects, and sometimes wishes to counteract. "You will perhaps be surprised to hear" (173) and "possibly you think" (399) are instances of this effort to second-guess, and to redirect, the actual reader's developing impressions of the characters. The narrator can be very direct in this attempt, as when she launches a defense of Adam's ill-advised passion for Hetty: "Before you despise Adam as deficient in penetration, pray ask yourself if you were ever predisposed to believe evil of any pretty woman—if you ever *could,* without hard head-breaking demonstration, believe evil of the *one* supremely pretty woman who has bewitched you. No" (198). This repetitive use of "you" in connection with Adam's most dangerous character flaw is the narrator's surest means of engaging the actual reader's empathy for "our friend Adam's" mistake. The narrator openly admits her intent to influence the narratee, shirking the use of "I" no more than that of "you." "I must remind you again" (209), she says, or "I assure you" (241), or "I beseech you to imagine" (242). The narrative "I" is present, personal, and insistent; she speaks directly to "you," bringing the actual reader's presence into the foreground as well.

Not every narrative intrusion in *Adam Bede* presupposes a specific response from the narratee. Some of the narrator's rhetorical questions seem genuinely to inquire into the actual reader's feelings or experiences, as if in conversation. "Have you ever seen a real English rustic perform a solo dance?" she asks, going on to suggest an answer: "Perhaps you have only seen a ballet rustic, smiling like a merry countryman in crockery, with graceful turns of the haunch and insinuating movements of the head. That is as much like the real thing as the 'Bird Waltz' is like the song of birds"

(324). Here the narrator appeals to the actual reader's experience of country dancers, real or artificial, and willingly fills in for the reader's possible ignorance with her amusing parallels.

In other instances, where the experience she asks the narratee about is less idiosyncratic, the narrator relies on the actual reader's own emotional memories to fill in the sentiment, as in the first scene in which Adam tentatively courts Dinah:

> That is a simple scene, reader. But it is almost certain that you, too, have been in love—perhaps, even, more than once, though you may not choose to say so to all your lady friends. If so, you will no more think the slight words, the timid looks, the tremulous touches, by which two human souls approach each other gradually . . . you will no more think these things trivial, than you will think the first-detected signs of coming spring trivial. . . . I am of opinion that love is a great and beautiful thing too; and if you agree with me, the smallest signs of it will . . . be like those little words, "light" and "music," stirring the long-winding fibres of your memory, and enriching your present with your most precious past. (537)

When she refers to "your present," the narrator evokes a consciousness of the moment at which the actual reader is reading that passage, absorbed in this budding love between Adam and Dinah. The "small signs" of their love should stir the actual reader's memory, bringing the "precious past" into a present response to Adam and Dinah. In the reader's experience, the past should momentarily enter the present: the personal memories should reinforce the reader's consciousness of his or her own genuine presence in the act of reading.[23] If the narrator can evoke the actual reader's complete empathy for the characters, then she will have taken a step toward educating the actual reader's faculty for sympathy. And to the extent that she can accomplish this, she aligns the reader even more specifically with her flawed hero, Adam, whose sympathies are educated through his contact with suffering and with Dinah. Significantly, the narrator does not generalize about the appropriate attitude to take toward these characters: instead she directs her remarks to "you." The technique parallels Dinah's strategy in her sermon when she exhorts Bess to imagine her own future sufferings in order to bring Jesus to life for her and to impress upon her a sense of what he has suffered for her. The device inspires belief.

This device of drawing on the actual reader's memory and imagination to fill in her descriptions and explanations hints at a lack of faith in any narrator's power to evoke a response without an actual reader's help. In this Eliot's narrator resembles the consistently self-deprecating narrator of *Mary Barton,* so dubious about her ability to transcribe imagined scenes, emotions, or even conversations "accurately." The narrator of *Adam Bede* expresses no misgivings about describing such fundamental elements of her story, but candidly admits other limitations to her narrative capacities. Her diffidence is never as extreme as the eighteenth-century conceit that a character such as Sophia Western or the Widow Wadman is simply too beautiful to be described in words and is expressed more sincerely than Fielding's or Sterne's. When in doubt, the narrator turns to "you" to explain:

> It is of little use for me to tell you that Hetty's cheek was like a rose-petal, that dimples played about her pouting lips . . . —of little use, unless you have seen a woman who affected you as Hetty affected her beholders, for otherwise, though you might conjure up the image of a lovely woman, she would not in the least resemble that distracting kitten-like maiden. I might mention all the divine charms of a bright spring day, but if you had never in your life utterly forgotten yourself in straining your eyes after the mounting lark . . . where would be the use of my descriptive catalogue? I could never make you know what I meant by a bright spring day. (128)

This is no hyperbolic trope, intended to imply that Hetty's beauty is so exceptional that it defies langauge, like Sophia's. Instead, it is a glimpse at the narrator's assumptions about the sources of actual readers' responses to realistic fiction. A reader who had never lived anywhere but Siberia, for instance, would obviously have no memories to correspond with the narrator's English "bright spring day"; but, more significantly, a British born and bred person who had never fully responded to the power of such a spring day, who had "never utterly forgot [him]self" through the season's romantic influence, could have no clearer idea of the narrator's "bright spring day" than the Siberian could.

Similarly, a reader who has never been affected by a woman "as Hetty affected her beholders" can only guess at what the narrator is trying to evoke in describing Hetty's attractiveness. This is particularly true in that the figurative language surrounding Hetty throughout the text—images of furry, heartless kittens, or rosy, juicy peaches with hard pits—is peculiarly repellent, in spite of all the narrator's reports of the compelling effect Hetty has upon those who see her. It may be difficult indeed to conceive of what the narrator means by saying of Hetty's beauty that "it is a beauty like that of kittens, or very small downy ducks making gentle rippling noises with their soft bills, or babies just beginning to toddle and to engage in conscious mischief—a beauty with which you can never be angry, but that you feel ready to crush for inability to comprehend the state of mind into which it throws you" (127). It is all very well for the narrator to use "you" in this passage, perhaps in the impersonal sense of "one," but can the device make actual readers feel that they have ever been thrown into a state of mind in which they would even momentarily want to crush a kitten, a duckling, or a baby with whom they could "never be angry"? "Unless you have seen" someone like Hetty, the narrator despairs of being able to make "you" see Hetty herself. The narrator recognizes the ambivalence of her own attitude toward Hetty, and in that ambivalence recognizes that the actual readers' mental images of Hetty, not to mention their emotional response to her, are outside the narrator's firm control.

This is inevitably true, of course, of the mental images and emotional responses that fiction evokes. A narrator's words can only begin to shape a reader's experience of a book: imagination and emotion make every actual reader's *Pride and Prejudice* or *Moby-Dick* different from any other actual reader's internalized versions of the novels.[24] This poses a particular problem for George Eliot's attempts at realism, a problem that the narrative technique both reflects and essays to remedy. Eliot's narrator, speaking from the author's own experience, tries to create a world that is a mirror, like the sorcerer's drop of ink, of a real, past world. She wants to distinguish it as much as possible from the "silly novels" that reflect only fantasy or other fiction, and she makes this desire explicit by mentioning the contrast between her homely characters and their fictional prototypes. She enlists the reader's sympathy for Dinah and Seth with elaborate mock solemnity: "We can hardly think Dinah and Seth beneath our sympathy, accustomed as we may be to weep over the loftier sorrows of heroines in satin boots and crinoline, and of heroes riding fiery horses, themselves ridden by still more fiery passions" (82). Similarly, she praises Hetty's beauty in the context of her oddly patched-together finery: "[Hetty's image in the mirror was] none the less lovely because Hetty's stays were not of white satin—such as I feel sure heroines must generally wear—but of a dark greenish cotton texture" (195). Such comments, particularly the reference to Hetty's lovely image in the mirror, should remind readers of the resemblance this mirror image of the Hayslope world is designed to bear to their own world.

The reflection is distorted; it differs from that which it represents, if only in that it surrounds the original with a frame. Still, the mirror, like the novel, reflects a representation of objects in the nonfictional world, and the narrator is particularly concerned that readers, unlike Hetty, should recognize the mundane reality of the originals. As a character, Hetty is not a representation of a real-world prototype, any more than she represents the idealized heroines in silly ladies' novels. The narratee, however, is meant to be a representation: in the mirror of "you" actual readers should see themselves, as in Hetty's mirror-image they should see resemblances to people they know. By mentioning the literary models she refuses to imitate, the narrator professes her unwillingness to idealize or to fantasize the way Hetty does, and requires actual readers to manifest their concurrence by becoming emotionally involved with these people whom they should see as so different from conventional literary figures, and so like themselves.

To be sure, the narrator's realism has limits, which she acknowledges even when it means she must depart from engaging strategies. One limit is the difficulty discussed above, namely, the problem of making actual readers visualize people or empathize with emotions for which they can find no parallels in their own experience. The narrator, sustaining her theme of the power of sympathy, would like to believe that a "realistic" emotional truth must be universal, until she tries to evoke an unconventional emotion— like the desire both to kiss and to crush Hetty—and must throw up her hands in defeat. Another acknowledged limit to her realism is the fact that though she claims that her characters are drawn from life, they nevertheless develop into extraordinary personalities. This comes to the surface of the narrative in one admonition to the narratee:

> Adam, you perceive, was by no means a marvellous man, nor, properly speaking, a genius, yet I will not pretend that his was an ordinary character among workmen; and it would not be at all a safe conclusion that the next best man you may happen to see with a basket of tools over his shoulder and a paper cap on his

head has the strong conscience and the strong sense, the blended susceptibility and self-command of our friend Adam. He was not an average man. (258)

The narrator proceeds to explain that some men like Adam do exist, but they are rare. The passage suggests the narrator's doubts that actual readers, unlikely as they are ever to have known or even heard of a man as admirable as Adam, may feel themselves to be in as remote a fantasy world as that of a silly novel while reading *Adam Bede*. For all her disclaimers of fantasy, the narrator is still creating a world where extremes do exist: Hetty's exaggerated attractiveness and selfishness, Dinah's limitless desire to give of herself, Adam's heroic emotional strength and capacity to learn forgiveness. The novel does operate on a more ideal plane than that of day-to-day occurrences, and such an intervention is tantamount to the narrator's admitting that fiction has to be more exceptional, less "average" than reality. The narrator's most engaging stroke consists of her two strategies in dealing with actual readers' potential doubt: first, by admitting openly that her characters and events might not always accord with the actual reader's experience, and second, by always keeping in mind the individual reader's capacity for disbelief. She keeps that awareness close to the surface of the narrative by addressing her arguments and advice personally to "you."

WHILE "THE STORY PAUSES," THE DISCOURSE CROSSES GENDER

For the narrator intent on reinforcing her reader's belief in the "reality" of the world she mirrors, nothing could be more audacious than to insert into the novel an extended commentary like chapter 17, "In Which the Story Pauses a Little." Opening the second book of the novel with an exclamation from "one of my lady readers" demanding that she make Mr. Irwine a more "edifying" example of a perfect minister, the narrator retorts, "Certainly I could, my fair critic, if I were . . . able to represent things as they never have been and never will be" (221). The chapter goes on to present the ostensible thesis of this novel: one can learn more of the deepest passions by close, sympathetic contact with real, lowly people than one can ever absorb from fantasy visions in life or in literature. The narrator claims "to give no more than a faithful account of men and things as they have mirrored themselves in my mind. The mirror is doubtless defective;

the outlines will sometimes be disturbed" but she feels "bound to tell you, as precisely as I can, what that reflection is" (221).

The chapter-long essay has become famous as a manifesto for all the points of realism that Eliot had earlier set forth in the *Westminster Review* and in her letters to Blackwood. It fills all the purposes that an author's theoretical preface or afterword to a novel could fill, while going one step farther. Not only does it force the actual reader to stand back from the fiction and consider its relation to reality, it makes him or her do so at a moment when the fictional world has already begun to be mirrored in meticulous detail. The chapter strives for a wrenching effect, analogous to the distancing effect of any metafictional narrative intervention, but multiplied in its intensity as it is in its length. The essay resembles the prefatory chapters in *Tom Jones,* except for one essential difference. Fielding's little essays occur regularly, at predictable intervals, and begin each of many books in the novel; they are only one part of an elaborate structure that works consistently to distance the actual reader from the fictional world. Eliot's chapter 17, appearing so unprecedentedly and unexpectedly at the beginning of only one of the six books in the novel, provides a jolt for any actual reader who does not skip it, a jolt the novel does not repeat.

What, then, could be the purpose of this jolt? Why would Eliot's narrator require her actual reader to abandon, if only momentarily, the illusion that the reasonably recognizable world she has begun to evoke is in some sense real? Why would she want the actual reader to remember that her characters' personalities are not fixed in reality, but are entirely the products of one person's authorial choices? Why, in other words, would she abandon the feminine novelistic project established by her engaging narrative techniques in the first sixteen chapters to signal a masculine, distancing acknowledgment that the fiction is really only fictional?

The answer, I think, is that this narrator—and by extension George Eliot—has tested the limits of the feminine, earnest stance and found them inadequate to her project. The pretense that the story is *real* can go only so far. After all, this narrator wants her actual readers to remember that they are merely reading, that the sympathy they are expending on Adam and Hetty, Dinah and Seth is only a model for what the actual reader could and should feel for real-world sufferers. Chapter 17, so personally and intently directed at "you" after its distancing first address, is explicit about the purpose of writing fiction that is realistic, but nevertheless admittedly not real:

> And I would not, even if I had the choice, be the clever novelist who could create a world so much better than this, in which we get up in the morning to do our daily work, that you would be likely to turn a harder, colder eye on the dusty streets and the common green fields—on the real breathing men and women, who can be chilled by your indifference or injured by your prejudice; who can be cheered and helped onward by your fellow-feeling, your forbearance, your outspoken, brave justice. (222)

If empathy for her characters helps develop the actual reader's capacity for sympathy, so be it, but reading the novel should, according to the narrator, be only an exercise for strengthening that capacity in the reader's life.[25] Whenever Eliot's narrator addresses a remark to "you," she is gradually building up her readers' awareness of their presence in the act of reading, of their actual relation to the characters, the narrator, and the author. With this chapter, she is expanding that awareness to force readers to recognize their necessary relation to characters that appear in their own real lives.

In this light, then, the *Adam Bede* narrator's shifting emphasis upon engaging and distancing techniques is not entirely paradoxical. The feminine insistence that the story is *real* works in tandem with the masculine acknowledgment that it is *really* a story. The combined narrative stances operate to redirect the actual reader's response to the fiction away from the text and into the extra-textual world. W. J. Harvey (who stops short of wholeheartedly endorsing intervention in Eliot's novels) has described this effect; "We do not leave the 'real' world behind when we are confronted with the world of [Eliot's] novels; in fact, George Eliot compels us to keep both worlds and their interrelationships firmly in our minds" (*Art of George Eliot* 79). The combination of engaging and distancing stances leads, however, to two slippery narrative moves that persistently point to paradoxes at the heart of any realist narrative text.

The first of these two moves is the narrator's insistence in chapter 17 that Adam Bede is a real person she knows. In the midst of defending the verisimilitude of her portrait of Pastor Irwine, the narrator quotes Adam's opinions on the minister, dramatizing a scene in which Adam and the narrator hold a conversation many years after the novel's main action (225–228). The device is blatantly inconsistent with the chapter's rhetoric. If, on the one hand, the narrator is supposed to be an individual capable of conversing with Adam, then the narrator's assertions about characters' thoughts and emotions must be subjective, conjectural; they must be the projections of one person's imagination onto other persons whose real feelings she could not know. If, on the other hand, the narrator is not supposed to be a person in the story—if her status is heterodiegetic, not homo-diegetic—then her discussion of the choices she has made in creating Pastor Irwine's character is consistent with her status, but her claim to have met Adam makes no sense at all.

Chapter 17 confuses the issue of the narrator's presence: she is present in a latter-day Hayslope, conversing with Adam, but she is also present in the extradiegetic situation in which she invents characters (such as Irwine) and tells "you" about them. The presence of the reader, too, becomes confused: the chapter presents the actual reader with both the distancing figure of a "lady reader" and the engaging "you" whom the narrator is so earnestly attempting to convert. The narrator's stance, then, oscillates between distance and engagement for the duration of the chapter.

The problem of the narrator's and the actual reader's position in chapter 17 finds a parallel in the second slippery move, another form of metalepsis. In two early passages of direct address the narrator places "you" upon the fictional scene. The conventional device of metalepsis is unusual for Eliot; its playful stance contrasts with the sober urgency of most of her interventions. In the tradition of Fielding's pretense that his narrator could "endanger the Reader's Neck" by picturing a reader-figure in a precarious position, the narrator positions "you" on the scene in two episodes, the introduction to Mr. Irwine's family and the first glimpse of the Poysers' home. In the latter passage, the narrator places "you" outside a window at the Hall Farm. "Put your face to one of the glass panes in the right-hand window," she urges, "What do you see?" (116). Under the influence of the repeated engaging interventions, the continual presence of "you" in this text, actual readers may find themselves simultaneously distanced and engaged by this maneuver. Sense tells them they are not at the Hall Farm: they are seated somewhere with a book in their hands, reading. And yet, the appeal to visual imagination, to the internal sensory experience of participating in the creation of a fictional world, directs the actual reader's attention to the physical, emotional reality of response. As the narrator puts it, "imagination is a licensed trespasser: it has no fear of dogs, but may climb over walls and peep in at windows with impunity" (115–116). The question to the narratee—"What do you see?"—brings the narrative focus back to sensation. It asks the actual reader to defy sense, to overlook the ontological paradoxes of a realist fiction, and to "*feel*" the story "*to be true.*"

Adam Bede's narrative discourse, then, represents an intermittent tug-of-war between sense and sensation, between engaging insistence upon the story's reality and distancing acknowledgments of its fictionality, between urgent feminine earnestness and metaliterary masculine playfulness. Considering George Eliot's position in the canon and her personal attempts to mask her gender in her public writing, the struggle is not surprising. Long considered among the great Victorian novels, her oeuvre has always been rated as comparable to the works of her male contemporaries. Eliot's reputation for brilliant, sophisticated manipulation of narrative technique is doubtless partly attributable to her willingness to incorporate the masculine effects of distancing narration into her novels. The flicker of masculinity that surfaces at those distancing moments in *Adam Bede* is congruent with the male pseudonym, the anxious desire not to be recognized by her Victorian audience as the "fallen" Marian Evans, and the wish to be taken seriously as an antitype of the Lady Novelist.

The fluctuation of gender in the novel's interventions resembles the apparent shift in the gender of the writer's first-person pronouns at the end of her essay on "Silly Novels." In the final paragraph, the referent of "we" oscillates between the masculine reviewer's editorial "we" and the "we" that speaks for women novelists.[26] The gender-versatility of George Eliot's written voice must be partly responsible for her high status in an androcentric canon. We would be underrating her centrality to women's novels and to the feminine Victorian tradition, however, if we were to overlook her novels' insistent reliance upon the engaging narrator.

6

Men's Narrators Who Cross Gender:

Can You Forgive Her? and *Bleak House*

BECAUSE they have pleased so many readers so well for so long a time, Trollope and Dickens can be said to have engaged many readers, but still their novelistic practices mainly fall under the matrix of distancing narration. To hold *Bleak House* (1853) and *Can You Forgive Her?* (1864) up against the models of engaging and distancing techniques is to recognize that Dickens and Trollope for the most part resisted the intimate relation between the narrative "I" and "you," the implied dynamic of actual readers' presence, the insistent and earnest "special pleading" that constitute the engaging narrator's characteristic moves. By inscribing distinctions between their narratees and actual readers, by pointing—subtly and explicitly—to the literary nature of their texts, both Dickens and Trollope participated in the masculine tradition of the distancing narrator. And yet each of them, at certain narrative moments and for reasons of his own, "borrows" the woman's move, direct address.

Without wishing to psychoanalyze either author (Dickens, at least, has already attracted plenty of attention along those lines), I want to point to signs in their texts that indicate a certain flexibility, a willingness to let their rhetoric be temporarily invaded by a trope that was encoded in their era as a feminine one. If they did not write earnest, engaging realist novels in the tradition of Gaskell and Eliot, it was because for both Dickens and

Trollope, the novel's status as aesthetic artifact took precedence over its rhetorical function. Their texts evince a preoccupation with the novel as an artifact, a literary construct taking its place among the productions of men of letters. Within the texts, this preoccupation finds expression in a self-consciousness about the process of novel writing.

In Trollope's case, the self-consciousness can be explicit, as in the passages in *Barchester Towers* where the narrator frets aloud over the fatiguing necessity of filling out a triple-decker novel to the end, or where the narrator promises the reader that Elinor Bold will not marry Mr. Slope, justifying the disclosure with a disquisition on the appropriate level of trust that should operate between a "novelist" and his "reader." Or, as we shall see in *Can You Forgive Her?*, Trollope's metaliterary musings can take a more implicit form, expressed in the story's structure through the playing off of one subgenre against another. In both respects, Trollope's expression of concern for literary questions closely resembles George Eliot's in *Adam Bede;* unlike Eliot, however, Trollope does not insist upon offsetting the metafictional features of his text by relying consistently on direct address.

"WE ARE ALWAYS WEAVING NOVELS": TROLLOPE'S METALEPSES

Can You Forgive Her? Is there, in the history of the English novel, a title more engaging—in my technical sense of the word—than this one? Read earnestly, it seems a sincere appeal to the individual reader's sympathy, a challenge that announces, even before one opens the book, a female character whose actions may or may not be forgiven, but whose plight will command "your" attention. This title is a bold stroke, because it insists upon addressing the actual reader, the person whose gaze falls upon the book's cover. Since the title is part of what Genette calls the "paratext," the apparatus that surrounds and defines the parameters of the text proper, its addressee cannot be located within the text.[1] The title in the form of a question enlists "you" immediately as its addressee, casting any casual consumer who happens to see the book (or one of its parts, in the original serial publication) in the role of reader. It draws you in.

And yet, as the text itself unfolds, the earnest applicability of the title seems to dissolve. Is the "her" whom we are to forgive—as the opening sentence of the first chapter asserts—Alice Vavasor, the young woman who throws over a seemingly ideal fiancé to accept a renewed marriage proposal from her cousin, a former lover whose inappropriateness as a mate is obvious even to Alice from the start? Or is it one, or both, of the women who form the apex of parallel love triangles in the novel's triple plot, Lady Glencora and/or Mrs. Greenow? If it is a generalized question—that is, can you forgive the female jilt, the flirt?—can the answer be the same for three such diverse women, who act from such completely different motives? Focusing on the acts of forgiveness dramatized in the story can only complicate the matter. Alice, for instance, is continually irritated by her relatives' gratuitous forgiveness for her refusal to bend to their collective and individual wills; after her worthy fiancé and friends have put Alice's mistakes behind them, the question seems to turn upon Alice, demanding of her whether she can forgive herself. Who, then, is the "you"; who is the "her"?

As one reaches the novel's conclusion, with its happy-ending resolution of the marriage plot it had exploded in its opening chapters, the title's question takes on even more complicated resonances. The narrative has so conscientiously depicted Alice's frustrated rage over being allowed to "do nothing" in politics, and has detailed with such precision the likelihood that as John Grey's wife, Alice can have little hope of exerting direct action on her own, that the question seems to stand upon its head: can you forgive Alice for marrying John Grey, which seemed at first to be the right thing, but which must in the end only exacerbate her frustration? (As is typical of Trollope, the proliferation of events and attitudes in the novel makes arrival at a definitive interpretation difficult if not impossible. John Grey's election to Parliament gives Alice the opportunity for the indirect political involvement she had hoped to gain, but had lost, through her cousin; still, John's dismissal of Alice's original anguish as symptoms of "illness" does not bode particularly well for her autonomous existence after she has become his wife.) The titular question is much less direct, and more ironic and perplexed, than at first it appeared to be.

So, too, is the relation that Trollope establishes between the narrator's "readers" and the actual reader. The title invites us to expect a recurring pattern of direct address; indeed, the title itself returns, refrain-like, in two passages where the narrator enlists his "reader's" sympathy for Alice. The second of these—"Oh! reader, can you forgive her in that she had sinned against the softness of her feminine nature?"—begins as an engaging appeal, but gets deflected into a passive construction that lets "you" off the hook: "I think that she may be forgiven, in that she had never brought herself to think lightly of her own fault" (730). The other repetition of the title phrase occurs in a frankly self-reflexive passage that points relentlessly to the fictional frame, even while pleading Alice's case before the potentially hard-hearted narratee:

> But can you forgive her, delicate reader? Or am I asking the question too early in my story? For myself, I have forgiven her. The story of her struggle has been present to my mind for many years,—and I have learned to think that even this offence against womanhood may, with deep repentance, be forgiven. And you also must forgive her before we close the book, or else my story will have been told amiss. (398)

Despite its direct-address structure, the intervention is distancing in two ways: first, by evoking a "delicate reader" who is prejudiced, quick to judge, and reluctant to sympathize (and then by professing his own conviction that such an attitude is not merited by Alice's "offence") the narrator creates a narratee with whom he implies the actual reader should not wish to identify; second, his references to the "story" (repeated three times in the passage), the "book," and his own responsibility for telling the reader about Alice all enforce a self-consciousness about the narrative's textual, fictional nature. These two interventions that repeat the title are not more straightforward instances of engaging direct address than the title itself, but models for the distancing moves Trollope's narrator typically makes.

As we have seen, a hallmark of the distancing narrator is to refer obliquely in the third-person to "the reader" or "my reader" rather than to "you," as though the figure being named were not present at the moment of the narrative transaction. Trollope's narrator refers so often to "the reader" in this novel that he seems to have been talking to himself while he composed, wondering aloud about what the future audience's reaction would be. In *Can You Forgive Her?* there are at least twenty-one such references to the reader. As he introduces his characters, for instance, the narrator seems to be making mental notes to himself: "Such had been Mr. Vavasor's pursuits and pleasures in life up to the time at which my story commences. But I must not allow the reader to suppose that he was a man without good qualities" (42), or "for Alice Vavasor when she will be

introduced to the reader had already passed her twenty-fourth birthday"
(43). This mode, quite distinct in its stance from conversational address,
persists throughout the text, as in "the attentive reader will remember"
(403), "It is hardly necessary to tell the reader that" (443), or "The reader is
not to suppose . . . it need hardly be explained to the reader" (632).
Granted, third-person references to "the reader" are a firmly entrenched
convention of nineteenth-century prose style, but we need only contrast the
preponderance of these references in Trollope's novel with their scarcity in
Adam Bede (which refers to "the reader" only twice) to recognize a significant difference in stance.

Trollope—who claims in his *Autobiography* not to have planned his
novels in advance, but to have composed rapidly and revised very little—
falls into certain formulas in his prose style, as several critics in his time and
ours have noted.[2] His notes to himself about "the reader" may be one such
tic; another is an interesting pattern by which his narrator constructs
passive sentences in order to avoid speaking directly to "you." I have already
mentioned a few of these passive constructions, for example, "I think that
she may be forgiven" (730) and "It need hardly be explained to the reader"
(632). Translated into the engaging mode of Gaskell or Eliot, these passages might read "I think you may forgive her" and "I hardly need to explain
to you." Trollope goes to some stylistic length to avoid this kind of direct
address, however. He writes the reader out of many remarks by inscribing
the figure within passive constructions, as in these examples: "Poor Alice! I
hope that she may be forgiven" (177); "It will be remembered" (600, 602);
"it must be owned" (537); "I beg that it may be also remembered" (490).
Despite the title's insistence upon evoking a present "you" before the text
begins, the novel suppresses "you" within the text; *Can You Forgive Her?*
contains approximately seventeen passages that describe the reader's potential actions and reactions in this passive mode.

By contrast, I have been able to find only five passages (in addition to
the title and its two refrains) that directly accost "you." In one case, the
narrator narrows the reference of "you" by endowing the narratee with a
gender: "Ah, my male friend and reader, who earnest thy bread, perhaps, as
a country vicar . . . hast thou never confessed . . . that Fate has been
unkind to thee in denying thee the one thing that thou has wanted?" (479).
That "one thing" is a seat in Parliament, a thing denied categorically to
women and specifically—it seems—to Trollope himself (of which I will say

more later in this chapter). Like the "delicate reader" whose exaggerated concern for offences "against womanhood" suggests that she is probably female, the "male reader" can stand in for only part of the actual audience, a part that is further circumscribed by the subsequent relative phrases, "who earnest thy bread . . . as a country vicar," "or sittest . . . at some weary desk in Somerset House," "or . . . rulest the yard behind the Cheapside counter." Only a few actual readers could answer this invocation.

The remaining four addresses to "you" are not limited in this way; by virtue of their general applicability and their scarcity within the text, their engaging impact is, I would argue, exceptionally strong. At the end of chapter 1, for example, as the narrator concludes his description of Alice, he seems to forget the aloof position he has adopted vis-à-vis his narratee, as though suddenly seized by the urgency of communicating his affection for his heroine: "I beg you, in taking her for all in all, to admit that she was a fine, handsome, high-spirited young woman" (45). The plea suggests an unusually antagonistic relation between the "you" and the "I" (since we are entirely dependent on the narrator for any opinion we can have of Alice at this point, why would we be unwilling to "admit" that she is what he describes her to be?). Still, for the moment, the "you" flashes onto the scene, and the narrator's concern that the actual reader should admire his heroine evokes the actual reader's presence as the story gets underway.

Appropriately enough, the first appearance of "you" within the text is on the first page, where the narrator refers directly to "your" role in the title: "Whether or no, she, whom you are to forgive, if you can, did or did not belong to the Upper Ten Thousand . . . I am not prepared to say. . . . Alice Vavasor, whose offence against the world I am to tell you, and if possible to excuse, was the daughter of [a] younger son" (39). Like the title, this opening sentence ushers "you" into the narrative. A definitive, if probably unintentional, symmetry contributes to the novel's closure, as the engaged "you" who enters the text departs in the distanced form of "my readers": "Probably my readers may agree with Alice. . . . But as [her friends] have all forgiven her . . . I hope that they who have followed her story to its close will not be less generous" (830).

In the juxtaposition of the first and final paragraphs of the novel, then, the opposition of distancing and engaging narrative breaks down. "My readers," they who "have followed [Alice's] story," are figures outside the narrative conversation, more distant from its contents than the initially (and thereafter occasionally) present "you." And yet, the final paragraph suggests, they occupy the same plane of existence as Alice's friends: their activity in forgiving Alice is exactly parallel to the characters' activity. The novel ends on a moment of metalepsis, in which the narrator is suggesting either that the "readers" are as fictional as the characters, or that the characters are as real as are the "readers," who, despite all the distancing strategies in the novel, have been established as figures for the rarely but pointedly present "you." By Trollope's own report, his characters *were* as real to him as his readers were. For him, the rhetorical issue of involving a real audience in the comings and goings of a fictional world was complicated by his passionate involvement in the imaginary world of his novels.

According to his *Autobiography,* Trollope "lived with [his] characters" (233). He asserts that the successful novelist "desires to make his readers so intimately acquainted with his characters that the creations of his brain should be to them speaking, moving, living, human creatures" (232):

> This he can never do unless he know those fictitious personages himself, and he can never know them well unless he can live with them in the full reality of established intimacy. They must be with him as he lies down to sleep, and as he wakes from his dreams. He must learn to hate them and to love them. He must argue with them, quarrel with them, forgive them, and even submit to them. (232−233).

For evidence that he took this attitude toward his own creations, Trollope cites his practice of returning to the same cast of characters over the course of many years of writing. "So much of my inner life was passed in their company," he says, that he could not resist being "allured back to [his] old friends" (319). Even after they had died in their fictional worlds, they lived on in his imagination; witness Trollope's legendary assertion that "I have never dissevered myself from Mrs. Proudie, and still live much in company with her ghost" (276).

According to Trollope, the process of conceiving narratives in fiction and the process of keeping track of the actual details of life were for him practically the same activity. On the subject of whether it would be more difficult to work simultaneously on two separate novels (as he once did) than to keep in mind the separate life stories of one's country friends and one's city friends, Trollope observes: "In our lives we are always weaving novels, and we manage to keep the different tales distinct" (155). From his perspective, the world of lived experience was in some respects as fictional as his novels, and the novels were nearly as real as his life. If we are to take his assertions about his own writing seriously, we must deduce that in his mind the line between the two worlds was deliberately and frankly blurred.

Small wonder, then, that his text blurs the lines as well. At different narrative moments, Trollope's narrator is equally capable of treating his characters and events as "real" and of reminding his "reader" that the same characters and events are fictional. (In this respect his practice resembles that of Thackeray, the contemporary novelist Trollope avowedly revered most highly.) Trollope's most persistently engaging strategy—that is, the technique his narrator most often uses to suggest the authenticity of his story—is a pretense that the narrator's information is imperfect. As in *Mary Barton,* the pose is not at all consistent: the narrator chooses seemingly arbitrary moments to suspend his omniscience and to claim that he does not have all the details. Frequently he repeats the phrases "I cannot say" or "I am not in a position to determine" (as on pages 46, 48, 52, 139, 140, 158), and he disavows knowledge of events, as well as of characters' motives. On the subject of what characters are thinking, he often raises questions rather than providing definitive information, characteristically introducing the questions with "I wonder" (pages 40, 73, 281, 604, 681, 685). These open-ended musings tend to militate against the closure of the text by suggesting that the narrator did not have complete access to all the "facts," and hence, that he did not invent the information he does report.

Similarly, the narrator opens out the text to invite the "reader's" participation in judging the characters' actions. Having detailed the awkwardness of Alice's decision to tour Switzerland, while still affianced to John Grey, with his rival, her cousin, the narrator turns to a narratee at the end of the paragraph to inquire, "Under these circumstances was not Lady Macleod right in saying that George Vavasor should not have been accepted as a companion for the Swiss tour?" (66). Much later in the novel, after examining Alice's assumptions about the gaming tables that have lured Lady Glencora, the narrator remarks, "Of course, she did not sift her suspicions. Who does at such moments?" (713). In the same vein, after narrating Kate's attempts to get the old Squire to listen to Bible chapters in the evening, the narrator appends a comment: "There may have been good produced by the small quantity to which he listened, as there is good from the physic which children take with wry faces, most unwillingly. Who can say?" (564). Who, indeed? When Trollope's narrator abdicates his claim to complete, definitive knowledge he takes a most engaging stance: he is not simply asking rhetorical questions, but genuine questions that enlist the actual reader's participation in filling out the narrative commentary.

And yet, despite his pretense of periodically allowing his characters to shield private thoughts from him, and despite his willingness to cede final judgments to the narratee, Trollope's narrator is far from consistently engaging in his stance toward the text itself. He continually alternates his claims for the narrative's reality with reminders of its fictive nature. When the Swiss tour takes place, for instance, the narrator suddenly foregrounds Trollope's authorial role:

> I am not going to describe the Vavasors' Swiss tour. It would not be fair on my readers. . . . and I should consider myself to be dishonest if I attempt to palm off such matter on the public in the pages of a novel. It is true that I have just returned from Switzerland, and should find such a course of writing very convenient. But I dismiss the temptation, strong as it is. Retro age, Satanas. (78)

Although this intervention somewhat audaciously focuses the narrative for the moment upon the way it is being written, it does not suggest that the narrator has invented the story. Other interventions are even more candid, however. One comes in the form of a footnote acknowledging that a character has been "borrowed" from a novel of Thackeray's (192). Another comes in the passage I have already cited, where the narrator wonders aloud about the possibility of adequately analyzing Alice's mind, in order to prompt his readers to forgiveness by telling the "story" well (397–398). Resembling the famous interventions in *Barchester Towers*, these spotlights on the narrator-as-creator recall the distancing effects of Thackeray's and Kingsley's metafictional meditations.[3]

PLAYING OFF THREE GENRES: THE METAFICTIONAL STORY

In *Can You Forgive Her?* Trollope's metafictional inclinations come across in the story, as well as in the discourse. As I have mentioned, the novel's pages are divided among three distinct plots, each one involving a woman with two rival suitors.[4] The two secondary plots are linked to the main plot by friendships among the characters: Alice Vavasor becomes intimate with Lady Glencora, the heroine of one subplot, and Alice's cousin Kate (who is closely involved in Alice's own story) spends much of her time with her aunt, Mrs. Greenow, the center of the second subplot. In addition to helping to vary the action and fill out the volumes of the novel, the two subplots operate as mirror images of the main plot. The mirrors reflect distortions of the main story, however; each of the three belongs to a separate subgenre of fiction, though all three find their comic/realistic resolutions in the end. By playing three kinds of story off against each other, and by privileging Alice's story as the focal point, the novelist implicitly raises the question: What kind of a novel will this be?

The subplots present two alternative fictional modes that contrast with the main plot, even as their action parallels its own. Trollope sets up the matrix for the plots in the titles for two of the chapters that deal with Alice's story, "John Grey, the Worthy Man" and "George Vavasor, the Wild Man." The terms are not applied in the text to the other two pairs of rivals, but their applicability is evident: Plantagenet Palliser is obviously the worthy man and Burgo Fitzgerald the wild man; Mr. Cheeseacre, ludicrous though he may be, earns the title of "worthy man" by being a substantial householder, while the freeloading Captain Bellfield aspires (through his shameless flirting and notorious irresponsibility) to the title of wild man. The resolution of each of the three stories depends upon the story's genre. In Glencora's story the worthy man wins the woman, but in Mrs. Greenow's, the wild man prevails. Both subplots are resolved far enough in advance of the novel's end to promote some suspense about which one Alice's story will imitate, or whether Alice might be the heroine to end up with no man at all.

Lady Glencora is at the center of a potentially tragic "silver spoon" novel, a story of romance among people with money and position, a situation whose potential consequences could affect many characters beyond the principals involved—indeed, could (and does) change the course of the (fictionalized) British Parliament. If Glencora were to abandon Plantagenet for Burgo, thus staining her husband's reputation, breaking his heart, and altering the course of his career, his prospects would be ruined, and he would never rise to become the prime minister. As it happens, Plantagenet's decision to accompany his wife to Europe has serious consequences, in that it postpones his promotion to chancellor of the exchequer. When Glencora wavers from her commitment to the "worthy man," she positions herself for a serious fall from her social position as well as her virtue, and threatens to join the ranks of tragic, sensational heroines along the lines of Mary Elizabeth Braddon's Lady Audley.

If Mrs. Greenow is not exactly low enough to be the heroine of a Newgate novel, she is enough lower than Glencora, socially speaking, to provide a sharply contrasting setting for the parallel plot. Mrs. Greenow's financial self-sufficiency and bourgeois self-satisfaction render her invulnerable to anything like a tragic fall. Her crocodile tears for her "dear departed Greenow" and her repeated assertion that the passionate part of her life is over, are—as the narrator likes to remind us—partly sincere. She has come too far in her life to be able to make any choices now that would have tragic consequences, even on a small scale. The subplot she dominates is a comic parody of the tragic plot concerning Glencora: Mrs. Greenow's story inverts the terms of Lady Glencora's, so that the "right" decision for her is to marry the attractive Captain Bellfield, the wild man, and to reject Mr. Cheeseacre, the ostensibly worthy man. The contrasts and similarities between these two plots provide a fertile ground for interpretation of Trollope's message, but that is not my present concern. What interests me here is the way the potentially tragic high-life plot and the relentlessly comic low-life plot point to the plot in between them, thus focusing attention on the nature of that main story.

Obviously, Alice is the heroine of a "realistic" novel, but her story plays with the conventional shape of such novels. Like Jane Austen's *Persuasion,* the novel begins at a moment somewhat later than the moment where realist novels typically end: with the heroine's engagement. Like Anne Elliott, Alice breaks off her commitment to her lover, but unlike Anne, Alice goes through the agonizing process of decision under the reader's eye, in the narrative present. As the story progresses and Alice experiences increasing panic at the thought of honoring her subsequent engagement to George, the novel turns its genre inside-out: whereas the conventional comic-realist novel (on the *Evelina*-model, for instance) traces the efforts of a heroine to get married, Alice's story follows her increasingly frustrating and painful attempts *not* to get married, first to John, then to George, then again to John (because she cannot forgive herself for having left him the first time). When, in the end, she consents to marry John, her plot aligns itself with the happy-ending closure of the other two—this is, after all, a comic novel. But in the contours of its story/ies, it is a novel that refuses to follow comfortably the shape that convention prescribes for its genre. In so doing, it draws attention to the question of genre itself, and becomes—on the level of its structure—a novel about novels, a work of subtly self-reflexive metafiction. Trollope's concern for literary questions—questions about what kind of novel to write and how best to write it—shows itself, then, in his novel's structure, as well as in the worries his narrator periodically expresses in interventions.

As I have argued, this self-conscious concern for the novel's literariness is a sign of masculinity in a narrator's stance (even, or should I say especially, when it surfaces in George Eliot's novels). In Trollope's case I think it signals his narrator's (as well as his own) identification with the tradition of male novelists, especially his beloved Thackeray. Alongside his predominantly distancing attitudes toward his fiction, however, a strain of engaging approaches—the few, potent examples of direct address and the implications that his characters are "real," which I have outlined above—persists. Other critics have argued that Trollope's "androgyny" surfaces in his treatment of women characters.[5] Looking to the realm of discourse rather than story, I see the rare but pointed engaging interventions as signs of "femininity" that enter Trollope's text; furthermore, I see parallel signs of feminine identification in Trollope's own account of his novel-writing activity in his *Autobiography*.

"IMPREGNATED WITH MY OWN CREATIONS": THE FEMININE TROLLOPE

First, let us look more closely at the terms in which Trollope frames his confession that he lived with his characters and thought of them as real. Describing the process by which he produced what he considered to be his best work, he says he would isolate himself from the responsibilities of his post-office job and his "household duties," in "some quiet spot among the mountains." "At such times I have been able to imbue myself thoroughly with the characters I have had in mind. I have wandered alone among the rocks and woods, crying at their grief, laughing at their absurdities, and thoroughly enjoying their joy. I have been impregnated with my own creations" (176). To be "impregnated with [his] own creations" is to take a decidedly feminine position in regard to their creation. Trollope's passionate emotional involvement with his characters, who moved him even to the point of "crying," also carries powerfully feminine connotations for a Victorian man.

For Trollope, creation itself, the process of bringing people—even fictional people—to life, is a female activity. The metaphor he uses clashes strikingly with Gilbert and Gubar's beautifully illustrated contention that the pen, for male writers, has usually been "a metaphorical penis" (3). The stance toward characters that Gilbert and Gubar describe as typically masculine applies to the distancing narrator: "Precisely because a writer 'fathers' his text, his literary creations . . . are his possession, his property. Having defined them in language and thus generated them, he owns them, controls them, and encloses them on the printed page" (12). Trollope, who (according to his own metaphor) saw himself as mothering his own text, is surely an exception to Gilbert and Gubar's rule. His engaging narrative attitude toward his characters' existence, which is not at all consistent, but nevertheless present in his text, acknowledges his feminine concept of the novelist's activity. Trollope departs the company of masculine artists who conceive of writing as a virile act.

I argue at length in Chapter 7 that a motivating force behind the engaging narrator's presence in female texts was the ban on women's public speech in the nineteenth century. I would not want to conclude this discussion of Trollope without noting that men, too, could feel publicly silenced, and could experience the urgency of expressing "real" sentiments through fictional texts. Trollope's narrator, addressing the male narratee of *Can You Forgive Her?* in a passage I mentioned above, refers to membership in Parliament as "the one thing that thou hast wanted" which Fate has denied. The *Autobiography* is very explicit about the novelist's own desire to sit in Parliament and his disappointment at finding he could not prove wrong the uncle who had taunted him for his boyhood ambition to be elected to the House of Commons. Trollope attributes his failure partly to his weakness as a public speaker: "I had no special gifts that way, and had not studied the art early enough in life to overcome natural difficulties" (296).

Whether or not his lack of success in his brief political campaign was entirely due to his difficulties with speaking, Trollope felt himself effectively silenced by his defeat. Twice in his *Autobiography* he asserts that his novels became the channel by which he made public statements about his private convictions: "As I was debarred from expressing my opinions in the House of Commons, I took this method of declaring myself" (that is, writing *Phineas Finn*) (317). Of Plantagenet and Lady Glencora, he writes,

> By no amount of description or asseveration could I succeed in making any reader understand how much these characters with their belongings have been to me in my latter life; or how frequently I have used them for the expression of my political and social convictions. They have been as real to me as free trade was to Mr. Cobden, or the dominion of a party to Mr. Disraeli; and as I have not been able to speak from the benches of the House of Commons, or to thunder from platforms, or to be efficacious as a lecturer, they have served me as safety-valves by which to deliver my soul. (180)

Evidently Trollope felt himself to be specifically barred from the locations of public expression—the M. P.'s bench, the lecturer's platform—that were theoretically available to men but generally forbidden to women. Unlike his female contemporaries, he focuses in his account of his frustration upon his own need to speak (as "a safety-valve by which to deliver my soul"), rather than on a desire to communicate a message to an audience, to effect some influence upon the world. Still, I think that his recourse to earnest, direct address in novels whose story and discourse are primarily distancing is a sign of his partial identification with all of the female voices that, like his own, could speak only through texts.

DICKENS AND THE POLYVOCAL NARRATOR

Anthony Trollope's access to the public ear, then, was confined to the utterances he made in his official capacity at the Post Office or in written texts. To find a contemporary whose standing as a public celebrity placed him in a contrasting situation, we need look no further than Charles Dickens. Dickens's passion and talent for oratory, public reading, and acting in melodramas are legendary; his own access to being heard in public was nearly unlimited.[6] His personal fame attests to a difference between his status and Trollope's. When Trollope visited the United States and called on Brigham Young, having "been vain enough to conceive that he would have heard my name," he was "properly punished" by the "great polygamist's" turning him away from the door and insisting that Trollope must be a "miner" (*Autobiography* 350). By contrast, when Dickens and his wife came to America for a tour of public readings, they were swamped with invitations and surrounded by adoring crowds who tried to touch the author or to take away souvenirs from among his clothes. Phyllis Rose has remarked that "in the annals of contemporary literary celebrity, there is nothing to which one can compare Dickens's reception in America in 1842"; his public reception resembled nothing so much as America's hysterical welcome to the Beatles in the early 1960s (157).

As his biographers have established, Dickens was extremely sensitive about his standing in the public regard.[7] He sometimes went to absurd lengths to maintain credibility in his relations with his audience—witness the preface he appended to *Bleak House,* arguing for the scientific reality of death by spontaneous combustion, after the serialized version of the novel raised controversy over the circumstances of Krook's demise. Dickens was a public figure; his opinions, his imagination, and even his body were regarded by his admirers and himself as public property.

In this respect, Dickens stands apart from all of the other authors in this study except (in her later life and in a comparatively modest way) Stowe. Kingsley, Thackeray, Gaskell, Eliot, and Trollope all enjoyed literary reputations of varying degrees of exaltation, and each of them (with the possible exception of Kingsley) was "lionized" in the middle of the nineteenth century as their works have been canonized since. But as Trollope ruefully acknowledges in his autobiography, no one else achieved the fame and popularity that Dickens did.

If we think about novels' narrative discourse in relation to their authors' historical situations, we can find significance in Dickens's singularity: the most publicly present of all these novelists, he was also the least given to using address to a "reader" in heterodiegetically narrated novels. The moments in Dickens's novels where an uncharacterized narrator addresses an audience directly as "you" are rare: one occurs in *Little Dorrit* (300), where the narrator advises the reader to have patience in waiting to hear of a character's fate; several mock-formal addresses to "my Lords and Gentlemen and Honourable Boards" appear in *Our Mutual Friend* during scenes concerning Betty Higdon; significantly, these distancing interventions include no engaging appeals to "you." The ending of *Hard Times,* which has frequently been compared to a sermon, is framed as direct exhortation to the audience: "Dear reader! It rests with you and me, whether, in our two fields of action, similar things shall be or not. Let them be!" (227).[8] But the most well known and most frequently discussed instances of direct address in Dickens's work is the scene in *Bleak House* where Jo, the illiterate crossing-sweep, dies.

Because of that scene's prominence, and because of the novel's chronological proximity to the others in this study, I choose *Bleak House* as my example of Dickens's narrative practice, even though its unique structure makes it atypical of Dickens's work. Everyone who has read *Bleak House* remembers the scene of Jo's death; the climactic moment of authorial address is often seen as prototypically "Dickensian" in terms of its exploitation of melodramatic, emotional impact. How strange, then, that Dickens at his most Dickensian—Dickens in an engaging intervention—is actually Dickens taking an uncharacteristic narrative stance.

In terms of narrative perspective, *Bleak House* is highly experimental for its era. The basic pattern of alternating narrators between Esther's homodiegetic viewpoint and the other, unnamed narrator's heterodiegetic perspective is complex in the first place. The multiplicity of voices within that "other narrator's" utterances complicates the structure even further.[9] It is not possible to determine who is speaking in *Bleak House* without first asking, When? In what chapter, what paragraph, what line? The interweaving of free indirect discourse with several recurring voices—among them a voice for the Fashionable Intelligence, and another voice that reports public occurrences at Tom-All-Alone's—produces a genuinely polyvocal novel that explodes the idea of an omniscient narrator-as-person. The narrative voice that alternates with Esther's is never a "who," but is rather a conglomeration of disparate languages and perspectives: it is, as Elizabeth Ermarth has called the realist narrators, "Nobody." The voice is bodiless, the perspectives are multiple, the strategies diverse. When the narrator suddenly asserts an intense personal presence through direct address during the scene of Jo's death, the moment's sharp contrast with the rest of the text draws special attention to the intervention's strategy.

Generally speaking, Dickens creates in *Bleak House* neither a distancing narrator nor an engaging narrator. It is not a "narrator" at all, in the sense that I have been using the term: a narrative voice representing a personal perspective that claims to parallel that of the novelist and that addresses an audience/auditor. To be sure, my concern here is not primarily with the dialogic discourse that Dickens produced in *Bleak House*. Before looking in detail at the scene of Jo's death, therefore, I will briefly illustrate the variety among the heterodiegetic narrative voices. In that the experimental nature of the text necessarily calls attention to its nature as text—for readers today as well as Dickens's contemporary audience—*Bleak House* is a self-reflexive, metafictional novel. Its narrative interventions do not evoke a personally present narrator, nor do they insist upon an identity between narratee and actual reader. In these respects, it is primarily distancing, rather than engaging, according to the models I am using. As such, the text is consistent with Dickens's identity as a man whose voice had extra-literary access to public attention. He could (and did) reach his audience from stages and lecterns, and thus was at leisure to use literary texts for other purposes. Within its context, the one passage of direct address—which W. J. Harvey has called the "controlled crescendo" of *Bleak House* (*Character and the Novel* 963–964)—is a shimmering example of the power this feminine trope could wield within a predominantly masculine narrative situation.

Let us look, then, at some of the variations in voice that Dickens's heterodiegetic narrator undergoes in *Bleak House*. The narrative stance moves freely among the thoughts and words of both major and minor characters, resulting in drastic stylistic shifts from one scene (or one part of a scene) to another. Some passages resemble pages from a reporter's notebook, as for example the scene in the street in front of Krook's shop after the death of Nemo. A beadle arrives, seeking information and witnesses for the inquest:

> Is immediately referred to innumerable people who can tell nothing whatever. Is made more imbecile by being constantly informed that Mrs. Green's son "was a law-writer his-self, and knowed him better than anybody"—which son of Mrs. Green's appears, on inquiry, to be at the present time aboard a vessel bound for China, three months out, but considered accessible by telegraph, on application to the Lords of the Admiralty. Beadle goes into various shops and parlours, examining the inhabitants; always shutting the door first, and by exclusion, delay, and general idiotcy, exasperating the public. Policeman seen to smile to potboy. Public loses interest, and undergoes reaction. Taunts the beadle, in shrill youthful voices, with having boiled a boy; choruses fragments of a popular song to

that effect, and importing that the boy was made into soup for the workhouse. Policeman at last finds it necessary to support the law, and seize a vocalist; who is released upon the flight of the rest, on condition of his getting out of this then, come! and cutting it—a condition he immediately observes. (195–196)

This short excerpt from the scene is narrated from a fairly consistent viewpoint, by an educated speaker whose evident contempt for the beadle comes across in such terms as "imbecile" and "idiotcy"; like all the heterodiegetically narrated chapters in *Bleak House,* it casts its verbs in the present tense. The speaker's relative sophistication can be inferred from the distance he establishes between his perspective and the antics of beadle, crowd, and policeman. Although he has access to words such as "exasperating," "innumerable," and "vocalist," his language is often invaded by that of the crowd. He can render their discourse directly ("'was a law-writer his-self'") or indirectly ("getting out of this then, come! and cutting it"), which blurs the margins between his own language and the crowd's. The ungrammatical sentences rely on predicates without subjects ("Taunts the beadle"), dangling participles ("choruses fragments of a popular song to that effect, and importing"), and misplaced relative pronouns ("which son of Mrs. Green's appears") to suggest the loose style of the speakers on the street and/or of someone noting their words and actions rapidly. Casual language mingles with terms from "officialese," perhaps the language of the beadle, or of the newspaper or institution for whom the reporter is taking notes ("appears, on inquiry, to be at the present time," "who is released upon the flight of the rest, on condition"). The resulting polyvocal rendition of the scene is presented to the narratee of *Bleak House* almost as though it were some kind of document. This is not a mimetic representation of a speaker's remarks to a personal addressee or even to a collective audience.

The narration of *Bleak House* continually shifts in style and perspective. The chapter following the one in which Nemo's death occurs depicts the Dedlocks in Paris. Here the narrator's voice undergoes appropriate alterations, exaggerating the superficial differences between the world of Lady Dedlock and that of her former lover:

Sooth to say, they cannot go away too fast; for, even here, my Lady Dedlock has been bored to death. Concert, assembly, opera, theatre, drive, nothing is new to my Lady, under the worn-out heavens. Only last Sunday, when poor wretches were gay—within the walls, playing with children among the clipped trees and the statues in the Palace Garden; walking, a score abreast, in the Elysian Fields, made more Elysian by performing dogs and wooden horses; between whiles filtering (a few) through the gloomy Cathedral of Our Lady, to say a word or two at the base of a pillar, within flare of a rusty little gridiron full of gusty little tapers—without the walls, encompassing Paris with dancing, love-making, wine-drinking, tobacco-smoking, tomb-visiting, billiard card and domino playing, quack-doctoring, and much murderous refuse, animate and inanimate—only last Sunday, my Lady, in the desolation of Boredom and the clutch of Giant Despair, almost hated her own maid for being in spirits.

She cannot, therefore, go too fast from Paris. Weariness of soul lies before her, as it lies behind—her Ariel has put a girdle of it round the whole earth, and it cannot be unclasped. (204–205)

Here, the elaborately literary diction contrasts with the casual language of the previous chapter. "Sooth to say," "poor wretches," "she cannot, therefore, go too fast"—the formal locutions align themselves with clichés ("bored to death," "under the worn-out heavens") to mimic the artificial stiffness of Lady Dedlock's existence. The literary allusions (to Ariel and to Giant Despair) and the use of personification (Boredom) combine with sardonic wordplay (the Elysian Fields "made more Elysian") to elevate the tone of the language. And yet even this passage is mixed in its voices. The long aside that occurs between dashes to depict "low-life" on a Sunday in Paris interrupts Lady Dedlock's insipid existence with a vivid string of activities. Dickens's famous penchant for list making comes into play, as the narrative voice contrasts Lady Dedlock's static list of occupations, all named by nouns ("Concert, assembly, opera, theatre, drive") with the life going on around her in exuberant participles and gerunds ("dancing, love-making, wine-drinking," etc.) The voice of the Fashionable Intelligence which reports on the Dedlocks' movements (56) gets interrupted and thrown off course by the voice of street life, even as Lady Dedlock's own world is soon to be thus disturbed.[10]

To look at every passage in *Bleak House*'s present-tense chapters in this much detail would obviously be to undertake a monumental task—and yet even this level of detail cannot begin to describe all the complexities with which the narrative voice plays off one kind of discourse with another. Without attempting to describe the subtleties of every passage or, indeed, of the novel as a whole, I want simply to emphasize that such narration does not mimic conversation, for the speaker's identity is constantly shifting, and the narratee's position is questionable and problematic. If we cannot establish *who* is speaking, how can we hope to know "to whom"? Unlike Esther's narrative, which manifests a strong awareness of a potential reading audience, the present-tense sections seem to be addressed to nobody in particular, to "nemo." The narratee, like the narrator, is "Nobody."

"AND DYING THUS AROUND US EVERY DAY": THE ENGAGING MOMENT

This shifting conglomeration of narrative voices and stances is what renders the moment of direct address at Jo's deathbed so memorable. All the force of the chameleon narrator suddenly consolidates into a voice that focuses itself outside the text for a unique moment of discursive contact between narrator and readers. The placement of the address at the end of a chapter seems to suspend narrative time, thus emphasizing the effect of extending the passage's point of reference outside the text. (Had the passage occurred at the end of a "number" in serial publication, the suspension of narrative time would have been even more strongly enforced, but as it happened, Dickens placed this chapter at the beginning of the fortieth installment of *Bleak House* [947–948].)

The chapter ends with Allan Woodcourt leading the dying boy in the Lord's Prayer, which Jo continually interrupts to ask "is the light a-comin', sir?" (705). Jo stumbles through the prayer's third line and expires:

> "Hallowed be—thy—"
> The light is come upon the dark benighted way. Dead!
> Dead, your Majesty. Dead, my lords and gentlemen.
> Dead, Right Reverends and Wrong Reverends of every order.
> Dead, men and women, born with Heavenly compassion in
> your hearts. And dying thus around us every day. (705)

Coming in the context of *Bleak House*'s narrative indeterminacy and relativity, this unabashedly didactic address has a peculiar power.[11] It begins in

153

the distancing mode, addressing a narratee with whom very few people can identify, "Your Majesty." This is not the first appearance of that narratee in the novel: the voice of the Fashionable Intelligence directs one snide remark to "Your Majesty" much earlier (55). This time, though, the voice moves on, to address the increasingly comprehensive groups of Parliament ("my lords and gentlemen") and Christian ministers ("Right Reverends"). The stance is still distancing, because only a minority of readers can answer personally to these addresses, and because the narrator ensures that many of them will refuse to identify with the next appellation he chooses, "Wrong Reverends of every order." The distancing stance implicitly places the blame for Jo's death on all of these public figures, with whom most readers would not identify themselves.

But then, in the modulation to "men and women, born with Heavenly compassion in your hearts," the narratee is suddenly transformed into "you" (through the phrase, "your hearts"): no adult reader can escape the address, or the implication of culpability. The final coda, "and dying thus around us every day," takes the ultimately engaging step of unifying the narrative "I" with "you" into the figure of "us"—this narrator, who up to now has had no unified voice, no identity to tie him to any personal perspective, is momentarily revealed to all of his readers as one of them, one of the "men and women" who are bound to take some action on behalf of Jo's memory. The action the narrator takes—of course—is to speak for the inarticulate Jo and to enlist the sympathy of actual readers for actual deaths.

Dickens's strategy at such a moment is melodramatic, sensational, sentimental. It is also engaging in the technical sense. For one instant in a very long novel it evokes the presence of actual readers, and it requires those readers to consider the relation of the book in their hands to the world they inhabit. Barbara Hardy says of the moment that "Dickens at last finds a perfect voice for death," in which "the individual experience is given a resonance and intensity, the reader's sympathy engaged through ritual or ritualistic appeals" (*Forms of Feeling* 73). Hardy attributes the passage's affective impact to "the generalization which attaches the emotion dramatized inside the book to a broader emotional experience": the experience, that is, of "you" and "us." The highly self-conscious literary frame that surrounds the moment is technically distancing. Still, in allowing his slippery narrator one personal manifestation, one instance of intimate contact with actual readers, Dickens was borrowing an engaging technique.

What did it mean for a Victorian male novelist to borrow a feminine narrative gesture? Women novelists had, after all, appropriated earnest direct address from the rhetoric of male preachers and politicians, transporting it from the public realm into the pages of their fiction. For women, this formed the most direct means of access to real-world political influence. Through women's novels, it also came to form part of the feminine literary tradition of manipulating literary rhetoric in order to effect real-world change. Dickens had more access than most men to the public's attention, because he could speak in his own voice and be assured of an attentive audience. (His famous public readings were to attest to his pleasure in commanding that public eye and ear.) As we have seen, the metaliterary structure of a novel such as *Bleak House* demonstrates the male novelist's resulting leisure to cavort through a text, to be—as S. J. Newman puts it, in reference to Dickens—"at play." When a male novelist felt a need to "get serious," if only momentarily, he could reach across the gap in gendered interventions to grasp the technique that women were devising for the purpose.

Cross-influence among male and female novelists has long commanded the attention of critics and reviewers. Dickens himself thought that Stowe, for example, borrowed too much from fellow novelists. In an 1852 letter, he wrote of his reaction to *Uncle Tom's Cabin:*

> She (I mean Mrs. Stowe) is a leetle unscrupulous in the appropriatin' way. I seem to see a writer with whom I am very intimate (and whom nobody can possibly admire more than myself) peeping very often through the thinness of the paper. Further I descry the ghost of Mary Barton. . . . [B]ut in spite of this, I consider the book a fine one. (quoted in Leavis 166)

The "writer with whom I am very intimate" must be Dickens himself. Playfully, he appropriate's Stowe's American dialect to frame the very phrase in which he accuses her of unscrupulously borrowing material from him. The timing of this letter suggests, however, that he may have been protesting too much: indeed, he may have borrowed from the intervention strategies of *Uncle Tom* and *Mary Barton* while composing the scene of Jo's death.

Bleak House was written in installments, beginning in November 1851 and ending in August 1853.[12] Dickens did not write the chapter containing Jo's death until the summer of 1853, after he had written the

1852 letter about *Uncle Tom*. The "ghost of Mary Barton" he saw in *Uncle Tom* could have been the spectre of presence evoked by the repeated passages of earnest direct address so characteristic of both women's texts. That ghost—the feminine presence that speaks earnestly to "you"—may have risen again for Dickens as he composed a scene whose purposes had so much in common with the two women's novels. When he needed to appeal to preachers and politicians and to the "men and women" who formed their audiences, he borrowed from the women novlists the technique that they had adapted from public speakers.

Critics have come to see Esther's narrative as the location of femininity in *Bleak House*.[13] The engaging moment after Jo's death, however, shows signs of the feminine carrying over into the heterodiegetically narrated parts of the novel, enabling Dickens to achieve his sentimental effects even within this multivalent, metaliterary structure. Like his female contemporaries, Dickens did not disdain the rhetoric of sensation: the power and popularity of his novels attest to the potential effectiveness of crossing the gendered boundaries of narrative intervention.

III

Reflecting upon the Model:
Gendered Interventions
in History

7

The Victorian Place of Enunciation:

Gender and the Chance to Speak

FOR THE nineteenth-century woman who had something to say, finding a safe space in which to say it was not easy. If she restricted herself to addressing her own domestic circle, her "true womanhood" could remain intact, but she would have to be content with the rather abstract prospect of influencing the public world indirectly through her personal impact on her husband, brothers, and sons.[1] If she tried instead to speak in public—as the American socialist reformer Fanny Wright began to do in the 1830s—she might extend her range of influence. She ran the risk, however, of endangering not only her feminine reputation, but also the public perception of her female sexuality.

Women were fully aware of the danger of speaking before a sexually mixed audience, or what journalists of the period liked to call a "promiscuous" gathering. Even in places where women were openly encouraged to speak, as in meetings of the American socialist movement, they suppressed themselves. One Owenite woman, trying to explain her silence, asked: "It being so novel a thing for females to speak in public assemblies, and the idea of all eyes being, at once, directed toward them, is it all that marvellous that . . . a sufficiency of courage is wanting to speak their sentiments?"[2] The woman's anxiety peeps through the shifting syntax of her question. The phrase "and the idea of all eyes being, at once, directed toward them" is grammatically unconnected to the first part of the sentence; it is a subject without any predicate, a state of "being" for which the consequences remain unspoken. What she cannot say is that the nineteenth-century female body toward which "all eyes [are] at once directed" must surrender its femininity.

Catharine Beecher, the elder sister of Harriet Beecher Stowe, dedicated her life to didactic writings and lectures on domestic science. She knew all about the immasculating potential of a woman's speech before a promiscuous audience. Teaching by word, if not by example, that women must devote themselves exclusively to their domestic responsibilities, Beecher covered the paradox of her own public activity by addressing chiefly female audiences and by attacking women who compromised their femininity by daring to speak before men. Consider her 1836 portrait of Fanny Wright:

> Who can look without disgust and abhorrence upon such an one as Fanny Wright, with her great masculine person, her loud voice, her untasteful attire, going about unprotected and feeling no need of protection, mingling with men in stormy debate, and standing up with bare-faced impudence, to lecture to a public assembly. . . . There she stands, with brazen front and brawny arms, attacking the safeguards of all that is venerable and sacred in religion, all that is safe and wise in law, all that is pure and lovely in domestic virtue. Her talents only make her the more conspicuous and offensive, her amiable disposition and sincerity, only make her folly and want of common sense the more pitiable, her freedom from private vices, if she is free, only indicates, that without delicacy, and without principles, she has so thrown off all feminine attractions, that freedom from temptation is her only, and shameful palladium. I cannot conceive any thing in the shape of a woman, more intolerably offensive and disgusting.[3]

Beecher's description transforms the woman orator into a thing, not just an object of derision, but also the object of the looks that Beecher beckons her readers to direct at Wright. The conservative political agenda of the attack is evident; Wright's socialist ideas threaten "all that is venerable and sacred . . . safe and wise . . . pure and lovely." But Beecher is careful neither to quote nor to allude to those ideas: they never take shape in her text. What emerges instead is Wright's "great masculine person"—Wright was uncommonly tall—"her untasteful attire," her "brazen front and brawny arms." If Wright's clothes are "untasteful," then she has abandoned the feminine duties and values of her middle-class status and has given the promiscuous audience licence to undress her; the body they find beneath

the attire is "masculine" and "brawny." The placement of Wright's figure—
"standing up with bare-faced impudence, to lecture to a public assembly,"
"unprotected and feeling no need of protection, mingling with men"—
further accentuates the vision of the nakedly masculine stance Wright
automatically adopts by mounting the stage.

Perhaps the most revealing move in Beecher's characterization of
Wright, though, is her handling of Wright's personal virtues. Conceding
the lecturer's "amiable disposition and sincerity," she demurs over Wright's
"freedom from private vices, if she is free." Beecher reasons that so immas-
culated a woman could not have avoided vicious sexual entanglements
through anything so feminine as "delicacy and principles." Instead, she has
"so thrown off all feminine attractions" that no man would want her. What
is "shameful" about Wright's "freedom from temptation" is that a feminine
Victorian woman, while she must repulse sexual overtures from men, is also
required to inspire them.

This vision of the incompatibility of public speaking with not only
feminine propriety, but also female sexuality, would surely have presented a
daunting picture to any "respectable" woman with ambitions of exerting a
public influence. To speak in public, Beecher implies, is to become a "thing
in the shape of a woman": to lose one's intrinsic sexuality as well as one's
outward gender, and worse, to become the object of the public regard.
Beecher's position is a startling one, given its context: she was herself
making a public utterance when she wrote the sketch of Wright for publication in her *Letters on the Difficulties of Religion* (1836). And Beecher did give
lectures on domestic economy—but not, if she could help it, to "promiscuous" audiences. The position from which Beecher writes is the ambitious
bourgeois matron's (or spinster's) compromise with the prevailing ideology
of domestic influence. She will speak to women of women's concerns, but
she will insist on remaining "in her place," out of that frightfully objectify-
ing public view.[4]

Catharine Beecher's verbal cartoon of Frances Wright recalls the gender arrangements in nineteenth-century caricatures of women orators.
Women speaking to groups of mixed or uncertain gender get stripped of
their femininity in Victorian-era cartoons, while women speaking to
women are marked as feminine, even if they are made to look foolish. The
French caricature on the frontispiece of this book shows a coarse-featured,
open-mouthed woman addressing amused women and distressed men from

The woman orator who speaks to women, thus maintaining
her femininity. (Courtesy of Harvard College Library.)

a pulpit (1871). The 1842 cartoon from *Punch* (*facing page*) makes an even
more masculinized thing of its subject, the "female Chartist," Mary Anne
Walker. Flat-chested, sharp-featured, wild-eyed, and speaking, the caricature of Walker is accompanied by *Punch*'s comments on her gender-
identity. "Miss Walker," *Punch* reports, "gave indications at a very early age
of a turn for public life, and from her decidedly masculine predilections, she
acquired the appellation of Tom-boy in her own immediate neighborhood"
(192). By contrast, the 1848 drawing of a woman addressing a working
women's club (*above,* attributed to "Beaumont" in Fuchs, 472) shows an
exaggeratedly feminine form, a delicately featured face, and an arm at-
tached to a hand by a decidedly limp wrist. Evidently, to speak to a group of
women was one thing; to speak to a "promiscuous" gathering was quite
another matter.

"Portrait of a Female Politician" from *Punch*. The female Chartist
with the "masculine predilection" for public speaking. (Courtesy of
Harvard College Library.)

Buried in these visual strategies for depriving women orators of their
gender is the attribute of the lecturer that poses the greatest threat to the
idea of true womanhood that Catharine Beecher shared with fellow domestic ideologues: "her loud voice." Against the background of the ban on
public self-expression, a woman with something to say was better off restricting her voice to the comparative silence of print. Indeed, by the
1870s, when Harriet Beecher Stowe toured New England and the Midwest,
reading her fiction aloud in an unsuccessful attempt to earn large sums of
money, a woman could appear on a stage without repercussions. Though
some reviews of Stowe's readings disparaged her voice for being weaker
than, for example, Dickens's (one review pointedly put her in her place,
remarking that "as a parlour reader Mrs. Stowe may be pleasant enough,
but as a public reader she furnishes forth dull entertainment"), no one

challenged the right of America's most famous woman author to read her work before a mixed audience.[5]

Nevertheless, Stowe herself cherished an idea, very similar to her sister Catharine's, about the gendered implications of addressing an audience from a stage. In Annie Fields's memoir of Stowe, she tells of the novelist's preparations before her first public reading in Boston. Fields reports that Stowe

> called me into her bedroom, where she stood before the mirror, with her short gray hair, which usually lay in soft curls around her brow, brushed erect and standing stiffly, "Look here, my dear," she said: "now I am exactly like my father, Dr. Lyman Beecher, when he was going to preach," and she held up her forefinger warningly. It was easy to see that the spirit of the old preacher was revived in her veins, and the afternoon would show something of his power. (299)

Granted, the phallic imagery of this description—the usually soft hair "erect and standing stiffly," the admonitory forefinger "held up," the father's spirit engorging the woman's veins with power—belongs to Fields, not to Stowe. But the fantasy of resembling the powerful male preacher is Stowe's, and Fields's avid participation in the fantasy shows that this woman of the 1870s had not strayed far from the ideas that Catharine Beecher had expressed forty years earlier about the immasculating potential of public speaking. To "preach" on stage was automatically to cross-dress.

Surprisingly enough, for some women, even to write for publication was to cross-dress. In spite of the firmly established tradition of eighteenth-century literary women, appearing in print in early nineteenth-century America was tantamount to appearing in drag. Mary Kelley relates a telling anecdote about Caroline Howard Gilman, who remembered in her old age that as a teenager she had been overcome with shame in 1810 when one of her poems (which a relative had secretly submitted for publication) was accepted. Gilman said she had "wept bitterly" and been "alarmed" to see herself in print—it was "as if I had been detected in a man's apparel" (180). What is interesting about Gilman's reaction is not just her youthful suppression of the generations of women who had written and published before her, but her intense identification of her poem with her own body. She explained the shame of publication as though it meant exposure of a hidden predilection: for the public to see her manuscript clothed, as it were, in print was the same for her as if they had seen her own female body clothed in a man's garb. The key word in her reflection on the experience is "detected": the shame was not in the writing or the cross-dressing, but in having been caught in the act.

Gilman's confession suggests that occupying herself with literary writing was still a transgression of gender roles, even for a woman of Gaskell's, Stowe's, and Eliot's generation. Public speaking and preaching, too, were off limits for the woman who was anxious not to transgress gender lines. What the women novelists did was to take two modes of potentially dangerous expression and combine them, forming a mode through which they could "speak" without exposing themselves. By taking up the strategies that men used in real-world discourse—the earnest exhortation, the personalized direct address to an audience, the insistence on speaking a *truth*—the women transformed those rhetorical moves into feminine codes in literary discourse. By moving preacherly rhetoric into print, they created a literary space where they could "speak" in relative safety. To write fiction with engaging narrative strategies was, for the mid-nineteenth century, to write as a woman: when Dickens or Trollope sometimes borrowed them, they, too, were cross-dressing. And yet for the men, novel-writing represented such a different choice in the realm of public utterances from what it meant for the women: it is not really surprising that feminine, engaging moves are more difficult to find in men's texts than are masculine, distancing moves in women's novels. Men had so many other public places in which they could, if they chose to, say something.

The difficulty, then, for the Victorian woman who wished to speak was to find the space where she could speak safely, the place of enunciation she could occupy without the humiliation of transforming herself into a "thing in the shape of a woman," or even a figure "exactly like [her] father." She could, if she would, speak up at an Owenite meeting, in a Quaker church, before a group of women students, at a religious revival, or as an evangelist buttonholing individual sinners: each of these alternatives, though, had the double disadvantage of giving the speaker access to only a small (and usually already converted) audience, and of requiring the woman's physical presence in a public arena.[6] If she was torn between ambition and the fear of immasculation and humiliation, if she wanted to reach large numbers with her voice without exposing her body to the general view, her only option was to write. The challenge was to find a mode of writing that could wield the kind of power that public speaking represented for men. Realistic fiction became that mode.

MAINTAINING A GOOD NAME: AUTHORIAL PRIORITIES IN THE FEMININE REALM

The fact that writing was the respectable middle-class woman's single opportunity for public self-expression has been firmly established in studies of gender's relation to authorship. Ellen Moers, for example, says that "the novel and the poem were women's only instruments of social action in the early nineteenth century: literature was their pulpit, tribune, academy, commission, and parliament all in one. 'I want to be doing something with the pen,' said Harriet Martineau, 'since no other means of action in politics are in a woman's power'" (*Literary Women* 20). Of American society, Kelley writes that "women were isolated from and generally denied participation in their country's public life. They were not statesmen or politicians, judges or legislators, entrepreneurs or merchants, or in any way simply prominent, public citizens" (111). And Vineta Colby writes of British women that "forbidden the pulpit, the university lecture platform, the seat in Parliament, they turned to an outlet in which they were welcome and through which they could express their ideas and wield an influence otherwise denied them" (6).[7] On both sides of the Atlantic, the ground where the respectable woman could speak authoritatively in public was strictly limited to the space within the covers of a book.

Under the circumstances, women who wrote were likely to regard their activity as being different from that of literary men. Robert A. Colby has said that when George Eliot referred "to herself in late career as an 'aesthetic teacher,' she was simply articulating what writers and readers had long accepted as the function of the man (or woman) of letters in society" (18). But did this parenthetical woman of letters necessarily regard her own function as identical to that of the man? And was the teaching that George Eliot's early novels tried to accomplish strictly of an "aesthetic" nature? (In the context of the letter where she uses the phrase, Eliot distinguishes between "aesthetic" and "doctrinal" teaching, in order to dissociate herself from novelists who concentrate on theological or political current events.) I think that Eliot's claim to be participating in the masculine tradition of aesthetic teaching, like her pseudonym and her use of distancing techniques in *Adam Bede,* is a sign of her self-conscious appropriation of a male role. Men, after all, could exert moral and political influence directly from pulpits, lecture halls, or parliamentary seats if they chose to. For them, literature was primarily an aesthetic realm, a space where texts and traditions could be played off against one another in an admittedly artificial form. Literature could serve the same purpose for women, but from the perspective of the female writer, literature also had to be the space of action and of public influence, difficult if not impossible for her to achieve in other spheres.

Women of the period certainly could recognize the potential for power that writing fiction represented. Dinah Mulock Craik is often quoted on this subject, for her striking boast that the novel is "one of the most important moral agents of the community. The essayist may write for his hundreds, the preacher preach for his thousands; but the novelist counts his audience by millions. His power is three-fold—over heart, reason, and fancy."[8] The novelist's power, then, is to be reckoned by the numbers he reaches as well as by the strategies—emotional, intellectual, and imaginative—he uses to move his enormous audience. What is odd about Craik's assertion, though, is the elision of gender that leads her to call the novelist, along with the essayist and preacher, "he." Whereas the essayist and the preacher would almost invariably be male, the novelist in Craik's day would have a fair chance of being female. Though a novelist herself, Craik seems to hesitate to claim publicly the novelist's power for her own sex. The implicit claim is there (along with the ironic fact that she is also for the moment included among the masculine group of "essayists"), but Craik's hesitation to overtly assign female gender to these groups of writers supports Kelley's contention that any mid-nineteenth-century woman who wrote for publication would have had to see herself as filling a male role.[9]

By taking on a public identity, by earning money, and by participating in the creation of culture, the woman writer, Kelley explains, assumed a "semblance of male status" (111). What Mary Poovey says of an earlier generation of English women writers was still largely true at mid-century: "The cultural pressure to conform to the image of proper (or innate) femininity directly contradicted the demands of professional authorship" (241). To be sure, authorship itself was not seen as intrinsically masculine. Caroline Howard Gilman, for example, expressed no sense of shame for having written a poem, but she agonized over being "detected" at it. It was the professional aspect of writing for publication—transporting a woman's words outside the domestic sphere—that endangered her feminine reputation in the public's view and in her own.

That Gaskell, Stowe, and Eliot—like the less celebrated "literary domestics" of their era—wished, at least at some level, to maintain their respectability has been well established by their various biographers. One sign of that desire was their reluctance to attach their names to their earliest work. Gaskell published *Mary Barton* anonymously; Eliot invented for herself a male pen name. And although Stowe did not suppress the fact that *Uncle Tom's Cabin* was her work, she did try to disavow responsibility for it (with her infamous claim that "God wrote it"). Almost perversely, Stowe adopted a masculine pseudonym, "Christopher Crowfield," for her most domestically oriented books, *House and Home Papers* (1865) and *Little Foxes, or the Little Failings which Mar Domestic Happiness* (1866). Perhaps Stowe felt that her fame as the author of *Uncle Tom* disqualified her from making feminine pronouncements in her own female name.

Both Gaskell's and Stowe's feminine "good names" were damaged by the reforming thrust of their literary efforts. For Gaskell, the temporary loss of her reputation as a proper woman came, as I have mentioned, with the publication of *Ruth*. For Stowe, the writing of *Uncle Tom's Cabin* precipitated attacks on her womanhood as virulent as the attacks on her artistry, especially from Southern reviewers. In a particularly memorable example, George F. Holmes in the *Southern Literary Messenger* made "a distinction between *lady* writers and *female* writers" to justify the vehemence of his condemnation of Stowe's novel:

> We could not find it in our hearts to visit the dulness or igno-
> rance of a well-meaning lady with the vigorous discipline which
> it is necessary to inflict upon male dunces and blockheads. But
> where a writer of the softer sex manifests, in her productions, a
> shameless disregard of truth and of those amenities which so
> peculiarly belong to her sphere of life, we hold that she has
> forfeited her claim to be considered a lady, and with that claim
> all exemption from the utmost stringency of critical punish-
> ment. (Ammons 7)

Ironically, although Holmes's reasons for denuding Stowe of the privileges of her sex are not intentionally complimentary, his action has the effect of distinguishing her work as deserving serious (albeit negative) attention. Stowe's use of the novel to extend her influence beyond "her sphere of life" meant that she gave up some of the feminine respectability due to a "lady writer," but it also meant she could be taken seriously. Stowe's family name was already a liability among Southern anti-abolitionists; in a flippant attack on *Dred* for its "profanity," the *Messenger* (speaking through an ostensibly female persona, a "young lady of New England") says of Stowe: "Were she a woman, we should blush for the sex—luckily she is only a Beecher" (Ammons 48). (I imagine this imputation would have nettled Catharine at least as much as it could bother her sister.)

For Eliot, too, a "good name" was a constantly nagging problem. Before she published her first novel, Eliot had already sacrificed her own feminine reputation to her relationship with George Lewes, not to mention having supported herself with professional, intellectual, literary work. On both counts, she "was no lady," and even after her fiction had been exposed as the work of a female writer, she was inevitably taken more seriously than any "lady writer" could be. Her insistence upon calling herself "Mrs. Lewes" throughout the twenty-two years that she lived out of wedlock with the man whose first name she borrowed for her pen name is a poignant sign of her desire to frame her personal life in terms of conventionally approved female roles. Biographers have speculated that Eliot's becoming "Mrs. Cross" so soon after Lewes's death signaled her eagerness to embrace that feminine role officially.

The personal positions Gaskell, Stowe, and Eliot took on female roles, then, were not particularly revolutionary. Indeed, critics who look through the plots of their novels in the hope of finding proto-feminist assertions of female power and subversiveness are, as often as not, disappointed.[10] Nevertheless, when these women wrote their first fictions, they embarked on the literary project in a distinctly feminine way, a way that was shaped by and appropriate to the positions they occupied as middle-class women torn between the irreconcilable desires to be publicly influential and to be irreproachably respectable. The narrative stance in their realist fictions is one sign of their feminine strategy for coping with the restrictions on their real-world discourse. By rejecting the model of self-referential narrative reflexiveness presented by the work of their male predecessors and contemporaries, and by using direct address to bridge the gap between strictly literary utterances and serious statements, they adapted the novelist's art to women's purposes. Engaging address to the reader is a sign of these women's conceptions of the purpose of art; as such, it signifies a gendered gesture.

The mid-nineteenth-century "feminine" idea of art is that fiction should be didactic in a particular way, with moral conversion as the novel's central goal. Men's novels of the period are also didactic, and their stories can trace the moral evolution of a central character (as in *Yeast, Great Expectations,* and *Phineas Finn,* for instance). The gendered difference, as I have argued for individual novels, is not one of story, but of discourse: feminine strategies for shaping the conversation between the narrator and narratee rely on the earnest mode of evangelical exhortation, while masculine strategies maintain a more conventionally literary structure of ironic, self-reflexive fictionality. Later in this chapter, I compare the feminine use of direct address in fiction to the rhetoric that nineteenth-century male writers use when they are speaking "in earnest," especially in sermons. First, though, I want to examine the idea of fiction's purpose that these female writers held when they began their novel-writing careers.

A perceived difference between the aims of Victorian men and women in writing novels already lurks behind critical summaries of the period, though the difference is not always explicitly announced as one of gender. To cite one prominent example: in his classic study of the genre of didactic novels, Robert A. Colby correctly assumes that "fiction with a purpose" had roughly the same purpose for male and female authors: to teach. If we look at Colby's characterizations of male and female novelists' purposes, though, we can detect signs of the gendered difference in his own descriptions. Colby quotes at length from Dinah Mulock Craik's essay on the novelist's power, remarking that Craik's declarations (for example, "Fiction forsooth! It is the core of all the truths of this world; for it is the truth of life itself. He who dares to reproduce it is a Prometheus who has stolen celestial fire; let him take care that he uses it for the benefit of his fellow mortals") "might have been written by George Eliot" (19). Thus yoking the purposes of two women writers, Colby adds Charlotte Brontë to their company, commenting that as novelists, Brontë and Eliot "enter not only their readers' homes but their minds and consciences. Miss Brontë, through Lucy Snowe, ministers to the soul in anguish. George Eliot, from a more detached viewpoint, becomes a guide to the perplexed in matters of faith and morality" (19).

Colby uses the same metaphor to describe the activity of male and female Victorian novelists: they penetrate the domestic circles of strangers to speak to their readers. Within his argument, though, Colby shows no sign of recognizing the distinction he is making between the women's purposes and the men's in entering readers' homes. Immediately preceding his characterization of Brontë and Eliot is a comment on one of their male contemporaries: "Dickens, as reporter turned novelist, exposes hidden shame and tries to shock his more affluent readers out of their smugness. Thackeray enters his readers' homes, bringing them cultural 'news,' advising the young on love and their parents on education and marriage prospects" (19). Colby's own phrasing points to a difference: the woman novelist "ministers to the soul," guides readers "in matters of faith and morality"; the man "exposes hidden shame and tries to shock," or dispenses advice on social relations and practical matters. The women's purpose is more personal, more individualized, more spiritual than the men's. When, in the same context, he quotes Trollope's remarks about "the low-heeled buskin of modern fiction" (18), which Trollope saw as filling a cultural need for "rational amusement" (17), Colby unintentionally emphasizes the gendered difference. The "low-heeled buskin" image draws attention to the artificial, staged nature of fiction, or its value as "amusement." Perfectly appropriate for the masculine literary pursuits of Trollope, Thackeray, Kingsley, and even (when he is "at play") Dickens, the formula seems oddly inapplicable to the feminine projects of Gaskell, Stowe, or Eliot.

Of the three women writers, Eliot was the one most concerned at the beginning of her career about the status of her work as art; she was, in this sense, the most "masculine." As we have seen, her preoccupation with aesthetic standards dominates her pseudonymous correspondence with her publisher on *Scenes of Clerical Life,* surfaces in her reviews of other writers' fiction (especially "Silly Novels by Lady Novelists"), and pervades the narrative interventions in *Adam Bede.* We should not forget that the letters, reviews, and even the novels were ostensibly signed by a man and contain textual codes to support the signature—her "readers," from John Blackwood to the *Westminster Review*'s audience to the narratees of *Scenes of Clerical Life,* were supposed to assume that they were being addressed by a man. (Blackwood apparently did assume it; his letters to Lewes about *Scenes* solemnly refer to the novelist as "he.")[11] Eliot was not scrupulously careful to gender all her published narrative "I's" as masculine: though many critics still assume that the *Adam Bede* narrator is a man, some contemporary readers found evidence that a woman must have written Eliot's first two novels, including, by their own report, Dickens and Stowe.[12]

In an even more revealing instance, Eliot shifts the gendered references of the pronouns in her essayist persona's impassioned call to "Lady Novelists" to stop writing silly novels. The essay's concluding paragraph begins with the "we" that stands for the essayist's masculine mask: "Happily, we are not dependent on argument to prove that fiction is a department of literature in which women can, after their kind, fully equal men." This "editorial we," the name of the presumably male reviewer, recedes later in the paragraph, as the writer includes herself among the ranks of potentially serious women novelists: "No educational requirements can shut *women* out from the materials of fiction, and there is no species of art which is so free from rigid requirements. Like crystalline masses, it may take any form, and yet be beautiful; *we* have only to pour in the right elements—genuine observation, humor, and passion" (*Essays* 324, emphasis added). Eliot's female identity, then, can slip through the male persona of her "editorial we" or her pen name. She flashed her adopted male name (or, alternatively, the anonymity of the reviewer) as though it were a license to write about aesthetic matters.

Nevertheless, in each of these fictional and nonfictional forums, the terms in which she writes about aesthetics place her in a feminine-gendered position in relation to art. Her interest in aesthetic form always comes back to questioning the artifact's relation to reality; for her, as for Gaskell and Stowe, that relation is only partly one of representation, of depicting a recognizable mirror of "truth" in the fictional world. Their novels' most intimate relation to the extratextual world inheres in their rhetoric—in the always complex, often contradictory messages about the world that the texts transmit, but even more in the appeal to actual readers to recognize themselves as the figures to whom those messages are addressed. The specific messages about social, political, or moral "realities" are less important than the medium, the interventions in these realist texts.

Eliot expressed this point directly in a late letter when she explained what it meant to her to be a novelist, in the famous passage that I mentioned above: "My function is that of the *aesthetic* not doctrinal teacher— the rousing of the nobler emotions, which make mankind desire the social right, not the prescribing of social measures, concerning which the artistic mind, however strongly moved by social sympathy, is often not the best judge." (*Letters* VII 44). For Eliot, the job of the *aesthetic* teacher is not so much to instruct an audience in the appreciation of art, as it is to "rouse the nobler emotions" of actual readers. As Stowe put it, the feminine novelist's function is to inspire readers "to see to it that *they feel right*" (*Uncle Tom* 624). And if a novel happened, as Gaskell expressed it, to "put the small edge of the wedge in" to a reader's consciousness of the problems it depicts, if it should manage to "make people talk and discuss the subject a little more than they did" (Letters 226), then that would be a sign that the text was serving its desired function. As we have seen, neither Stowe nor Gaskell is much more concerned than Eliot with "the prescribing of social measures," and their first novels propose no practical answers to the social dilemmas they raise. Like Eliot, Gaskell and Stowe use their first novels as a means to "make mankind desire the social right"—in other words, to do what preachers and politicians ostensibly tried to do.[13] Except in evangelical circumstances, earnest public exhortation was a masculine prerogative. To use fiction for the same ends was a feminine alternative.

Clearly, these women exploited the novel's moral potential self-consciously. Stowe wrote in a newspaper column that the novel's "concentration on 'the great question of moral life' was becoming 'one of the features of the age,'" and emphasized a change from a literary past she imagined, when "the only object of fictitious writing was to amuse" (quoted in Kelley 250). In picturing such a past, Stowe was suppressing the entire tradition that had come into the history of the novel through Cervantes and Fielding from Horace, the tradition which claimed that the function of imaginative writing was always "to instruct and delight." The fact that Stowe was wrong about the past "object of fictitious writing" is less important, however, than her statement's implication that she saw herself and her contemporaries as using the novel toward new and unusual ends.

SEEING THE VOICE IN THE FACE: THE PRESENCE OF THE WOMAN WRITER

Although Gaskell and Eliot might not have endorsed Stowe's vision of literature's past, the three women apparently saw themselves as constituting a literary community. Their earliest correspondence with one another (and their public and private remarks upon one another's novels and personalities) reveal each woman's desire to emulate the other two. Their comments also show that each of them was "taken in" by the others' engaging narrators. They all tended to conflate the narrative persona of a novel with its author's identity, a tendency which hints at their own desire to project their personalities—in some important sense, their selves, their presences—through the narrative voice of a novel into the reader's world. Each claimed an intimate acquaintance with the others through having read their novels, and each appears to have believed that the narrator was identical to the woman who created it, and that novels of the earnestly engaging type genuinely expressed their authors' individual subjectivity.

Since neither Stowe nor Gaskell ever met Eliot (whose living arrangements made her an unsuitable acquaintance for respectable married ladies), and since Stowe and Gaskell (who did meet) lived on different continents, their community existed only metaphorically. Established originally through their novels, the relationships developed in letters that expressed the women's sense of affinity with one another. Certainly, ambivalence entered into their expressed feelings: for example, Gaskell could not resist alluding to her disapproval of Eliot's unmarried liaison with Lewes, and Eliot's first outbursts of warmth in her correspondence with Stowe cooled somewhat in later years. But their respective epistolary friendships represent a literary subset of what Carroll Smith-Rosenberg has called "the female world of love and ritual. . . . [A] world built around a generic and unself-conscious pattern of single-sex or homosocial networks" (60). Solidarity among women was not to be taken for granted—for evidence we need only look to Catharine Beecher's position on Fanny Wright, or to the outspoken criticism of women to be found in the writings of Eliza Lynn Linton and Dinah Mulock Craik. But the novelistic goals of Gaskell, Stowe, and Eliot bound them into a verbal version of the "community of women" that Nina Auerbach has described, one that "freely offers the work that must be wrenched grudgingly out of the 'real' world of Victorian patriarchy" (21). In the present case the "real" world is not only the public world of men's work and men's discourse, but literally the *real* world, that is, the world outside the fictional texts: the three women shared a belief in the genuine work they could accomplish through their fictions.

Though each of the women held specific reservations about some features of the others' lives, all three publicly and privately admired one another's work. As I have mentioned, their comments in letters and memoirs reveal evidence that each identified the other two authors with the narrators of their respective novels. I think, too, that their relations with one another suggest "influence" in the traditional literary-critical sense: admiring one another's books, seeing their personal concerns reflected in their own and the others' narrative voices, they made their mutual affinities explicit in both public and private statements.

Stowe's memoirs show that she had probably read *Mary Barton* before she wrote *Uncle Tom's Cabin* in 1851. During her 1853 visit to London, when *Uncle Tom's* phenomenal success ensured Stowe's reception into British literary circles, she met Gaskell at a party. Stowe's later account of the meeting implies previous familiarity with Gaskell's novels: "Mrs. Gaskell [was there], authoress of Mary Barton and Ruth. She has a very lovely, gentle face, and looks capable of all the pathos that her writings show" (*Sunny Memories* 224). The "pathos" in those two novels is largely a function of the earnest narrator's voice; Stowe read the narrator's voice into the author's face.

In fact, when Stowe met her, Gaskell was no longer writing novels with engaging narrators. Perhaps reading *Uncle Tom's Cabin,* with its energetic crossings from feminine earnestness to masculine irony, as well as its dire consequences for its author's feminine reputation, reinforced the effect of *Ruth*'s reception on Gaskell's narrative technique. In any case, after 1852 she abandoned direct address in novels altogether. Gaskell liked Stowe personally, and entertained her for several days in Manchester in 1856 (Forrest Wilson 432). After their first meeting in London, Gaskell wrote of Stowe to a friend, "I was 4 or 5 hours with her, and liked her very much indeed. She is short and American in her manner, but very true and simple and thoroughly unspoiled and unspoilable" (*Letters* 237). From Gaskell, who was concerned on her own account about the dangers of being spoiled by those who "lionized" her after *Mary Barton*'s popular success, this is a compliment to Stowe's feminine integrity. Whether Gaskell meant to imply that Stowe was short in her manner as well as short in person (the American author was diminutive) is not easy to determine; clearly, though, she honored the woman she could call "true and simple."

Though Gaskell left no written record of her reaction to Stowe's novels, she did write letters praising *Scenes of Clerical Life* and *Adam Bede* to George Eliot, whom she never met in person. The correspondence between Gaskell and Eliot emphasizes the interests and approaches that the two novelists had in common. Not surprisingly, during the period after *Adam Bede*'s publication, when one of literary London's favorite pastimes was guessing the identity of "George Eliot," Elizabeth Gaskell's name came up. Gaskell herself had been among the early supporters of a Mr. Liggins's claim to have based George Eliot's first two novels on his experiences in the Coventry neighborhood where Mary Ann Evans grew up. At the time when her own name was proposed, however, Gaskell seems to have believed that the Dean of Bristol, Gilbert Elliot, was the actual author (Haight, *George Eliot* 287).

The addressee of Gaskell's first letter to Eliot is, then, male: she sent it to "Gilbert Elliot" and signed it "Gilbert Elliot," playfully offering to take the credit for having written the novels. Gaskell frames her compliment to the novels in almost flirtatious language. She begins the letter, "Since I came from Manchester to London I have had the greatest compliment paid me I ever had in my life. I have been suspected of having written 'Adam Bede.' . . . [I]t would be very pleasant for me to blush acquiescence." Going on in the same vein, she exclaims, "Well! If I had written Amos Barton, Janet's Repentance, and Adam Bede I should neither be to have nor to hold with pride and delight in myself—so I think it is very well I have not" (Eliot, *Letters* III 74). Gaskell's adaptation of the phrasing of the marriage ceremony (each spouse takes the other "to have and to hold") is interesting. If she had written those books, she seems to be saying, she would be too proud and delighted with herself to remain a married woman, or at least to go on behaving as a respectable married woman should behave. The feminine modesty implicit in this declaration (and in her expressed pleasure at the thought of "blushing acquiescence") suggests Gaskell's assumption that she is writing to a man.

Gaskell's surprise at learning that the author was Marian Evans did not diminish her admiration for the novels, though it did color her next letter to George Eliot. In a more serious mode, she wrote in 1859 to the woman novelist, declaring of Eliot's first two novels, "how earnestly fully, and how humbly I admire them. I never read anything so complete, and beautiful in fiction, in my whole life before." She tempers her praise with a frank but forgiving allusion to Eliot's personal life:

Perhaps you may have heard that I upheld Mr. Liggins as the
author for long. . . . But I never was such a goose as to believe
that such books as yours could be a mosaic of real and ideal. I
should not be quite true in my ending, if I did not say before I
concluded that I wish you *were* Mrs. Lewes. However, that can't
be helped, as far as I can see, and one must not judge others.
(Gaskell, *Letters,* 586–587)

To say that "one must not judge others" is certainly not the same as saying "I
accept your having chosen the life you have"—the gesture at the end of
Gaskell's letter falls somewhat short of an embrace. And yet, Gaskell's letter
apparently pleased George Eliot, who was very sensitive to adverse criticism but usually indifferent to kind words from enthusiastic readers. Eliot's
reaction suggests that she respected Gaskell's feminine preoccupation with
propriety enough to overlook it in her answer.

In 1856 Eliot had written respectfully (though anonymously) in
"Silly Novels" of Gaskell's status as a serious writer. Accordingly, Eliot was
fervent in her personal thanks for Gaskell's letter and for the influence that
Gaskell's first two novels had held over her while she wrote her own first
two books:

I shall always love to think that one woman wrote to another
such sweet encouraging words—still more to think that you
were the writer and I the receiver.

I had indulged the idea that if my books turned out to be
worth much, you would be among my willing readers; for I was
conscious, while the question of my power was still undecided
for me, that my feeling towards Life and Art had some affinity
with the feeling which had inspired "Cranford" and the earlier
chapters of "Mary Barton." That idea was brought the nearer to
me, because I had the pleasure of reading Cranford for the first
time in 1857, when I was writing the "Scenes of Clerical Life,"
and going up the Rhine one dim wet day in the spring of the
next year, when I was writing "Adam Bede," I satisfied myself
for the lack of a prospect by reading over again those earlier
chapters of "Mary Barton." I like to tell you these slight details because they will prove to you that your letter must have
a peculiar value for me, and that I am not expressing vague
gratitude towards a writer whom I only remember as one who
charmed me in the past. (Eliot, *Letters* III 198–199)

Evidently Eliot did not focus on the personal allusions in Gaskell's letter, but was drawn instead to the "sweet encouraging words" about her work. She makes it clear, furthermore, that the words' having come from Gaskell made them more valuable; the letter implies that she thought of Gaskell as a literary mentor.

Pauline Nestor puzzles over the appeal that Gaskell's *Cranford* would have held for Eliot, "since as [Eliot] made clear in 'Woman in France' and . . . in the priorities in her fiction, the prospect of a community of women without men held little charm for her" (147). Similarly, Barbara Hardy has remarked that what Eliot meant by the "feeling towards Life and Art" she shared with Gaskell "is a matter for guessing" ("Mrs. Gaskell and George Eliot" 182). Comparing the narrative stances of Eliot's first two novels with Gaskell's (as I have done elsewhere) can help solve part of the puzzle: Eliot's eye may have been drawn to the discourse, more than the story, of Gaskell's fiction. Just as the nameless male narrator of *Scenes* and Mary Smith of *Cranford* occupy parallel textual positions as minimally characterized, homodiegetic narrators, some of the similarities between the engaging narrators in *Mary Barton* and *Adam Bede* can probably be attributed to Eliot's having reread Gaskell's novel while working on her own.[14]

George Eliot and Harriet Beecher Stowe also enjoyed mutual professional admiration and carried on a long, warm correspondence on literary and personal matters, although they were never to meet. Eliot reviewed *Dred: A Tale of the Great Dismal Swamp* for the *Westminster Review* in the fall of 1856, and though by that time she no longer shared the Christian faith that motivates so much of Stowe's fictional vision, she nevertheless approved of Stowe's exalted tone. Eliot's review praises Stowe for having "*invented* the Negro novel," and points to the source of its power: "She seems for the moment to glow with all the passion, to quiver with all the fun, and to be inspired with all the trust that belong to her different characters; she attains her finest dramatic effects by means of her energetic sympathy, and not by conscious artifice" (*Essays* 326, 329). The referent of "she" in this statement is Stowe the novelist, but the "glow," the "quiver," the inspiration describe the narrator's voice. By setting Stowe's "energetic sympathy" off against "conscious artifice," Eliot conflates the narrator and the novelist.

The review of *Dred* does criticize Stowe for oversimplifying the complexities of slavery by idealizing her black characters. Eliot's first letter to Stowe, written in 1869 to answer an unexpected fan letter from the American novelist, does not mention artistic differences, however; it stresses instead the spiritual purpose that the two novelists held in common:

> I believe that religion too has to be modified—"developed," according to the dominant phrase—and that a religion more perfect than any yet prevalent, must express less care for personal consolation, and a more deeply-awing sense of responsibility to man, springing from sympathy with that which of all things is most certainly known to us, the difficulty of the human lot.

The letter acknowledges the risk of being misunderstood when writing on such "wide subjects," but Eliot confidently concludes, "I trust your quick and long-taught mind as an interpreter little liable to mistake me" (Eliot, *Letters* V 29–31). Of course, Eliot's familiarity with Stowe's mind was limited to what she had seen in one letter and in Stowe's novels. In the narrative voices of those texts she had recognized the concepts of sympathy, of a sense of responsibility to others, and of an awareness of "the difficulty of the human lot" that informed her own novels. This striving to achieve sympathy, to turn away from the pursuit of "personal consolation," and to inspire readers to widen their circle of personal responsibility is, of course, the impetus behind the engaging authorial address that both authors practise in their first full-length fictions.

Of the three novelists Stowe is the one who came closest to expressing the bond of narrative technique that connects them. When Eliot wrote her congratulations to Stowe on the success of *Oldtown Folks* (1869), Stowe responded with thanks, and asked Eliot in passing, "Is it not true that what we authors want is not praise so much as sympathy?" Kelley (who quotes the letter from Stowe's unpublished correspondence) interprets the remark in the context of the literary domestic's conflict-ridden life. She says Stowe's impulse "was to focus on the quandary of the person rather than the quality of the book; regarding the latter as a genus [Stowe] said, 'A book is a hand stretched forth in the dark passage of life to see if there is another hand to meet it'" (283–284).

Perhaps Kelley is right. In their correspondence, both Eliot and Stowe often turned to each other for personal comfort. But if, in writing a book, a novelist stretches forth a hand to meet the hand of a sympathizing reader, the engaging narrator—extending her appeals for sympathy through direct address to a narratee—reproduces that metaphorical gesture within the text. The "sympathy" that "we authors want" is only partly personal: the authors of *Mary Barton, Uncle Tom,* and *Adam Bede* may have craved sympathy for themselves, but the novels operate to inspire a more generalized sympathy that would originate in egocentric self-involvement ("how fast could *you* walk?") and would spiral outward to engulf fictional protagonists, their antagonists, the narrators who tell their stories, the real world the stories are meant to resemble, and finally (but by no means exclusively) the authors who created them. They wanted readers' sympathy, and they wanted that sympathy to spill over from the realm of the fiction and transform the world through the same kind of feminine "influence" that domestic ideology promoted.

In this respect, Gaskell, Stowe, and Eliot were emulating evangelical techniques of "buttonholing" sinners, singling out individual members of an audience and attempting to work on their feelings. All three had experienced such techniques in revivalist circumstances, and all three had been exposed to and influenced by more formal Protestant sermonizers. Daughter of Lyman Beecher, sister of Henry Ward Beecher, and wife of Calvin Stowe, Harriet Beecher Stowe lived a life suffused with powerful preaching and lecturing. Gaskell's husband was a Unitarian minister. And, as a young girl, Mary Ann Evans had been moved to imitate the evangelical examples of her schoolmistress-friend Maria Lewis and her Methodist aunt, Mrs. Samuel Evans. Though Eliot renounced her Christian faith in her early twenties, and though Stowe converted her allegiance to Episcopalianism from the sterner Calvinism her father represented, both of them shared with Gaskell the memory of the powerful influence of preachers. They all were familiar with the strategies and cadences that mid-nineteenth-century men used in speaking publicly and urgently.

BEING "UP TO PAR IN MANLINESS": THE PRESENCE OF THE PREACHER

"If you are not a man, what business have you in the ministry?" Speaking in 1871 to a group of male seminarians at Yale Divinity School, Henry Ward Beecher uttered this question in the context of the increasing female influence upon churches that Ann Douglas has described as part of the "feminization of American culture." The clergy's growing dependence upon influential female parishioners and the pastor's inevitable collaboration with the woman whose primary responsibility was her family's moral education contributed to the emasculation of religious institutions. As if in defense against this feminine onslaught, Beecher seized upon the immasculating power of public speaking to bring "manliness" more squarely into the center of the minister's identity. If you are not a man and you wish to be a preacher, he warned the seminarians, "You have mistaken your vocation. You may do to make some other things, but you will not be a maker of men. It takes a *man* to refashion men. You cannot do it unless you have some sort of vigor, vitality, versatility, moral impulse, and social power in you" (*Lectures* 192). A woman might have a hand in the physically procreative process of making men in the first place, but only a man can spiritually "refashion men."

And what of the woman who felt herself sufficiently in possession of the qualities of "vigor, vitality, versatility, moral impulse, and social power" to be a preacher? She was doomed. George Eliot's fictional Dinah Morris has a relatively easy time of it, gradually moving out of the fields where she preaches and into interior, personalized spaces such as the prison cell where she comforts Hetty, or the Bedes' home where she ministers first to Lisbeth by sweeping the floors and later to Adam by becoming his wife. The treatment Dinah received from nineteenth-century illustrators of *Adam Bede* suggests that the image of an attractive, feminine, woman orator in the act of preaching was to some degree unimaginable. Queen Victoria commissioned Edward-Henry Corbould in 1861 to depict the scene of Dinah's preaching from the second chapter of the novel. In the resulting painting (reproduced in Laski, 60), Dinah stands elevated among her audience, arms and hands open to the crowd of men and women, and mouth firmly shut. The line drawing that serves as frontispiece to the nineteenth-century illustrated edition of *Adam Bede* follows Corbould's precedent (Figure 3). Whereas Dinah's sermon takes up nine full pages of text and serves as the first dramatic action in the novel, F. T. Merrill's frontispiece shows her as she is described before she begins to speak ("with an egg-like line of cheek and chin, a full but firm mouth, a delicate nostril, and a low perpendicular brow" [67]). Dinah's primary role in the first part of the novel is to preach, unabashedly, unselfconsciously, powerfully, and publicly. But Dinah is to become the novel's heroine, and the femininity of her ultimate image required that she be drawn as silent. Real women who insisted on public ministries fared much less well than Dinah. According to historian Leonard Sweet, American "women preachers in the first half of the nineteenth century paid an incredible price in tattered nerves, shattered reputations, and psychosomatic ailments. Their autobiographies are tortured testaments to the psychological abuse heaped on women who dared to preach" (143). Preaching, more than any other kind of public speaking, was perceived as an inalienable right of men.

Henry Ward Beecher's advice to aspiring ministers, collected in his *Lectures on Preaching,* can help illuminate the assumptions that operated to bar women from Victorian pulpits. In accord with Victorian theological views of "Christian manliness," Beecher sees preaching as a function of a man's body, as much as a product of his mind and heart.[15] For Beecher, a preacher's appearance and physical stance are as essential to his effectiveness as his enthusiasm and earnest faith. A truly manly minister enters into a frankly physical relation with his audience when he mounts the pulpit. His primary responsibility to his congregation is to serve as the physical presence, the literal embodiment, of Christian faith: his body must be an appropriate object for the audience's observation, and it must become their source of inspiration. When a sermon works, the preacher's own joy is orgasmic:

> I have had youth and middle age, and now I am an old man. I have seen it all, and I bear witness that, while there are single moments of joy in other matters that, perhaps, carry a man up to the summit of feeling, yet for steadfast and repetitious experience there is no pleasure in this world comparable to that which a man has who habitually stands before an audience with an errand of truth, which he feels in every corner of his soul and in every fiber of his body, and to whom the Lord has given liberty of utterance, so that he is pouring out the whole manhood in him upon his congregation. (192–193)

How could any respectable Victorian woman hope to emulate the habitual, public, and promiscuous act of ejaculation that Beecher evokes with that suggestive phrase, "pouring out the whole manhood in him upon his congregation"? No wonder Beecher's sister Harriet transformed herself into their father before she tried to face that Boston audience.

F. T. Merrill's frontispiece for *Adam Bede:* Dinah at the scene of the
preaching, with her mouth firmly closed. (Courtesy of Harvard
College Library.)

Beecher's Yale lectures cover the material one might expect in an
experienced preacher's advice to beginners.[16] In addition to many practical,
professionally specific disquisitions, one of his ten lectures is devoted to the
preacher's body, or "Health, as Related to Preaching." He provides "practical hints" on "the art" of eating, sleeping, regulating one's work, and

getting enough exercise, though he cautions against the excessive emphasis on sports training characteristic of the "muscular Christians": "Now if you undertake, as scholars, very violent exercise, according to the exaggerated idea of muscular Christianity, you will very soon use up all the vitality of your system in the bone-and-muscle development, and it will leave you, not better, but less fitted for intellectual exertion" (194). The preacher must conserve the "vitality of his system" in order to maintain his ecstatic experiences in the pulpit, but "you cannot expect either these exceptional, higher consummations, or the strong, steady flow of a joyful relish for your work, unless you cultivate a robust and healthful manhood" (193). The man's drive to preach is like an extension of his virility: it results, as does his sexual drive, from the proper care of his masculine body. [17]

His healthy body is more to the preacher than the source of his sermons' power: it is also the locus of his relation to his audience. Beecher objects to "barrelled pulpits" that obscure the preacher's body from the public view, for "a man's whole form is part of his public speaking. His feet speak and so do his hands" (*Lectures* 71). So, too, do the parts of his body that Beecher leaves unnamed. The speaker who would move his auditors must be visibly and even physically accessible to them, close enough to allow his "magnetic influence" to reach them (71). "There is a force—call it magnetism or electricity, or what you will—in a man, which is a personal element, and which flows from a speaker who is *en rapport* with his audience. This principle should be utilized in the work of preaching" (73). The phrasing suggests that the preacher must exploit animal magnetism, a "personal element" inextricably bound up with sexuality. And Beecher's suggestion for exploiting the physical connections between speaker and audience hints at the forbidden implications of a "promiscuous" gathering. Literal, physical contact among the listeners will heighten the effect of the electrical magnetism emanating from the speaker: "I can speak just as well to twelve persons as to a thousand, provided those twelve are crowded around me and close together, so that they touch each other. . . . [C]rowd your audiences together, and you will set them off with not half the effort" (73). As performer, as orchestrator of his own and his audience's visceral experience of the sermon, and as the one who must "set them off," inflame and excite them, the preacher is in the position of sexual aggressor.

The line between religious and sexual ecstasy has always been a blurred one, and the resemblance of revivals to orgies is obvious enough to any post-Freudian observer. And, too, the preacher who carries the role of seducer out from the pulpit and into his personal life is treading on dangerous territory. American culture is full of fictive and historical emblems of such scandal, working back in time from Jim Bakker to Elmer Gantry to Henry Ward Beecher himself. What is remarkable about Beecher's characterization of the preacher's task is not his equation of preaching with masculine sexuality, but the unselfconscious way in which he makes that equation so explicit while firmly restricting the minister's seductive powers to the pulpit.

Beecher's vision of the virile minister's relation to his congregation recalls the astonishing sketches Charles Kingsley made before his marriage, as a wedding present for his fiancée (Chitty 64ff). The drawings, made during the period when Kingsley was most absorbed in his own rigorous training for "muscular Christianity," show the young minister and his bride nude, copulating in postures suggesting the consummation of Christian suffering and joy. In one of Kingsley's sketches the two bodies are bound together on a cross tossed by a turbulent sea, in another they ascend to heaven on the strength of the man's broad, muscular wings. In Kingsley's fantasies, all the energy of the ecstatic experience inheres in the man; the woman is limp, passive, even unresponsive. The drawing of their joint ascension is a particularly apt example. His eagle-wings contrast with her transparent ones, which resemble those of an inert moth; he supports her body with his strong hands, arms, thighs, and phallus, while her smooth, flaccid form hangs from him in a posture that suggests death. In an era when (as Douglas has shown) Protestantism was unquestionably undergoing "feminization," when the success of congregations and of individual pastors depended vitally on the support of female parishioners, and when women were increasingly taking on the responsibility for moral reform toward a more Christian culture, Beecher's and Kingsley's equation of religious leadership with virility is significant—and also a bit sad. It suggests a self-protective defensiveness in the minister's conception of his own function. In the drawing, the man's body is all that prevents the woman from falling; in the pulpit, the man's body should support his congregation in their efforts to avoid a Fall from grace.

Beecher undoubtedly felt that his body provided his congregation's access to grace, especially when he stood before them, speaking extemporaneously. Invariably he ranks spontaneous, enthusiastic speech over reading written words, whether the written texts are biblical or generated by the preacher.[18] As Beecher puts it in his *Lectures*, "every preacher should be able to *speak*, whether with or without notes. Christ *'spake'*" (214). Speech is preferable to reading aloud, because "a written sermon is apt to reach out to people like a gloved hand. An unwritten sermon reaches out like the warm and glowing palm, bared to the touch" (215)—again, the electricity of physical contact is invoked. Speech is present the way a living body is present: in Beecher's view, that presence is the essence of a minister's calling. The effective preacher must deliver original, orally composed interpretations of biblical verses: "The reason why reading the truths that are just as plainly stated there [in the text] has sometimes so much less effect than stating them in your own way, is that the truth will gain a force when it becomes part of you that it would not have when merely read as a text" (7). That force is entirely a product of presence:

> A preacher is in some degree a reproduction of the truth in personal form. The truth must exist in him as a living experience, a glowing enthusiasm, an intense reality. The Word of God in the Book is a dead letter. It is paper, type, and ink. In the preacher that word becomes again as it was when first spoken by prophet, priest, or apostle. It springs up in him as if it were first kindled in his heart, and he were moved by the Holy Ghost to give it forth. He *is* so moved. (3)

Transcending textuality—the inertia of the "dead letter," the "paper, type, and ink"—is a resolvable problem for the preacher. In personally delivering the word, he reenacts the origination of the word, and the truth to which it refers is reincarnated in him. In voice and person, he becomes the embodiment of the truth he speaks, and re-creates divine presence in mortal form. As in the crucifixion and resurrection fantasies of Kingsley's drawings, the preacher steps in for Christ: he becomes the Word made Flesh. Beecher's preference for speech over text, his faith in spontaneous oral expression as the unmediated means of access to thought, and his conviction that divine truth could be made manifest in a preacher's words beautifully exemplify the logocentrism that Derrida has identified as the heart of any Western "metaphysics of presence." Beecher, along with the world to whom and for whom he spoke, participated fully in the fantasy of presence, unsuspecting of the moves that philosophers were soon to take toward dismantling the tenets of his faith.

The minister's corporeal, gendered presence, then, was the sine qua non of Victorian preaching. In this respect, the male body played a similar role for political public speakers. If the minister's body gave corporeal form to God's word, the body of the Chartist agitator, for instance, was the vehicle that carried the word of the people. Martha Vicinus reports that "Thomas Cooper described himself as 'the people's instrument, rather than their director,' claiming a leader to be one whose 'temperament, nature and powers fit him by quick sympathy, and strong, energetic will, to become the people's mouthpiece, hand, or arm, either for good or evil'" (489–490). The speaker's body becomes a location for the voice of something larger than himself, whether that voice is God's or the people's. To become the "mouthpiece, hand, or arm" the body has to be positioned publicly, in close proximity to the audience to whom and for whom the voice speaks. Only a male body could be so publicly displayed with impunity; saying something in public was therefore both an expression and a function of the speaker's masculinity.

The speaker's virility extended beyond his appearance and stance, to include his rhetorical strategies for wooing his audience, for trying to "set them off." Vicinus has detailed the strategies that the speakers for the three Chartist factions exploited toward this end (490–500). As for the minister's tactics, I will turn again to Beecher's own report for suggestions that he saw his relation to his audience in terms of his gender. In describing his preaching strategies, Beecher frequently employs similies comparing preaching to hunting, fishing, or warfare. As in poetic conventions that pit man against woman in venal pursuit, Beecher's tropes place the preacher in the role of aggressor and the congregation in the role of prey. As far as rhetorical ethics are concerned, Beecher's attitude might be summarized as "all's fair in love and war—and preaching."

Eschewing "mere trickery," Beecher nevertheless endorses "preaching which produces a *sensation*," because "the legitimate use of real truth is all right, no matter how much people get stirred up; the more the better. In this matter you will not err if you are *up to par in manliness,* neither above it nor below" (*Lectures* 237). Being "up to par" may mean feigning the passions one is hoping to induce: "In addressing a congregation, a man may use the language of a feeling for the sake of getting and propagating the feeling. Indeed, when it comes to preaching, I think it would be a great deal better to act as though you had the feeling, even if you had not, for its effect in carrying your audience whither you wish to carry them" (126). Faking arousal, then, is an acceptable act if it leads to consummation. "Getting and propagating the feeling" is another of the preacher's masculine sexual duties; as long as he believes his rhetoric is motivated by enthusiasm for the truth, he is free to use any tactics that will work to move his listeners.

The preacher's primary vehicle for encouraging individual listeners to participate in this process is, not surprisingly, direct address. Beecher calls the tactic "taking aim," and recalls anecdotally how he developed the strategy by studying the apostles' sermons when he was trying to hit upon an effective preaching style. He subjected each of the biblical sermons to rhetorical analysis, asking himself What were the circumstances? who were the people? what did he [the preacher] do? (*Lectures* 11). Concluding that the apostles typically made an appeal to common knowledge before applying its implications to their message, Beecher worked out a model of sermonic direct address:

> First, I sketched out the things we all know. "You all know you are living in a world perishing under your feet. You all know that time is extremely uncertain; that you cannot tell whether you will live another month or week . . . ." and in that way I went on with my "You all knows" until I had about forty of them. When I had got through that, I turned round and brought it to bear upon them with all my might; and there were seventeen men awakened under that sermon. I never felt so triumphant in my life. I cried all the way home. I said to myself: "Now I know how to preach." (*Lectures* 11–12)

Taking aim at attitudes and experiences he presumed his audience could recognize and acknowledge, Beecher thus drew them in. Later, he reports, he learned to aim at individuals, or at specific faculties within an individual, by addressing the audience in general and avoiding the eye of the intended receiver of the message. Direct address to the crowd works in these instances, he explains, because his unsuspecting prey do not realize that he is shooting at them, but lower their defenses. Reflecting on the sermon later, "They take it to heart, and it is blessed unto them" (*Lectures* 168).

In Beecher's lectures as in his sermons, direct address pervades the rhetoric. Lectures and sermons alike were originally delivered extemporaneously, as Beecher—true to his tenets—preferred to speak from notes, rather than to read. When he spoke, his frequent references to "you" drew continual attention to the situation in which he was speaking. In the Yale lectures, the youthful, eager, doubting, earnest male audience's presence in the "you" is as manifest as the preacher/lecturer's presence is in the "I." In the original delivery of the lectures, this was as literally true as it can ever be in matters of language: preacher and audience were really there. In the printed transcripts of the sermons and lectures, the recurring "you's" evoke a shadow of the historical audience's presence. As Beecher himself was so quick to point out, the text is only "paper, type, and ink," and can provide only a pale imitation of the truth it seeks to represent—in this case, the actuality of the speaker's interaction with his listeners.

Beecher's reliance on direct address was by no means idiosyncratic, nor was it restricted to preaching in the revivalist mode. Charles Kingsley's sermons, written in a staunchly Anglican vein, frequently and repeatedly speak to "you." Typically, Kingsley begins his discourses by establishing the situation in which he speaks. He may introduce part of his sermon by justifying its relevance to his audience:

> Before I can explain what this text has to do with the Church
> Catechism, I must say to you a little about what it means.
> Now if I asked you what "salvation" was, you would
> probably answer, "Eternal life."
> And you would answer rightly. (15)

Or he might begin with exhortation, then support his demands upon the congregation by means of illustration and reasoning throughout the rest of the sermon: "Have any of you here ever stood godfather or godmother to any young person in this parish who is not yet confirmed? If you have, now is the time for you to fulfill your parts as sponsors. . . . It really is your duty. It will be better for you if you fulfill it. . . . Let me try to show you what I mean" (59). Such introductory addresses establish the presence of speaker and audience and cement the relation in which they are to stand to each other: the paternal, authoritative speaker has access to the truth, which he undertakes to transmit to his auditors.

Within the body of each sermon, Kingsley uses "you" to stand for the receiver of rhetorical questions, the actor in hypothetical situations, and the subject of such reassuring phrases as "you know," "you see," "you understand." In the sermons, the "you" is continually present, always there to be buoyed up by the preacher's spiritual, intellectual, and physical strength, and thus to take the minister's message to heart.

When novelists import earnest, exhortative direct address from preaching techniques into fictional discourse, they are employing the idiom of the minister. Just as the minister seeks to convert sinners by evoking memories and emotions they can recognize as their own, the novelist tries to transform readers' attitudes through the same technique. The "you" in the sermon is, strictly speaking, an "addressee," a figure the speaker creates and projects through his sermon's language; similarly, the "you" in the novel is a narratee, a textual construct. But when the minister "takes aim" at a living audience by addressing them directly, he hopes that individual listeners will take the address personally and seriously. He believes that his words can work real change, and that "his people" can experience spiritual transformation through his presence. The engaging narrator is the sign that some novelists believed that their words could have a similar effect.

Evidently Gaskell, Stowe, and Eliot felt that they were present in their fictional texts. When they looked at one another, they saw their novels' narrators: to identify another woman with her narrative voice was to declare one's identification with the narrators in one's own novels. Their strategies show a desire to accomplish the kind of moral and spiritual influence that preachers claimed to wield from the pulpit, but they wished, too, for feminine respectability. They could not afford the price that Fanny Wright (or even Catharine Beecher) paid for becoming a public presence; their feminine bodies could not occupy the space a public speaker stands in without undergoing immasculation in the public view as well as in their own. They relied instead on the influence of their narrative "I" over the "you" invoked in their texts, and they counted on the conventions of verisimilitude to lend the aura of truth to the "dead letter" that they found themselves producing when they conceded to men the privilege of speaking aloud in public.

The postmodern philosopher might reflect that the project of these Victorian women novelists was impossible to achieve, that the "I" and the "you" of realist fiction can never really refer to individual subjects, that they are only the products of *"différance"* among signifiers in these and other texts, that the authors and readers themselves are merely constructs born of reading. And yet, the postmodern perspective would also see the preacher's faith in presence and in the manifestation of truth as a nostalgic illusion, a project just as doomed as that of the earnest women writers. The preacher's presence is, after all, only a substitute for the divine reality he hopes to transmit to his listeners: his body, like the fictional narrator's voice, is only a signifier standing in for the presence of the Real Thing.[19] What links the feminine realist novelist and the masculine preacher is their shared hope that the signifier might be enough, that it might enable them to convey truth by hitting one's audience "below the fifth rib." For both kinds of speakers, the audience's emotional reaction metaphorically represents a moment of physical contact. Both preacher and novelist want to "touch" the audience. The Victorian male preacher does so by using his voice as an extension of his body; the Victorian female novelist shields her body by placing her voice in a text. Whether or not it could ever be possible to make real contact with an audience through a fictional text, that was what novelists who used engaging strategies were earnestly trying to do.

8

Direct Address and
the Critics:

What's the Matter with "You"?

WHAT IS IT about "you" that literary critics and theorists find so embarrassing? Commentators on texts can manifest embarrassment in diverse ways: we can express irritation or impatience, make apologies and excuses, or rise above the source of our discomfort by denying it, ignoring it, or imagining it to be something other than the thing we find so problematic. Earnest direct address has been both vilified and defended in commentaries on particular realist novels, but in theories of literature and theories of reading it has, for the most part, been suppressed.

To examine in detail all of the reasons for each literary theory's means of avoiding this trope would require writing another book. In this concluding chapter, then, I simply sketch out some possible sources for the critical discomfort over earnest direct address in literary texts. I situate the problem at the intersection of three locations of anxiety. The first source of anxiety centers on literary-theoretical disagreements about whether "literary" and "nonliterary" language must necessarily occupy separate realms. The second producer of anxiety is the discomfort critics and theorists seem to experience when they are confronted with texts that gesture toward moments of intensified presence. And finally, I look at the way these anxieties are aggravated when that presence is coded as feminine.

"IT SHOULD DO NOTHING":
MODERN PROBLEMS WITH VICTORIAN ART

The problem of "you" begins, I think, with the tradition of distinguishing between literary and nonliterary language. The differentiation of two distinct kinds of language, functioning independently and uniquely, propels twentieth-century critical practices as diverse as Russian formalism, New Criticism, and narratology. Most modern literary criticism operates on the assumption that the two kinds of language, poetic and nonpoetic, are distinct from each other in terms of their "truth-status"; the two categories are supposed to function differently in that nonpoetic, non-literary language presents itself as referential—claiming to be related to the real world—whereas poetic, literary language makes no such claims. According to this line of thinking, literary writing does aspire to a "higher" truth, transcending the mundane limits of the nonpoetic.

Stanley Fish has ingeniously exploded the opposition between literary and nonliterary language by arguing that there is nothing ordinary about "ordinary language" at all. Distinguishing literary language from ordinary language defies reason, he points out, since "ordinary" (that is, "literal," "scientific," "propositional," "logical," "denotative," "neutral," "mathematical," "serious [as opposed to fictional]," "metaphorical," "representational," "message-bearing," "referential," "descriptive," or "objective") language does not exist (97). No use of language enjoys the direct, unproblematically representational relation to reality that nonliterary language has been presumed to have: "*There is no such thing as ordinary language,* at least in the naive sense often intended by that term" (106).

Fish rightly points out that literature is not distinguished by intrinsic formal or linguistic properties. On the contrary, "literature" is always that subset of writing which the dominant culture agrees to call "literature"—and nothing more. "The one disadvantage in all of this," Fish observes, "is that literature is no longer granted a special status, but since that special status has always been implicitly degrading, this disadvantage is finally literature's greatest gain" (108).

Literature, then, stands to gain from its reintegration into the realm of ordinary language; surely we cannot harm literature by broadening our understanding of the ways that literary texts can work. For the literary/

nonliterary opposition necessarily breaks down in specific applications to certain fictional genres that gesture toward (limited) referentiality, such as the realist novel. Under the modernist rubric, any text that is "referential," "ordinary," or "serious" in its use of language must be nonliterary: it must not be literature. But surely, when some aspects of a realist novel are presented as referential (such as place names, for instance, or dates, which may be rendered in full or "disguised," as in "the city of L——, in the year 183—") the critic cannot in good faith approach every detail of the novel as though it could *not* be referential, as though it were absolutely without connections to the "real world."[1] One possibility for such a connection in realist fiction is the implication that the pronoun "you" might sometimes be as referential—as "serious," in John Searle's sense of the word, as "London" or "1836." Of course, as Fish reminds us, the word's referentiality is problematic, like that of any word: its relation to "the world" is not as simple as Searle's system would make it out to be. Nevertheless, in engaging texts, the pronoun's relation to the world—its claim for reference—is different from that of the distancing "you," or of such signifiers as "Dorothea Brooke" and "Yoknapatawpha County."

The possibility that a fictive text might be seriously addressed to an audience it calls "you" raises another difficulty, closely related to anxieties over the poetic or nonpoetic functions of language. Many theories of literature take for granted a split between genuine "literature" and "rhetoric"—the first being language that functions entirely for art's sake, the second being language with designs upon the extratextual world. In earlier periods, when formal distinctions between literature and rhetoric were less strictly drawn than they have been since the early nineteenth century, an address from within a text could be taken for granted as one of the many means a writer could use to gain access to an audience's emotional or intellectual response. For the past two centuries, however, idealist literary theory has been devising ways to separate authorial address to readers from actual communication.[2]

How has this happened? Lionel Gossman hypothesizes that the divorce between literature and rhetoric can be traced to the mystification of poetry that began during "the final phase of neoclassicism" in the eighteenth century:

> The term "literature" gradually became more closely associated
> with poetry, or at least with poetic and figurative writing, and,

especially among the Romantics and their successors, took on the meaning of a corpus of privileged or sacred texts, a treasury in which value, truth, and beauty had been piously stored, and which could be opposed to the world of historical reality. (5–6)

According to Gossman, "literature thus ceased to be thought of as an art by which ideas could be conveyed effectively and elegantly, and which could be pursued with varying degrees of skill and success by all people" (6). This "fetishizing" (as Gossman calls it) of the literary work entails a belief that a poem should never accomplish ulterior goals, because it must exist as art for its own sake. Culminating in the late Victorian and fin de siècle emphasis upon the uniquely "real" quality of the work of art, this idealist, aestheticist line of thinking suppresses the manipulative, transactional, or rhetorical potential inherent in "literary" writing, as in all writing. Jane Tompkins has amplified the implications of this attitude for contemporary criticism: "The imputation that a poem might break out of its self-containment and perform a service would disqualify it immediately from consideration as a work of art. The first requirement of a work of art in the twentieth century is that it should *do* nothing" (*Reader-Response Criticism* 210).[3] Tompkins suggests that recent critics have perpetuated this assumption by treating literary texts as repositories of meaning waiting for interpretation, rather than viewing them as authors' instruments for provoking real-world action.[4]

If the split between literature and rhetoric originated with Coleridge and Kant, then Victorian novelists were working in a post-"divorce" era; still, as we have seen, they tended to view their activity as an act of communication between themselves and a living, breathing audience. Novelists who relied heavily upon the engaging narrator to persuade audiences on matters of morality and politics would have been horrified at the thought that a novel should "do nothing" in order to aspire to the status of art. The renewed emphasis on "art for art's sake" at the beginning of the modern period is, to some extent, a reaction against the eagerness of earnest Victorians to promote a remarriage between literature and rhetoric. Accordingly, modern criticism of Victorian fiction has frequently operated to suppress, denigrate, or deflect the properties of the novels that try to do something, including exhortative passages of direct address.

One way to express discomfort with Victorian novels' attempts to "do something" has been simply to object, as did the majority of British and American nineteenth-century reviewers, to the didactic, preachy, or condescending tone of a narrator's accosting a reader as "you." [5] Another way has been to assume—with Percy Lubbock, his Impressionist contemporaries, and his New Critical heirs—that authorial "intrusions" are flaws in the fabric of the fictional illusion, and hence are offensive on aesthetic grounds. In defense of the Victorian novels they unblushingly admire, more rhetorically-minded Anglo-American critics such as W. J. Harvey, Barbara Hardy, and Wayne Booth have rehabilitated authorial intervention as essential to certain novelists' "art," but they, too, treat authorial address as something the novelist must regulate, something that can hurt a text if it is allowed to get out of control. Each of these generations of critics has turned its collective back upon the implied presence of actual readers in authorial intrusions. They all presumably consider such a presence inappropriate in a text that could be upheld as belonging to the category of literature.

From the point of view of the literary critic eager to defend a work's position in the canon, direct address bears a damaged reputation, attributable to the rhetorical company it keeps: the trope has been tainted by its wide use in advertising, television, and journalism. Commentators anxious to maintain distinctions between "legitimate art" and other, more overtly manipulative or rhetorical forms of discourse tend to view direct address with exaggerated suspicion. Barbara Kruger, writing in *Artforum,* decries television's dominance of the American consciousness in the 1980s, declaring that "television, perching in our living rooms like a babbling, over-controlling guest, is deeply embroiled in the authoritative declarations and confessionals of 'direct address.'" Particularly conscious of its use in advertising and in "nonfiction" broadcast genres such as news and talk shows, Kruger maintains that "direct address dominates and lets the viewers think they know who's doing the talking and to whom" (7). Direct address on television is misleading, she implies, because the talking head belonging to the news anchor does not originate the words that issue from his or her mouth; when distraught people tell the "hidden camera" their troubles with headache, dandruff, or fabric softener, the individual viewer finds him- or herself fictively placed in the position of addressee. Viewers less astute than Kruger are presumably fooled into accepting a mock communication as a genuine one.

Bruce Morrissette, the only critic who has attempted to survey the modes of "narrative you," is even more insistent that direct address can be misleading or harmful in nonliterary applications. After quoting advertising copy that relies heavily on personal pronouns, Morrissette warns "that 'you' . . . can be a dangerous pronoun that advertising and journalism may corrupt so badly as to render it virtually useless to 'literature'" (112). Making no distinction between lyric poetry's uses of "you" in apostrophe and in direct address, Morrissette is much stricter in his definition of appropriate prose examples for his analysis: "Obviously, we must eliminate all uses of 'you' in oratory or elsewhere that are addressed frankly to an audience" (115). This restriction passes without further remark, showing Morrissette to be among the critics who separate literary and rhetorical writing in the way that Gossman has identified.

What evidently distinguishes the "you" in advertising and oratory from the literary use of "narrative you" is that the more manipulative mode of direct address requires the addressee to take the pronoun personally. When a McDonald's ad says "you deserve a break today," when a public broadcasting auctioneer pleads, "you must call and make your pledge if you value the quality programming we are bringing you," when a preacher warns "you will go to hell if you disobey the word of God," each listener is meant to apply the statement to his or her own situation. When an utterance is "addressed frankly to an audience," the referent of its second-person pronoun is both plural and singular: "you" stands for the group and for each member of the group who could conceivably take the utterance to heart. Some advertisements inscribe their "you" more narrowly than others: an ad for a "gentle laxative" begins, "As a woman, you do so much for so many people. You don't have time for irregularity." Many viewers (female and male) will fail to see themselves in that "you," but any woman who is prompted, consciously or unconsciously, by that ad to buy that product will have at least momentarily identified that "you" as herself. A statement containing "you" that really means *you* has the potential power to make something happen. And if "legitimate art" must be kept separate from discourse that attempts to spark action—advertisement, oratory, propaganda, or preaching—one way to maintain that separation is to insist that the "you" in truly literary texts has no extra-literary referent.

By transforming the reader who is hailed in literature into a fictional construct, something whose existence is strictly circumscribed within art, reader-centered critics and structuralists—from Booth to Iser to Genette to Riffaterre—have developed sophisticated ways of talking about the "you" in texts by deflecting any implication that the pronoun might ever be a signifier for real persons. The race of "readers" they have spawned serve as models for the way actual people might read, but in the critical discourse where they are born, they do not represent actual readers. The textual reader may be conceived as an Implied Reader (Booth and Iser), a Model Reader (Eco), an Average Reader/Superreader (Riffaterre), an Informed Reader (Fish), a Competent Reader (Culler), a Strong Reader/Mis-Reader (Bloom), a Perverse Reader (Barthes), a Deconstructive Reader (Derrida), a Feasting Reader (Hartman), a Resisting Reader (Fetterley), a Created Reader (Preston), a Determined Reader (Peterson), or, as Robert Rogers (whose witty list of "readers" I have incorporated into this catalogue) calls it, the Amazing Reader. Whatever the term (and whatever its longevity—theorists are nearly as prone to disavowing their "readers" as to creating them), it never stands for the person who holds the book and reads.

A notable exception is Peter J. Rabinowitz's essay, "Truth in Fiction: A Re-Examination of Audiences," which moves beyond theories that posit a single "reader" to propose four separate roles that readers play. Rabinowitz suggests that when we read novels we must position ourselves in relation to four figures: the Actual Audience (real people who buy and read the book, in any era); the authorial audience (the group the author presumably had in mind while writing); the narrative audience (a conglomeration of characteristics to be inferred from the narrator's assumptions about the readers' knowledge and attitudes); and the ideal narrative audience (an entity defined by its willingness to accept the author's evident intentions). The first three correspond to narratologists' distinctions among "the actual reader" (see Suleiman, *Of Readers and Narratees*), the "addressee," and the "narratee" (see Prince, "The Narratee Revisited"), respectively. Narratology has no term for the "ideal narrative audience," probably because, like the implied reader or the virtual reader, its existence depends entirely upon an act of interpretation that cannot always appeal to "empirical textual evidence" among the words on a page.

According to Rabinowitz, "the narrative and authorial audiences are closer together in some novels than in others" and "the distance between these audiences is a major element in any novel's structure" (131). He points out that "the wider the gap, the greater the effort required to bridge it" (131–132); a great effort leads to emotional distance from the fiction. Rabinowitz's theory can help elucidate the distinction between Victorian realist texts with engaging and distancing narrators. Both kinds of novel share the same actual and authorial audiences. Their narrative audiences diverge: whereas the engaging narrator's "you" is in complete sympathy with the characters and the narrator's assertions about them, the distancing narrator's "you" (like Jones at the Club) demurs. Both narrators' ideal narrative audiences are the same: they sympathize unstintingly with the characters. The difference is one of irony. The distancing narrator distinguishes between the narrative audience and the ideal narrative audience, but for the engaging narrator, the two groups are identical.

It seems to me that all of these critics (with the exception of Rabinowitz) share an implicit answer to a question they do not raise in any explicit form. That question is: "What is the referent of 'you' in a literary text?" They have raised and answered the question about the literary "I," concluding through various lines of reasoning that it stands for the textual construct known as the narrator or the narrative voice. In novels where homodiegetic narrators speak to narratees who share their level of diegesis, the referents of "I" and "you" are hardly problematic. The "I" is the character-narrator and the "you" is a figure who is more or less explicitly inscribed in the text. (Wolfgang Müller has taken significant steps toward outlining the possible identities for the *"unbestimmtes Du"*—the "unspecified you"—in such texts.) In texts with heterodiegetic narrators, as we have seen, the questions of reference become more complex. The speaker is a creature in and of the text. No "real person" speaks in such a literary transaction; in a serious sense, it is the text itself which speaks. But unless a real person picks the text up and reads it, no interaction can occur. Indeed, the texts themselves do not even minimally dramatize an interaction in the way that Müller's study examples do. To assign every occurrence of the literary "you" a parallel function to that of the literary "I," to assume that every "you" is simply a textualized narratee just as every "I" is a narrator, is to overlook the complex differences between the two kinds of nineteenth-century novels, those with intradiegetic situations of narration and those with heterodiegetic situations. Novels with engaging narrators point to a difference between two possible and distinct referents for "you": the "you" that is utterly the product of the text's internal structures, and that other "you," the one that is inextricably tied to systems of signification outside the text, to real persons who find their social beings engaged by the narrator's address.

As Emile Benveniste has painstakingly demonstrated, the personal pronouns "I" and "you" are peculiar in their relationship to their referents. As "shifters," they have no fixed referents; they can be assigned meaning only in the context of the "present instance of discourse" (253). Unlike "he/she/it," which substitute for entities and items existing outside the situation in which an utterance is being made, the first- and second-person pronouns refer only to a "reality of discourse." It is the act of speaking that assigns the value "speaker" to "I," and the value "addressee" to "you" (252–253).[6] In each individual instance of literary discourse, the "I" stands for the addressor, the narrator, a function of the language on the page, a figure which may or may not correspond to the real-world author. (In the early novels of Elizabeth Gaskell and George Eliot, as we have seen, the narrator's "I" evokes a strongly personal presence who closely resembles the author's expressed idea of her own best self.) But as the discursive event in certain novels requires the presence of an actual reader, the referent of "you" may change according to the circumstances of the "present instance of discourse." In some literary cases—notably, the case of the engaging narrator—the "reality of discourse" determines that the referent of "you" is the actual reader him- or herself.[7]

Indeed, I do not mean to undermine the importance of the rich and diverse reader-centered theories of the past two decades. Demonstrating theories of reading fiction always requires the theorist to create fictions of reading. The "reader" becomes the hero of their fictions: for example, Iser's implied reader, who bravely adjusts his idea of the "real" as he reads, or Fish's reader, who is continually experiencing the adventure of surprise when he encounters patterns that disrupt his experience of literary conventions or his sense of "self." In narrating possible ways to receive narratives, these theorists self-consciously focus attention on the circularity of the theoretical enterprise, as well as on the subjective nature of the reading experience. And, too, for nineteenth-century novels with distancing narrators, the various constructions of Readers have proven to be useful tools for describing fictional conventions, as well as for theorizing the process of literary reception. But they are not particularly helpful in accounting for the one convention of nineteenth-century realism with which I am most concerned: the engaging narrator's use of "you" to stand for the actual reader. In the presence of earnest direct address, contemporary theorists avert their eyes, as though to avoid the sign of something shameful.

APOSTROPHE, EMBARRASSMENT, AND DIRECT ADDRESS

When I call the engaging use of "you" embarrassing, I borrow the adjective from Jonathan Culler's investigation into apostrophe in lyric poetry. Culler asserts—and Barbara Johnson concurs—that critics of lyric poetry are typically made so uncomfortable by apostrophe that they either ignore it or treat it in their criticism as though it were a mode of description (*Pursuit of Signs* 136). Although Johnson locates apostrophe's discomfiting power in its self-contradictory claims to be able to breathe life, through poetry, into inanimate entities, Culler concentrates instead on the "moment of apostrophe" as an event. When a lyric poet invokes an abstract, inanimate, or absent figure, the poet invests that figure with being by naming it "you." As Johnson emphasizes, the subjectivity of the apostrophized being in romantic poetry is only an illusion, a product of the poem. But I think Culler is right to trace critical discomfort with the trope to doubts over "the power of poetry to make something happen" (140).

As Culler explains, apostrophe differs from other rhetorical moves in that it "makes its point by troping not on the meaning of a word but on the circuit or situation of communication itself" (135). Apostrophe shifts the address of a text in such a way that the speaker stops talking to the reader/listener, and turns to speak to an absent third party. To evoke and animate that other entity is to make something happen. What's more, that "something" happens in "real time" (as a computer scientist would call it), the time of writing and/or reading, Benveniste's "reality of discourse," rather than the lyric time or narrative time depicted in the text. Culler borrows the terms of narratology to explain the "now" that apostrophe brings to life: "This is the time of discourse rather than story" (149). He sums up the disconcerting power of the trope: "Apostrophe is not the representation of an event; if it works, it produces a fictive, discursive event" (153).

The recent critical interest in apostrophe provides a useful context for looking into reasons why literary critics have so persistently evaded and avoided the related but different trope, direct address. First, this attention to apostrophe—as opposed to earnest, direct address—suggests that the new practitioners of poetics are still most comfortable concentrating on the literary, created figures in texts, rather than on the actual "circuit of communication" an author might try to establish with a reader. Second, earnest direct address exactly parallels apostrophe in its status as an event, a trope that "makes something happen" in real time. And finally, the issues of presence and absence that Culler identifies as the source of embarrassment over apostrophe are even more crucial in considerations of direct address, complicated as they are by the addressee's literal presence in the act of reading.

Even though both Culler and Johnson attend carefully to the potential impact of apostrophe upon a "reader," each of them concentrates on the trope's evocation of a third party whose existence depends entirely upon the text. The stress in Culler's formulation of apostrophe as "a fictive, discursive event" is on the "fictive." Johnson overtly distinguishes apostrophe from direct address: "Apostrophe is both direct and indirect: based etymologically on the notion of turning aside, of digressing from straight speech, it manipulates the I/Thou structure of *direct* address in an indirect, fictionalized way" (30). True enough: this is precisely why I have placed apostrophe under the matrix of the distancing narrator. Apostrophe is a "fictive," "fictionalized" manipulation of address. The "you" to whom it speaks, whether the West Wind, the Muse, a deceased and honored poet, or the hero of *Yeast*, is indisputably a literary construct.

But what about the other "you," the "you" that need not be named in situations of apostrophe but that must be present in any act of reading, the "you" that really means "*you*, reader"? In the disarming but revealing introduction to his essay, Culler plays with an example of apostrophe:

> If we posit for this essay, "Apostrophe," a communicative process linking an "authorial voice" and the readers of *The Pursuit of Signs,* an apostrophe seems to mark a deflection of the message: O mysterious apostrophe, teach us to understand your workings! Show us your varied talents here!
>
> Such apostrophes may complicate or disrupt the circuit of communication, raising questions about who is the addressee, but above all they are embarrassing: embarrassing to me and to you. (135)

Here Culler illustrates his point about apostrophe's discomforts beautifully, but he raises one more question "about who is the addressee" than he answers. His essay questions the status of the apostrophe's addressee, but remains silent about the identity of the second of those two pronouns, "to me and to you." If we simply plug into these variables the values (in the algebraic sense) he supplies, that phrase would read, "embarrassing to [an authorial voice] and to [the readers of *The Pursuit of Signs*]."

Such a statement would be within the etiquette prescribed by structuralist and semiotic analysis, but does it really make any sense? Can an authorial voice experience embarrassment? Must I really conceive of myself as an anonymous member of a group of readers while I am working my way through Culler's essay? Or do the "me" and the "you" actually serve here as the personal pronouns they appear to be? I read the phrase, "embarrassing to me, [Jonathan Culler] and [I presume] to you, [Robyn Warhol or whoever you may be]." Since an expository essay is primarily an act of communication, there can be no grounds for shame over the text's attempt to "do something," in this case, to convey ideas persuasively. And yet, even here, the critic hesitates to acknowledge that the text represents his personal attempt to persuade individual readers to his position.

When it is used earnestly and engagingly in fiction, direct address is, like apostrophe, "not the representation of an event." It "produces" an event, but the event is a genuine one, not a fictive one. When the distancing narrator sets up conversations between himself and "Miss Bullock," or when he addresses a narratee while taking pains to ensure that the actual reader will resist identifying with that narratee, he is representing a fictive event, an act of communication between one persona and another. When the engaging narrator speaks to a "you" that stands for the actual reader, however, the text produces a real event, an exchange of ideas that the novelist hopes will result in real consequences.

In this respect, earnest, engaging direct address differs from apostrophe: the verbal exchange it instigates is "real," because the receiver of the message, the actual reader, is present at the moment of reading, not absent, as is the addressee of apostrophe. Culler points to the ways in which apostrophe is particularly appropriate to a lyric mode that operates outside of empirical time: "Apostrophe resists narrative because its *now* is not a moment in a temporal sequence but a *now* of discourse, of writing" (152). Apostrophe plays with the opposition of presence and absence by shifting the two terms away from the time of story and into the time of discourse; the dead poet invoked in an elegy, the abstraction apostrophized in an epic poem are "not there" on the level of story, but they achieve existence in the discourse. Hence, according to Culler, apostrophe represents "the attempt to produce in fiction an event by replacing a temporal presence and absence with an apostrophic presence and absence": the poem "knows its apostrophic time and the indirectly invoked presence to be a fiction and says so but enforces it as event" (153–154).

Culler's point is that apostrophe may be experienced as disruptive to narrative, since it produces a fictive, discursive event that competes with the fictive events depicted in a story. Direct address, like apostrophe, shifts a text's emphasis from the time of story to the time of discourse, if only momentarily. For the duration of a narrator's address to "you," be it a single phrase or several paragraphs long, the actual reader's attention is necessarily drawn away from the fictive events being narrated and toward the real situation of narration. To be reminded that a given story is embedded in discourse is to be reminded that it is "only a story." What engaging direct address attempts to do that neither distancing address nor apostrophe can do is to insist that it is "only a (*true*) story" by alluding to the presence of the actual reader in the engaging "you," a presence that is literally real as long as someone is perusing the passage of address and receiving the message. As I have suggested in Chapter 7, the engaging narrator is also working to promote a sense of the author's own presence in the text, through the earnest "I" that parallels the engaged "you." And as my reading of *Mary Barton*, for example, demonstrates, the engaging narrator can use the author's and reader's discursive "presence" to reinforce the narrative's claim to being realistic, by implying or even asserting that author, reader, and characters are all present simultaneously on the same diegetic plane.

Perhaps this is one source for our embarrassment about earnest, direct address: the engaging narrator's claim that the story is as real—not only as "realistic"—as the discourse that conveys it. The claim is absurd, naive, patently untrue, as Stowe's and Eliot's narrators emphasize when they complicate their engaging methods with distancing ones. And yet, as actual readers' emotional reactions to *Uncle Tom*, for instance, attest, the strategy can nevertheless be an effective means of stirring up readerly sentiments. It works. The strategy's very effectiveness points to another potential source for embarrassment similar to one Culler proposes for apostrophe. If achieving powerful effects depends on something as mechanical and easily manipulated as addresses to "you," then the effects must be cheap ones—and can they have anything to do with legitimate art? Up to now, even the most progressive theorists and critics have replied, no.

THE INTRUSION OF THE FEMININE

Another, and perhaps more profound, source for embarrassment about earnest direct address in literature is its association (for the nineteenth-century novel, at least) with femininity. Indeed, the implicit assumption that it is a woman's strategy, to be applied at moments when a reader's emotional receptivity should be most sensitive, and to be avoided by practitioners of self-referential "high art," must be at least partly responsible for critics' assumption that direct address is somehow an illegitimate technique. Direct address is "sensational," lacks "genuineness," "holds a strong implication of judgment, of moral or didactic" aims, according to Morrissette's summary of twentieth-century critics' attitudes toward the trope (124, 132). In the hands of nineteenth-century female novelists who use it to emphasize a feminine presence behind the narrative "I" and to exert female influence over the moral condition of the reading audience, direct address does operate upon the sensations toward didactic ends. And if, in 1929, Clifton Fadiman felt that rewriting a novel addressed to "you" into "the straightforward pattern of a direct third-person narrative" would help it "gain in genuineness" (Morrissette 124), who is to say whether or not his anxiety over the perceived deviousness of direct address could be traced to a distrust for feminine wiles?

Throughout this study, I have tried to show that earnest, direct address came to function in Victorian novels as a sign of feminine presence and as a gesture of connection between the worlds inside and outside the text. If playing with presence and absence through rhetorical tropes inspires discomfort in the first place, that discomfort must only be aggravated for androcentric or more extremely misogynist critics when the authorial presence is coded as feminine. I think that this is one way to account for the traditional critical hesitation over whether George Eliot is really in control of her art, for the long-standing dismissal of *Uncle Tom's Cabin* as propaganda too popular and too manipulative to be called art, for the placement of Gaskell on the margins of a canon she occupies more comfortably later in her career, when her techniques rely less heavily on direct address. It can account, too, for objections to signs of the feminine that surface in moments of direct address in men's texts: the oratorical sentimentality of Dickens and Thackeray, the "intrusive" chattiness of Kingsley and

Trollope. For each of the texts in this study, direct address has been a feature for critics to condemn, to ignore, to defend, or to apologize for. What attracts the critics' opprobrium—and what draws my own interest to the trope—is the resonance of gender that it evokes.

Perhaps direct address in nineteenth-century novels is a subtle case of the phenomenon that Joanna Russ has outlined in *How to Suppress Women's Writing:* when it is not possible to deny a woman's agency behind a literary text, critics have simply devalued the features that the woman's text displays. Since a primary feature of Victorian novels by women is the urgent need for the novel to *do* something, to break the barrier between literature and rhetoric, to become a platform from which the woman could speak, women's novels may have been one inspiration for the perpetuation of the "divorce" Gossman and Tompkins describe. To use a Victorian novel as a vehicle for public speech is to write as a woman, and to write as a woman is—as Russ has so ably illustrated—to write substandard "art." Therefore, to rely on direct address is to produce illegitimate novels. The twentieth-century appropriation of direct address by the media has only aggravated a bias that became entrenched before anyone had even imagined a television commercial.

Notes

CHAPTER 1

1. In her detailed discussion of the drawbacks inherent in structuralist and formalist systems which, like Genette's, omit "questions of value and context," Susan Sniader Lanser has pointed out "the complete disregard of gender in the formalist study of narrative voice" (*The Narrative Act* 39, 46). According to Lanser, "Nowhere in modern narrative theory is there mention of the author's or narrator's gender as a significant variable . . . [but] surely the sex of a narrator is at least as significant a factor in literary communication as the narrator's grammatical person, the presence or absence of direct address to a reader, or narrative temporality" (46–47). In her more recent work, Lanser has begun to rectify the situation she describes, asking "whether feminist criticism, and particularly the study of narratives by women, might benefit from the methods and insights of narratology and whether narratology, in turn, might be altered by the understandings of feminist criticism and women's texts" ("Toward a Feminist Narratology" 342). Lanser's article also addresses the reasons why feminists have avoided narratological research in the past.

2. See, for instance, Bal's recent work on the Bible, e.g., "Sexuality, Sin, and Sorrow: The Emergence of Female Character (A Reading of Genesis 1–3)" and "The Rape of Narrative and the Narrative of Rape."

3. Miller borrows the terms for her two types of novel—"euphoric" and "dysphoric"—from the work of male writers in French semiotics, particularly Greimas. Miller herself correctly observes, however, that the terms are not restrictive, but flexible in her hands: "This distinction [between "euphoric" and "dysphoric" texts] is primarily a heuristic device meant to serve as a frame of reference within which individual narratives can be delineated in their specificities" (xi).

4. Meese outlines her position on Eagleton's formulation of the relation between feminism and literary theory in her chapter "In/Conclusion" (136–140).

5. According to Culler, "In recent French writing 'woman' has come to stand for any radical force that subverts the concepts, assumptions, and structures of traditional male discourse" (*On Deconstruction* 61).

6. Genette has acknowledged, for example, that the emphasis on temporal structures in his *Narrative Discourse* arises from Proust's preoccupation with time; he confesses, too, to being biased in that his "curiosity and predilection went regularly to the most *deviant* aspects of Proustian narrative, the specific transgressions or beginnings of a future development" (265). Suleiman recognizes that "the danger that the cases chosen may be too 'special' to be generalizable always haunts the enterprise of the structural anthropologist [and] . . . the theorist of genres who works on a limited corpus" (*Authoritarian Fictions* 16). Fish (who, like the structuralists, insists that his methods are "oriented *away* from evaluation and toward description") admits that "this is not to say that I do not evaluate. The selection of texts for analysis is itself an indication of a hierarchy in my own tastes" (51).

7. Genette illustrates this idea with reference to Proustian narrative's specificity (22–23).

8. Brownmiller's history of body hair occurs in her chapter on "Skin" (138–148); Ronald Pearsall, illustrating his assertion that "the Victorians were transfixed by feminine beauty" (141), mentions that William Etty (a "great and underestimated . . . painter of womanly flesh") "conformed to the unwritten code that specified no pubic hair . . . [the delineation of which] was the prerogative of the artists who specialized in pornography" (142).

9. For linguistic studies of differences in men's and women's language, see Hiatt, Henley and Thorne, Thorne and Henley, and Jarrard and Randall.

10. Lanser investigates gendered implications of "public" and "private" narration, proposing to add them to Genette's model for narrative situations. Her emphasis upon "the difference between purely formal and contextual approaches to meaning in narrative" ("Toward a Feminist Narratology" 354) points to the new emphasis on context in the recent work of narratologists such as Suleiman (*Authoritarian Fictions*) and Prince ("Narrative Pragmatics").

11. I borrow the sense of this phrase from Suleiman, who has used it to refer to acts of enunciation that make serious referential or didactic claims.

12. As Culler points out, this kind of reading does not require biological womanhood, but rather what Showalter has called a "hypothesis of a female reader" (*On Deconstruction* 50). This approach has been pursued in recent studies of gender and reading; see especially Flynn and Schweikart.

13. In addition to feminist studies of deconstruction's notion of *différance,* studies of sexual difference based in psychology have led to fruitful literary applications, e.g., Chodorow's theory of object relations, Dinnerstein's model of male and female children's relations to the mother, Gilligan's distinctions between male and female constructions of morality and maturity, and Keller's recent moves toward transforming traditional gender categories. See also Miller (*Poetics of Gender*) and Abel.

CHAPTER 2

1. Tompkins observes that "Reading, for [Prince] . . . consists of discovering what is already there on the page. His narratees, like Wayne Booth's narrators, belong to the text" (*Reader-Response Criticism* xii).

2. I am thinking of the kind of reading Barthes performs on brief literary passages in *A Lover's Discourse,* where he strikes a pose of personal response to the affective implications of texts.

3. The assumption also pervades the Anglo-American tradition of rhetorical criticism, which treats "the reader" as a figure created by the text. As Walker Gibson put it in an influential 1955 essay, "There are two readers distinguishable in every literary experience. First, there is the "real" individual upon whose crossed knee rests the open volume, and whose personality is as complex and ultimately inexpressible as any dead poet's. Second, there is the fictitious reader—I shall call him the "mock reader"—whose mask and costume the individual takes on in order to experience the language. The mock reader is an artifact, controlled, simplified, abstracted out of the chaos of day-to-day sensation." (2) The idea of the mock reader survives in Booth's "implied reader" and in the reader that Ong asserts is "always a fiction," existing only as a persona that the writer imagines and the actual reader may or may not adopt. This critical tradition removes the "actual reader" from the discussion of literary works, avoiding the "affective fallacy" and focusing more or less exclusively on describing or interpreting the text. See Suleiman and Crosman; Tompkins, Introduction to *Reader-Response Criticism;* and W. Daniel Wilson.

4. Direct address to a narratee in a text where the narrative situation is intradiegetic (e.g. *Wuthering Heights*) or where the narrator is homodiegetic, that is, a character within the narrative (e.g., *Jane Eyre* or *Great Expectations*) has a different rhetorical effect because it mirrors what speech-act theorists call "the natural narrative situation" (see Pratt 45). For an insightful analysis of direct address that fits this category, see Monod ("Charlotte Brontë and the Thirty 'Readers'").

5. *Distancing* and *engaging* are my terms. Very few critics have analyzed the effects of engaging intervention in fictional texts. For a debate that focuses on engaging technique without using the term *narratee,* see Gmelin's, Auerbach's, and Spitzer's arguments about Dante's use of direct address in the *Divine Comedy.*

6. All three novelists make their intentions explicit, both within and outside their fictional texts. See Gaskell's Preface to *Mary Barton* (37); Stowe's "Concluding Remarks," in *Uncle Tom's Cabin* (618–629); Stowe's *A Key;* and Eliot's "In Which the Story Pauses a Little," *Adam Bede* (150).

7. Stang has shown that many mid-nineteenth-century critics and reviewers in England disapproved of narrative intervention; Baym (*Novels, Readers, and Reviewers*) makes the same observation about American critics. Novelists of the period would have been aware of the theoretical objections to the convention. Eliot,

in particular, was self-conscious about typical attitudes toward authorial commentary. See her observations on Sterne's narrative irregularities (*Essays* 446).

8. Tompkins identifies similarities between the forms of address in *Uncle Tom* and the Old Testament models for the American jeremiad (*Sensational Designs* 139−141).

9. I am grateful to Cynthia Bernstein for suggesting this example in her response to the first published version of this study.

10. Obviously not every reader can identify with the narratee. Evidence of the distanced response in hostile readers of *Uncle Tom* surfaces in reviews of the novel by Stowe's contemporaries; see Ammons.

11. See Conrad and Ford Madox Ford for further evidence that modern novelists, to avoid distancing effects, try to stay out of the text. As Ford puts it, they intend "to keep the reader entirely oblivious of the fact that the author exists—even of the fact that he is reading a book" (76). Ferguson demonstrates, however, that even the most scrupulous of the impressionists cannot avoid some narrative intervention.

CHAPTER 3

1. Wright, though eager to demonstrate that Gaskell "thought seriously about her work and was a conscious craftsman," nevertheless concedes that "she is not a literary critic, not much—in her surviving correspondence—of a self-critic" (8).

2. See Craik's assertion that in Gaskell's fiction "the circumstances and settings and details that attend them are vividly actual because they are those common to their kind. Her success in combining historical fact and documentary detail with her invented story is virtually complete" (18). David Smith, by contrast, has challenged the notion that social-problem novels can be evaluated according to their "accuracy . . . in particulars" (98).

3. Jordan has demonstrated "the irruption into the text of discourses other than that of sympathetic observing realism" (48). Gallagher, too, sees competing literary modes at work in *Mary Barton,* which she attributes to "an ambivalence about causality that finds its way into Gaskell's tragedy and creates an irresolveable paradox there," resulting in the introduction of "other narrative forms, primarily melodrama and domestic fiction" (*Industrial Reformation* 67). Lucas sees the too-easy solutions of the plot as interfering with the social-problem novel's goals; Ricchio has analyzed the role of utopian mythic patterning in realist novels as central to the formal problems *Mary Barton* raises.

4. Jordan points out that Gaskell's narrative is vague even about the details of Chartism (56).

5. Gerin quotes A. W. Ward's "Biographical Introduction" to the Knutsford edition of *Mary Barton*. See Gerin for an account of the birth and death of William Gaskell, Jr. (71−75).

6. This authorial insistence upon a personal, rather than an overtly political, interest in social unrest recalls the assertions of critics such as Tillotson and Wright who think of Gaskell as primarily a "Christian" novelist, proselytizing for a change of heart, a reborn sympathetic zeal, among her audience. See David Smith's refutation of Tillotson's suggestion that *Mary Barton,* in the universality of its theme, has no "social, extra-artistic purpose" (Tillotson 210, Smith 100); see also Wright's argument that the "particular aspect of the condition [she was] hoping to treat" was "the religious" (29).

7. Wright has also noted that Gaskell's account of her decision shows that she "felt compelled to write of what was close to her and observable," which makes her "a social novelist" (11).

8. See treatments of allusion, quotation, and intertextuality in *Mary Barton* by Jordan, Wheeler, and Easson.

9. Whereas Lansbury argues that the narrative voice in Gaskell's novels probably reflects a projected idea of the middle-class reader's opinions rather than Gaskell's own, Fryckstedt identifies the narrator's views with those of Gaskell's Unitarian faith and shows the ways in which Gaskell's first two novels pose a challenge to received middle-class religious notions.

10. Furbank's essay concentrates on the narration of *North and South,* in which "the author allows herself for certain purposes to be a false witness" (53). Citing a passage that depicts the heroine's thoughts and behavior in one scene, Furbank remarks, "Now here we really cannot take Mrs. Gaskell literally, and must be meant to realise that she is telling a fib. Margaret's reason for standing still is clearly not just what we are told it is. What passes through her mind is something less simple, and more natural" (53). Furbank objects to Gaskell's "mendacity," attributing it to an excessive identification between author and heroine (51).

11. Wright points to Gaskell's "identifying herself with the reader, and both herself and the reader with humanity at large" as typifying the authorial stance in her "novels of religious and social purpose" (241).

12. I borrow the phrase from Meese, who applies it to Celie's last letter in Alice Walker's *The Color Purple.* Like engaging interventions, Celie's address to "dear everything" "opens the significance of the novel as it closes this particular fiction" (127).

13. Wright notes with particular relief the disappearance of direct address from Gaskell's later work. Listing some early examples in which Gaskell's narrative "I" addresses "you," Wright remarks, "This is probably the most naive form of narrative comment, and disappears from her work as she gains control of her medium" (242). In her enthusiastic defense of Gaskell's novels, Craik, too, concedes that Gaskell "sometimes over-exerts herself to make the way plain for the reader. . . . [S]ometimes she feels compelled to state her position—a dispassionate one . . . with unneeded emphasis" (10). Yet Craik concludes that Gaskell is "for her time and with her aims, very sparing of addresses to her reader." Given the sheer number of addresses to the reader in *Mary Barton* (of which I have quoted only

a portion), perhaps Craik's impression that Gaskell's narrator, "although not self-effacing," is "unobtrusive" (29) could be attributed to the engaging nature (rather than the frequency) of the narrative interventions.

CHAPTER 4

1. The phrase comes from Justin McCarthy's description of Charles Kingsley, which is on the whole a sneering one, and probably not a fair characterization. I use it merely to evoke Kingsley's image, not his real personality.

2. Gallagher links narrative technique in *Alton Locke* with Kingsley's "ambivalence about causality" and says that the novel "undermines faith in the possibility of referential, realistic fiction" (*Industrial Reformation of English Fiction* 89).

3. See, for example, Kestner, Cazamian, Hartley, and Uffelman. Recently, *Alton Locke* has been the subject of more literary consideration; see especially Gallagher's *Industrial Reformation of English Fiction*.

4. See Chitty (111) for an account of the reaction to *Yeast* among Kingsley's friends. His honored mentors, Ludlow and Mansfield, detested it. His wife, however, was so fond of her husband's first novel that she requested that a copy of it be buried with her. The parts that appealed to her were apparently those treating the love affair of Lancelot and Argemone, which was loosely based on the Kingsley's courtship. She, too, disapproved of the novel's political contents.

5. I take up this point in Chapter 7, where I look in more detail at direct address in nineteenth-century sermons.

6. Swanson locates the irony in a disjunction between the world the author has created and the comments the narrator makes on that world. He argues that Thackeray's irony can be decoded into a moral message: e.g., "It is the ambiguity of the narrator toward Becky that most clearly defines Thackeray's critical method: the narrator questions her innocence, but the author confirms her guilt, thereby condemning the narrator for judging by a false standard" (140). Rawlins, by contrast, sees no obvious way to decode the irony: "Thackeray undercuts his own rhetoric as well as the rhetoric of his characters, and in ways for which we cannot offer explanation except in the general terms of an habitual ironic perspective" (155). For other treatments of irony in *Vanity Fair,* see, for instance, Wilkinson, Mauskopf, and Sheets.

7. Olmsted outlines this debate in the preface to his bibliography of twentieth-century Thackeray criticism. Segel ("Thackeray's Journalism") mentions "the characteristic bugaboo of Thackeray's readers— . . . the tendency to simply miss the presence of the persona or mask and to attribute both commentary and its implied values directly to Thackeray the author" (25).

8. This question arises particularly for Segel ("Thackeray's Journalism") and Mauskopf, who analyze Thackeray's early journalism for his position on fiction.

9. The equation of Thackeray's techniques with realism can be traced back to

nineteenth-century critics of his novels (Flamm 3). As recently as 1983, Sinha was still arguing that Thackeray's "excellence," like Fielding's, depends on "the authorial commentaries which go to establish an intimate relationship between the novelist and the reader" (233). Wilkinson sees the reader's position as that of "accomplice" to the gossiping narrator (372–373). See also Polhemus on the intimacy between narrator and reader (152). Blodgett, in contrast, argues that "while Fielding's narrator may deepen in intimacy with his reader, Thackeray's narrator instead gives the sense of his own growth as he draws with anecdotal geniality . . . on various parts of his own history in order to associate himself with the tale" (214).

10. See Wilkenfeld for an analysis of "Before the Curtain" that differentiates some of the narrator's roles in the preface, particularly those of "Manager" and "Man" (314). See also Stevens for questions about the audience's position vis-à-vis the puppet stage, e.g., "Where, then, are *we?*" (394).

11. Sheets has catalogued half a dozen instances where the narrator claims authentic sources for his information, counterbalancing them with an equally long list of passages in which the narrator claims not to have been able to ascertain the pertinent facts. Sheets concludes that these inconsistencies leave "us with the question, 'What after all, *did* happen?'" (426–427). Of course, literally nothing "*did* happen": it is all invented, and—as Morton Bloomfield has pointed out—so many references to "authenticating devices" in the text merely call "attention to the need for authentication and hence to the inauthenticity of the work of art" (quoted in Segel, "Truth and Authenticity" 56).

12. The impulse behind some critics' claims for *Vanity Fair*'s realism comes from a New Critical desire to find coherence and unity in any great novel. See, for example, Blodgett's assertions that "*Vanity Fair* succeeds because of its narrator, not despite him" (211), that "the many roles of the narrator's 'pose' interact harmoniously, making the novel coherent" (215), and that "what he claims is right for the novel and what he demonstrates through his novel constitute a unity" (217).

13. Praz treats Thackeray's narrator as a preacher, emphasizing that he has in mind a kind of preaching which operates upon logic, rather than emotional appeal (49). Carlisle insists that "no matter how indirect, the role of the preacher, a voice expounding on our fallen human nature, is central to Thackeray's fiction" (40). And Segel concludes her defense of *Vanity Fair*'s seriousness by arguing for Thackeray's attempt "to bring together for the reader's instruction the real world and the fictional world, so widely separated in conventional novels of his time" ("Truth and Authenticity" 58).

14. Ferris concludes that Thackeray "risks the entire narrative enterprise to assert—briefly and obliquely—a limited freedom for the human imagination" (303). Sheets says Thackeray came to realize that "the novelist can no longer be a historian or a preacher lecturing to his fellow citizens. He is a lonely man who sees himself in his novels, and he must therefore develop a subjective narrative technique that will acknowledge his imperfection and alienation" (430). Rawlins

decides that Thackeray "seems to have created a context for his fiction that allows the universal moral relevance that Richardson erroneously claims" (176).

15. My description of Thackeray's project as "play" draws upon Huizinga's definition of a "game," which Lynette Hunter summarizes: "First, it is a freedom and marked by voluntary activity; second, it lies outside real life in a disinterested world of its own; and third, it is secluded and limited, isolated from reality in fixed time and absolute order. Because of that isolation it denies any moral aspects, claiming neutrality not on the basis of truth but from its autonomy" (92–93).

CHAPTER 5

1. Traditional histories of the sentimental novel traced the genre's flowering to the romantic period; see Herbert Ross Brown, and Allen.

2. "Sentimentality" is one element in the Victorian domestic feminine ideal; see Parker. In "The Silence is Broken," (McConnell-Ginet, et al.), Donovan analyzes the rhetoric of women's sentimental novels. Some critics defend *Uncle Tom* as a "serious" women's novel which is not "sentimental" (see Zeman), but Tompkins shows that even on the level of plot, "the tears . . . which we find easy to ridicule are the sign of redemption in *Uncle Tom's Cabin;* not words, but the emotions of the heart bespeak a state of grace" in the story (*Sensational Designs* 131).

3. Gribble looks into the role of literary sentimentality in "the education of the emotions." Hardy (*Forms of Feeling*) discriminates among the particular emotional lessons that classic Victorian novels were meant to transmit.

4. See Hirsch's account of *Uncle Tom*'s public reception. For evidence of Eliot's unsentimental reputation, see Harvey's assertion in *The Art of George Eliot* that Eliot's "intrusive comments are generally neither dramatic gestures, [nor] rhetorical embellishments demanding an overwrought emotional response from the reader" (82–83). Not all critics agree that Eliot always rises above sentimentality; see Oldfield and Oldfield on the "flaw of sentimentality" in *Scenes of Clerical Life* (9–14). See also Mann, for a detailed analysis of the figurative language Eliot's narrators use to generate "laughter and tears in the reader," excluding direct address (168–199). Benson has shown that Eliot valued more highly reviews that showed emotional receptivity to her work than those praising her technique, and he does not respect her for it: "It is tempting to say that this emotionalism is a lapse, and that George Eliot knows better, but to do so would be a falsification" (440).

5. Hardy (*Forms of Feeling*) observes that Eliot's novels shift in their designs upon readers' sympathies, from a simple attempt to rouse pity in *Scenes,* to an effort to prompt readers to "particularize and analyze" their feelings (152). Later in her career Eliot was to become impatient "with the solicitations of text as well as the facile readiness of response" (155). Ermarth ("George Eliot's Conception of Sympathy") and Doyle have further elucidated Eliot's position on sympathetic response.

6. As Bell has argued, sentiment and realism are not mutually exclusive in nineteenth-century novels.

7. Ammons has collected some vehement examples: see "Anon." (1852), Holmes (1852), Thompson (1852), and Woodward (1853) in *Critical Essays*.

8. Levin looks into the specific problems of trying to mine *Uncle Tom* for "historical evidence."

9. Stowe's biographer specifies that Stowe "invented the text" of at least one slave-advertisement in the *Key*, though "she had seen similar ones in Cincinnati" (Forrest Wilson 333).

10. Forrest Wilson lists half a dozen titles of these "counter propaganda" novels (325).

11. Holmes (see Ammons) was only one of many who assumed that Stowe derived her ideas from other novelists: Dickens himself believed Stowe had "appropriated" material from his novels and Gaskell's (Leavis and Leavis 166). The persistence with which critics have always referred to "Little Eva," as if in imitation of "Little Nell" (though the narrator calls the character only "Eva" or "Evangeline") has perpetuated the idea that Stowe copied Dickens inordinately.

12. See, for instance, Moers (*Harriet Beecher Stowe*), Adams, Gillian Brown, Crumpacker (in Fleischmann), Fiedler, Joswick, Tompkins (*Sensational Designs*), and the essays by Yarborough, Yellin, Halttunen, and Ammons in Sundquist.

13. Tompkins has observed that *Uncle Tom* resembles an American jeremiad (*Sensational Designs* 139). Stowe was to break with Calvinist doctrine later in her life (Forrest Wilson 435, 621), and she developed a critique of the Presbyterian church as an institution (see Hovet). I am tracing the Edwardsian influence upon the rhetoric of Stowe's writing, rather than upon its theological content.

14. The plot provides models for individual upper- and middle-class bereaved mothers to see as mirrors for themselves (for example, Mrs. Bird).

15. Yellin (in Sundquist) emphasizes that Stowe seeks to inspire individual sympathetic responses to slaves, rather than collective public action (101). Alexander makes a similar point about the primacy of individual moral action in George Eliot's fiction.

16. The classic study of Eliot's early realism is Knoepflmacher's (*George Eliot's Early Novels*); Ermarth (*Realism and Consensus*) outlines the historical and philosophical "premises of realism" for Eliot and her contemporaries. Adam, Henberg, and Cottom each explicate Eliot's conception of realism; Wittig-Davis and Mansell compare Eliot's views with Ruskin's. Examining limitations of and conflicts within Eliot's realism, Levine (*The Realistic Imagination*) compares her ideas with Ruskin's and looks into the problems of combining artistic and scientific notions of reality (255–274). For studies of Eliot's changing conception of realism throughout her novelistic career, see Levine ("Realism, or in Praise of Lying") Laurence Lerner, McGowan, and Gallagher ("The Failure of Realism").

17. Critics generally assume that the narrator of *Adam Bede*, like that of *Scenes*, is male. Hardy (*The Novels of George Eliot*, 155–157) cites passages in which the *Scenes* narrator refers to having been a "boy," but gives no evidence for the *Adam Bede* narrator's masculinity except that "he—though the sexual reminders have

ceased to be persistent—holds a conversation with Adam Bede about Mr. Irwine" (157). I see no reason to doubt that a female narrator could "hold" such a conversation.

Hayles identifies the narrative voice of Eliot's next novel, *The Mill on the Floss*, as feminine because it participates in Gilligan's "female ethic of care . . . and a habitual plea for tolerance" (26). Though Hayles accepts Hardy's characterization of the *Adam Bede* narrator as masculine, Hayles's description of the female-ethic-inspired narrative stance in *The Mill* describes the strategy in *Adam Bede* equally well: "The strategy is to invite judgment, then to forestall it by broadening the context so that we see the connection between our faults and those of the characters" (25).

18. Ermarth (*Realism and Consensus*) argues persuasively that Eliot's narrator is "a protean figure . . . [who] shuttles between extremes of personalization and abstraction" (237). Accepting her point that the narrator can speak sometimes as "nobody . . . a kind of generalized historical awareness hardly distinguishable from our own," I am concentrating—as did Ermarth in an earlier piece ("Method and Moral")—on the "personalized" aspect of Eliot's narrator and narratees.

19. As Hardy has pointed out, Eliot's novels changed over the course of her career in their conception of the narratee: "In the earlier novels, George Eliot's narrator may imagine a reader below the reasonable level of expectation, flattering the sympathetic response by singling out an exemplary unexemplary reader in the manner of Sterne and Thackeray [i.e., distancing strategies], but in *Middlemarch* there is refusal to praise the average sympathetic reader" [i.e., a suspension even of engaging strategies] (*Forms of Feeling* 155).

20. Anderson demonstrates at length that Blackwood was the "reader" Eliot had in mind while composing chapter 17. Despite Knoepflmacher's dismissal of the idea as an "unlikely conjecture" ("George Eliot" 256), my reading of the chapter supports Anderson's thesis.

21. In the 1940s and 1950s this disruption of the illusion was the primary critical objection to Eliot's novels. See Bennett and Van Ghent, for examples. Harvey disputes the critics' theoretical biases, but assumes that disruption of illusion is a problem which the defender of Eliot's art must justify (*Art of George Eliot* 66–68).

22. Watson demonstrates Dinah's "authenticity" as a female Methodist preacher by comparing her language with that of Eliot's aunt, Mrs. Samuel Evans.

23. See Lee for an analysis of the similar role memory plays in reading *The Mill on the Floss*.

24. This is particularly true at the level of interpretation, as Holland and Bleich, among others, have shown.

25. See Alexander's analysis of the relation of Eliot's realism to her didactic, humanistic goals.

26. I take up this question in more detail in Chapter 7.

CHAPTER 6

1. Genette explores the paratext in *Seuils*.

2. One reviewer identified Trollope as the author of the anonymously published *Nina Balatka* because he had "found the repeated use of some special phrase which had rested upon his ear too frequently when reading . . . other works of mine" (*Autobiography* 205). More recently, Davies has noted Trollope's stylistic habit of balancing two statements about a character on either side of a "but" or "still" (99). For an exhaustive analysis of Trollope's characteristic language and style, see Clark.

3. Kendrick has tackled the question of Trollope's narrators' ambivalence toward the production of texts that can draw readers into an imaginative world but must simultaneously leave them outside (32).

4. McMaster has outlined the basic parallels among the novel's subplots.

5. See especially Wijesinha, who claims that Trollope presents "a more realistic as well as a more sympathetic portrayal of the woman of the day" than do Dickens, Thackeray, and Kingsley (21, 338).

6. See Schlicke's account of the element of "popular entertainment" in Dickens's career; see Worth's tracing of melodramatic influence upon the novels.

7. Rose focuses on this aspect of Dickens's personality; see also Edgar Johnson.

8. See Green's treatment of sermonic rhetoric in *Hard Times*.

9. For a more complete analysis of the sections not narrated by Esther, see Hough (who details the style of the "other narrator" 52–59) and Hornback. Hornback locates the novel's "other portion" in the activity of the reader: "It is the portion that you and I, as Esther's 'unknown friend,' have to write" (195). For recent discussions of the effect of the double-narrative in the novel, see Daldry; Blain; Moseley; Frazee; and Kearns.

10. The interventions made by the Fashionable Intelligence voice resemble those in the final chapter of *Our Mutual Friend*, the "Voice of Society."

11. Horton has persuasively described Dickens's rhetoric of uncertainty from a reader-response perspective.

12. The dates come from the "Chronology" in Ford and Monod's edition of *Bleak House* (883–884).

13. For the standard argument about Esther's femininity (and sentimentality), see Monod ("Esther Summerson") and Dunn. More recent feminist-inspired readings see Esther's position as a positive embodiment of Dickens's feminine ideal; see Kennedy and, especially, Senf.

CHAPTER 7

1. Welter defines "The Cult of True Womanhood"; for recent discussions of domestic ideology, see Kelley (308) and Gallagher (*The Industrial Reformation of English Fiction* 118, 148).

2. The question is quoted anonymously by Taylor (220).

3. Eckhardt quotes this sketch in her biography of Wright to illustrate the abuse the speaker often received as her celebrity increased (249–250). Even women who spoke for temperance or abolition with the explicit or implicit sanction of the church, such as Abby Kelley or the Grimké sisters, were subject to criticism. For details on the careers of the Grimkés, who began lecturing nine years after Wright, see Gerda Lerner.

4. Beecher was not always successful in avoiding censure: she inevitably suffered consequences for stepping outside the domestic realm. As Gossett puts it, "In spite of her taking the position that women ought not to agitate publicly the questions of the day, Catharine was obliged to some extent to do this herself. . . . In spite of her efforts to state her ideas modestly and to work through influential men, Catharine herself was often written off as a busybody and as a querulous old maid" (48). See Beecher's *Essay on the Education of Female Teachers, Principles of Domestic Science,* and *The True Remedy for the Wrongs of Women* for exposition of her views on women's proper sphere. For details of Beecher's life against an informative backdrop of domestic ideology, see Sklar.

5. Stowe's two tours and their reception have been detailed by Trautmann and Kirkham. Drawing on newspaper reviews and the Stowe family's correspondence, Kirkham traces the Midwestern tour. Trautmann's two articles report on that one and the previous tour of New England; his two essays, however, follow exactly the same outline and make precisely the same points, varying only in illustrative details.

6. For details of women's activity in the socialist movement, see Taylor. Smith-Rosenberg describes female participation in revivalist activities (130); Sweet depicts women speaking in Methodist congregations (115). Even in Protestant churches, however, women could face severe penalties for speaking "out of turn." The trial of Rhoda Bement, excommunicated from her Rochester, New York, Presbyterian congregation in 1843 for publicly criticizing her minister, illustrates the dangers. The historians who have recorded the case remark: "When women such as Abby Kelley, the Grimké sisters, and Rhoda Bement [all of them abolitionists] asserted their right to be heard and to act in public, they did violence to one of the most powerful traditions of their time. . . . However unarticulated or unconscious her acts, [Bement] stood for the right of women to be heard publicly, and thus ran athwart one of the strongest traditions of nineteenth-century society" (Altschuler and Saltzgaber 57, 18).

Some women nevertheless continued to participate in what Smith-Rosenberg calls "disorderly conduct." Hewitt provides a critical summary of historians' assumptions about the rise of female activism and its relation to the women's rights movement (1–39). See Nestor (8–11) for a brief and specific survey of English women's collective activity in publishing and social reform; see Kanner for more detailed documentation and bibliographic references. For accounts of American women's efforts at mid-century, see especially Smith-Rosenberg (109–164), Ryan (83–98, 105–144), and Conway.

7. See Basch for a discussion of limitations on women's professional options (103–109).

8. Nestor (3) and Robert A. Colby (10) are among the critics who cite this passage from Mulock Craik's "To Novelists—and a Novelist," *Macmillans Magazine,* (April 1861): 442.

9. Kelley specifies that the female novelists she studies (the "literary domestics") "were women of the home who simultaneously came to assume the male roles of public figure, economic provider, and creator of culture" (111).

10. See, for instance, Kelley, Douglas, Basch, and Newton. According to Newton, even Gaskell's novels of protest reveal an implicit endorsement of the cult of true womanhood: in *North and South* Newton perceives an "acceptance of the ideology of woman's sphere" (165), which she attributes to Gaskell's "conservative relation to ideology" (168). In the novels of Burney, Austen, Charlotte Brontë, and Eliot, Newton sees a substitution of female "ability" for the dominant model of feminine "influence": "These novels delineate a line of covert, ambivalent, but finally radical resistance to the ideology of their day" (10). Gilbert and Gubar argue for a similar line of covert resistance in women's literature.

11. Blackwell was responding to explicit textual hints of masculinity in the narrative interventions in *Scenes*. Two of the specifically gendered self-references that the narrator of *Scenes* makes occur in "Janet's Repentance," where he recalls himself as a little boy, misbehaving in church, making his little sister cry by imitating a preacher's "yoaring" at her (292), and wearing coattails for the first time (256).

12. Dickens claimed that he immediately recognized a feminine eye for domestic detail in *Scenes:* "'If the tale were not by a woman,' he wrote, 'I believe no man ever before had the art of making himself, mentally, as like a woman, since the world began'" (Edgar Johnson 483). Stowe wrote to Eliot in 1869 that she had first read Eliot's work "supposing you man," but that she had based her final conviction that Eliot was a woman on "internal evidence": "No, my sister, there are things about us no *man* can know and consequently no man can write" (Kelley 252).

13. Peterson argues that evangelicalism was partly responsible for this emphasis on moral teaching in nineteenth-century novels (11).

14. See my "Letters and Novels 'One Woman Wrote to Another': George Eliot's Responses to Elizabeth Gaskell," *Victorian Newsletter* 70 (1986): 8–14.

15. See Vance for a recent history of this connection in Victorian literature and religious attitudes.

16. According to Buell, divinity school lectures on the art of preaching were increasingly common in America during the first half of the nineteenth century; they usually centered on strictly rhetorical or oratorical topics (172).

17. Muscular Christians were not the only Victorian group to fetishize the "healthy body"; see Haley.

18. Beecher's emphasis on extemporaneous sermonizing set him apart from the mainstream of Unitarian and Congregationalist preachers, whose sermons were usually more polished literary constructions; see Buell (179).

19. The minister's belief that he is a mouthpiece for the voice of God survives in fundamentalist sects, particularly in the tradition of orally composed sermons called "American spiritualist preaching," where the "preacher is only lending Him his mouth and lips and tongue" (Rosenberg 9).

CHAPTER 8

1. Sandy Petrey adapts J. L. Austin's theory of speech acts to develop a subtle approach to the problem of referentiality in realist fiction. Petrey's work exemplifies the way in which speech-act theorists can approach literary language without trying to differentiate it from language in general; it does not take up the referentiality of the reader-figure in realist texts.

2. A case in point: Boris Gasparov, modeling "The Narrative Text as an Act of Communication," proposes numerous formulas for "the connotative parameters" of narrative texts at a very high level of abstraction. His structures describe texts as utterances, or messages encoded by a sender; the only observation he makes about the receiver is that a sender's "attitude toward the addressee may either be 'familiar' (as is appropriate in 'practical discourse') or 'neutral' (as in 'official discourse')" (248). The literary narrative text "belongs to the neutral type. This feature results from the nonspecific and nondirect character of the addressee, by virtue of which familiar appellation is rendered impossible" (249). Gasparov focuses throughout on the encoding of the message, not its decoding, as though a literary act of communication in fact involved only an utterance, independent of a receiver.

3. Tompkins's tone, as usual, suggests that she is exaggerating. Her hyperbole not only amplifies her point, but also excludes from her narrative of modern criticism any movements which have—for instance—taken seriously the work of G. B. Shaw or Bertolt Brecht. Still, the phenomenon she describes certainly exists; moreover, it has extended beyond theories of literature to inspire theories of reading. Louise Rosenblatt, for example, has proposed a "Transactional Theory" that shifts the emphasis from dividing up literary and nonliterary *texts* to distinguishing between literary and nonliterary *reading*. For Rosenblatt, the "poem" is a function of a reader's interaction with a text: a reader produces a poem through "aesthetic" reading, in which "the reader's attention is centered directly on what he is living through during his relationship with that particular text" (24). "Efferent" reading, by contrast, is what a reader does to glean information. Appealing and effective as the theory is for describing readerly activity in encounters with lyric

poetry, it stops short of accounting for texts that are to be read simultaneously from aesthetic and efferent perspectives, such as the didactic novel or the *roman à thèse*.

4. Until recently, structuralist narratology has eschewed thematic interpretation of the texts it describes, and as a result has participated in perpetuating the boundaries between text and world. Lately narratologists have been calling for more attention to external context as being essential to describing narrative, as well as to interpreting it. See Prince, "Narrative Pragmatics, Message, and Point" and Lanser, "Toward a Feminist Narratology."

5. For documentation of nineteenth-century reviewers' disapproval of "preachy" authorial address, see Stang (for British examples) and Baym (*Novels, Readers, and Reviewers,* for American examples).

6. Jakobson concurs with Benveniste's analysis and employs the term "shifter" in his further elucidation of deixis (132).

7. I depart here from speech-act theories that propose universally applicable formulas for the truth status of literary discourse. Barbara Hernstein Smith and Richard Ohmann treat fictional discourse as a pretense of uttering real statements, whereas Mary Louise Pratt approaches fictive discourse as a real narration of fictive statements. According to Smith, "The essential fictiveness of novels . . . is not to be discovered in the unreality of characters, objects, and events alluded to, but in the unreality of the alluding themselves. . . . In a novel or tale, it is the act of reporting events, the act of describing persons and referring to places that is fictive" (29).

For Pratt, on the other hand, the "natural narrative" or real-life narrative situation and the situation of literary narration are exactly the same: both are real instances of articulating a "narrative display text," regardless of the "truth" of the events and circumstances they express. Pratt insists that literary and nonliterary discourse should be subjected to the same kind of linguistic analysis, since "fictive or 'imitation' speech acts are readily found in almost any realm of discourse, and our ability to produce and interpret them must be viewed as part of our normal linguistic and cognitive competence, not as some special by-product of it" or as "'poetic deviance'" (200).

Different kinds of novels, I think, make different kinds of claims; even among realist novels, actual narrative practices diverge. The distancing narrator, by continually drawing attention to the novel's textuality, points to the fictiveness of his utterance, supporting Smith's claim; the engaging narrator strains against that convention, however, by insisting upon the reality of the narrative situation, the communication between "I" and "you." Novels with engaging narrators provide strong supporting evidence, therefore, for Pratt's hypothesis.

Works Cited

Abel, Elizabeth, ed. *Writing and Sexual Difference*. Chicago: U of Chicago P, 1982.

Adam, Ian. "The Structure of Realisms in *Adam Bede*." *Nineteenth Century Fiction* 30 (1975): 127–149.

Adams, J. R. "Structure and Theme in the Novels of Harriet Beecher Stowe." *American Transcendental Quarterly* 24 (1974): 50–55.

Alexander, William. "Howells, Eliot, and the Humanized Reader." *The Interpretation of Narrative: Theory and Practice*. Ed. Morton W. Bloomfield. Cambridge: Harvard UP, 1970. 149–170.

Allen, Richard. "If You Have Tears: Sentimentalism as Soft Romanticism." *Genre* 8 (1975): 119–145.

Altschuler, Glenn C., and Jan M. Saltzgaber. *Revivalism, Social Conscience, and Community in the Burned-Over District: The Trial of Rhoda Bement*. Ithaca: Cornell UP, 1983.

Ammons, Elizabeth, ed. *Critical Essays on Harriet Beecher Stowe*. Boston: Hall, 1980.

Anderson, Roland F. "George Eliot Provoked: John Blackwood and Chapter Seventeen of *Adam Bede*." *Modern Philology* 71 (1973): 39–47.

Auerbach, Erich. "Dante's Addresses to the Reader." *Gesammelte Aufsätze zur romanischen Philologie*. Bern: Rancke, 1967. 145–155.

Auerbach, Nina. *Communities of Women: An Idea in Fiction*. Cambridge: Harvard UP, 1978.

Bal, Mieke. *Narratology: Introduction to the Theory of Narrative*. Toronto: U of Toronto P, 1985.

———. "The Rape of Narrative and The Narrative of Rape: Speech Acts and Body Language in Judges." *Literature and the Body: Essays on Populations and Persons*. Ed. Elaine Scarry. Baltimore: Johns Hopkins UP, 1988.

———. "Sexuality, Sin, and Sorrow: The Emergence of Female Character (A Reading of Genesis 1–3)." *The Female Body in Western Culture: Contemporary Perspectives*. Ed. Susan Rubin Suleiman. Cambridge: Harvard UP, 1986. 317–338.

Baldwin, James. "Everybody's Protest Novel." *Partisan Review*. 16 (1949): 578–585.

Banfield, Ann. *Unspeakable Sentences: Narration and Representation in the Language of Fiction*. London: Routledge, 1982.

Barthes, Roland. *A Lover's Discourse: Fragments*. Trans. Richard Howard. New York: Hill, 1978.

Basch, Francoise. *Relative Creatures: Victorian Women in Society and the Novel*. New York: Schocken, 1974.

Baym, Nina. *Novels, Readers, and Reviewers: Responses to Fiction in Antebellum America*. Ithaca: Cornell UP, 1984.

————. *Woman's Fiction: A Guide to Novels by and about Women in America, 1820–1870*. Ithaca: Cornell UP, 1978.

Beauvoir, Simone de. *The Second Sex*. Trans. H. M. Parshley. 1952. New York: Vintage, 1974.

Beecher, Catharine. *An Essay on the Education of Female Teachers, Written at the Request of the American Lyceum and Communicated at Their Annual Meeting in New York, May 8, 1835*. New York: Van Nostrand, 1835.

————. *Principles of Domestic Science as Applied to the Duties and Pleasures of Home: A Textbook for the Use of Young Ladies in Schools, Seminaries and Colleges*. New York: Ford, 1870.

————. *The True Remedy for the Wrongs of Women, with a History of an Enterprise Having That for Its Object*. Boston: Phillips, 1851.

Beecher, Henry Ward. *Lectures on Preaching*. New York: Ford, 1872.

————. *Sermons: Plymouth Church, Brooklyn; Selected from Published and Unpublished Discourses, and Revised by their Author*. 2 vols. New York: Harper, 1868.

Bell, Michael. *The Sentiment of Reality*. London, Allen, 1983.

Bennett, Joan. *George Eliot*. Cambridge: Cambridge UP, 1948.

Benson, James D. "'Sympathetic' Criticism: George Eliot's Response to Contemporary Reviewing." *Nineteenth Century Fiction* 29 (1975): 428–440.

Benveniste, Emile. *Problèmes de linguistique générale*. Vol. 1. Paris: Gallimard, 1966.

Bernstein, Cynthia. Letter to "Forum." *PMLA* 102 (1987): 218.

Blain, Virginia. "Double Vision and the Double Standard in *Bleak House*: A Feminist Perspective." *Literature and History*. 11 (1985): 31–46.

Bleich, David. "The Logic of Interpretation." *Genre* 10 (1977): 363–394.

————. "The Subjective Character of Critical Interpretation." *College English* 36 (1975): 739–755.

————. *Subjective Criticism*. Baltimore: Johns Hopkins UP, 1978.

Blodgett, Harriet. "Necessary Presence: The Rhetoric of the Narrator in *Vanity Fair*." *Nineteenth Century Fiction* 22 (1967): 211–223.

Booth, Wayne C. *The Rhetoric of Fiction*. 2nd ed. Chicago: U of Chicago P, 1983.

Brown, Gillian. "Getting in the Kitchen with Dinah: Domestic Politics in *Uncle Tom's Cabin*." *American Quarterly* 36 (1984): 503–523.

Brown, Herbert Ross. *The Sentimental Novel in America: 1789–1860.* Durham: Duke UP, 1940.

Brownmiller, Susan. *Femininity.* 1984. New York: Columbine-Fawcett, 1985.

Buell, Lawrence. "The Unitarian Movement and the Art of Preaching in Nineteenth-Century America." *American Quarterly* 24.2 (1972): 166–190.

Carlisle, Janice. *The Sense of an Audience: Dickens, Thackeray, and George Eliot at Mid-Century.* Brighton, Sussex: Harvester, 1981.

Cazamian, Louis. *The Social Novel in England, 1830–1850.* 1904. Trans. Martin Fido. London: Routledge, 1973.

Chatman, Seymour. *Story and Discourse: Narrative Structure in Fiction and Film.* Ithaca: Cornell UP, 1978.

Chitty, Susan. *The Beast and the Monk: A Life of Charles Kingsley.* London: Hodder, 1974.

Chodorow, Nancy. *The Reproduction of Mothering.* Berkeley: U of California P, 1978.

Clark, John Williams. *The Language and Style of Anthony Trollope.* London: Deutsch, 1975.

Colby, Robert A. *Fiction with a Purpose: Major and Minor Nineteenth-Century Novels.* Bloomington: Indiana UP, 1967.

Colby, Vineta. *The Singular Anomaly: Women Novelists of the Nineteenth Century.* New York: New York UP, 1970.

Conrad, Joseph. Preface. *The Nigger of the 'Narcissus.'* By Conrad. Ed. Robert Kimbrough. New York: Norton, 1979. 705–717.

Conway, Jill Ker. *The Female Experience in Eighteenth- and Nineteenth-Century America: A Guide to the History of American Woman.* Vol. 1. New York: Garland, 1982.

Cottom, Daniel. "The Romance of George Eliot's Realism." *Genre* 15 (1982): 357–377.

Craik, W. A. *Elizabeth Gaskell and the English Provincial Novel.* London: Methuen, 1975.

Culler, Jonathan. *On Deconstruction: Theory and Criticism after Structuralism.* Ithaca: Cornell UP, 1982.

———. *The Pursuit of Signs: Semiotics, Literature, Deconstruction.* Ithaca: Cornell UP, 1981.

Daldry, Graham. *Charles Dickens and the Form of the Novel.* Totowa: Barnes, 1987.

Davies, Hugh Sykes. "Anthony Trollope." *British Writers.* Vol. 5. Ed. Ian Scott-Kilvert. New York: Scribner's, 1982. 89–103.

De Lauretis, Teresa. *Alice Doesn't: Feminism, Semiotics, Cinema.* Bloomington: Indiana UP, 1984.

Derrida, Jacques. *Of Grammatology.* Trans. Gayatri Spivak. Baltimore, Johns Hopkins UP, 1974.

Dickens, Charles. *Bleak House.* 1853. Ed. Norman Page. Harmondsworth: Penguin, 1971.

———. *Hard Times.* 1854. Eds. George Ford and Sylvère Monod. New York: Norton, 1966.

————. *Our Mutual Friend.* 1864–1865. Ed. Angus Calder. Harmondsworth: Penguin, 1971.

Dinnerstein, Dorothy. *The Mermaid and the Minotaur: Sexual Arrangements and Human Malaise.* New York: Harper, 1976.

Donovan, Josephine. "Feminist Style Criticism." *Images of Women in Fiction: Feminist Perspectives.* Ed. Susan Koppelman Cornillon. Bowling Green: Bowling Green State UP, 1972. 339–352.

Douglas, Ann. *The Feminization of American Culture.* New York: Knopf, 1977.

Doyle, Mary Ellen, S.C.N. *The Sympathetic Response: George Eliot's Fictional Rhetoric.* Rutherford: Fairleigh Dickinson UP, 1981.

Dunn, Richard J. "Esther's Role in *Bleak House.*" *The Dickensian* 62 (1966): 163–166.

Eagleton, Terry. *Literary Theory: An Introduction.* Minneapolis: U of Minnesota P, 1983.

Easson, Angus. *Elizabeth Gaskell.* London: Routledge, 1979.

Eckhardt, Celia Morris. *Fanny Wright: Rebel in America.* Cambridge: Harvard UP, 1984.

Edwards, Jonathan. "A Careful and Strict Inquiry into . . . Freedom of Will." *The Works of Jonathan Edwards.* Vol. 1. London: Ball, 1840.

Eliot, George. *Adam Bede.* 1859. Ed. Stephen Gill. Harmondsworth: Penguin, 1980.

————. *Essays of George Eliot.* Ed. Thomas Pinney. New York: Columbia UP, 1963.

————. *The George Eliot Letters.* Ed. Gordon S. Haight. 5 vols. New Haven: Yale UP, 1954.

————. *Scenes of Clerical Life.* 1858. Ed. David Lodge. Harmondsworth: Penguin, 1977.

Ermarth, Elizabeth. "George Eliot's Conception of Sympathy." *Nineteenth Century Fiction* 40 (1985): 23–42.

————. "Method and Moral in George Eliot's Narrative." *Victorian Newsletter* 47 (1975): 4–8.

————. *Realism and Consensus in the English Novel.* Princeton: Princeton UP, 1983.

Felman, Shoshana. "Woman and Madness: The Critical Phallacy." *Diacritics* 5.4 (1975): 2–10.

Ferguson, Suzanne. "The Face in the Mirror: Authorial Presence in the Multiple Vision of Third-Person Impressionist Narrative." *Criticism* 21 (1979): 230–250.

Ferris, Ina. "Realism and the Discord of Endings: The Example of Thackeray." *Nineteenth Century Fiction* 38 (1983): 289–303.

Fetterley, Judith. *The Resisting Reader: A Feminist Approach to American Fiction.* Bloomington: Indiana UP, 1978.

Fiedler, Leslie. *What Was Literature? Class Culture and Mass Society.* New York: Simon, 1982.

Fielding, Henry. *The History of Tom Jones, a Foundling.* 1749. Ed. Sheridan Baker. New York: Norton, 1973.

Fields, Annie. *Authors and Friends.* Boston: Houghton, 1897.

Fish, Stanley. *Is There a Text in This Class?* Cambridge: Harvard UP, 1980.

Flamm, Dudley. *Thackeray's Critics: An Annotated Bibliography of British and American Criticism, 1836–1901.* Chapel Hill: U of North Carolina P, 1966.

Fleischmann, Fritz, ed. *American Novelists Revisited: Essays in Feminist Criticism.* Boston: Hall, 1982.

Flynn, Elizabeth A., and Patrocinio Schweikart, eds. *Gender and Reading: Essays on Readers, Texts, and Contexts.* Baltimore: Johns Hopkins UP, 1986.

Ford, Ford Madox. "Impressionism and Fiction." *Critical Writings of Ford Madox Ford.* Ed. Frank Macshane. Lincoln: U of Nebraska P, 1964. 33–103.

Ford, George, and Sylvère Monod, eds. Chronology. *Bleak House.* By Charles Dickens. New York: Norton, 1977.

Frazee, John P. "The Character of Esther and the Narrative Structure of *Bleak House.*" *Studies in the Novel.* 17 (1985): 227–240.

Fryckstedt, Monica Correa. *Elizabeth Gaskell's* Mary Barton *and* Ruth: *A Challenge to Christian England.* Uppsala: Studia Anglistica Upsaliensis, 1982.

Fuchs, Eduard. *Die Frau in der karikatur.* 1906. Frankfurt: Verlag Neue Kritik, 1973.

Furbank, P. N. "Mendacity in Mrs. Gaskell." *Encounter* 40.6 (1973): 51–55.

Gallagher, Catherine. "The Failure of Realism: *Felix Holt.*" *Nineteenth Century Fiction* 35 (1980): 372–384.

———. *The Industrial Reformation of English Fiction: Social Discourse and Narrative Form, 1832–1867.* Chicago: U of Chicago P, 1985.

Gaskell, Elizabeth. *The Letters of Mrs. Gaskell.* Eds. J. A. V. Chapple and Arthur Pollard. Cambridge: Harvard UP, 1967.

———. *Mary Barton.* 1848. Ed. Stephen Gill. Harmondsworth: Penguin, 1976.

———. *Ruth.* 1853. Ed. Alan Shelston. Oxford: Oxford UP, 1985.

Gasparov, Boris. "The Narrative Text as an Act of Communication." *New Literary History* 9 (1978): 245–261.

Genette, Gérard. *Narrative Discourse: An Essay in Method.* Trans. Jane E. Lewin. Ithaca: Cornell UP, 1980.

———. *Nouveau discours du récit.* Paris: Seuil, 1980.

———. *Seuils.* Paris: Seuil, 1987.

Gerin, Winifred. *Elizabeth Gaskell: A Biography.* Oxford: Clarendon, 1976.

Gerson, Noel B. *Harriet Beecher Stowe: A Biography.* New York: Praeger, 1976.

Gibson, Walker. "Authors, Speakers, Readers, and Mock Readers." *Reader-Response Criticism.* Ed. Jane P. Tompkins. Baltimore: Johns Hopkins UP, 1980. 1–6.

Gilbert, Sandra M., and Susan Gubar. *The Madwoman in the Attic: The Woman Writer and the Nineteenth-Century Literary Imagination.* New Haven: Yale UP, 1979.

Gilligan, Carol. *In a Different Voice: Psychological Theory and Women's Development.* Cambridge: Harvard UP, 1982.

Gmelin, Hermann. "Die Anrede an den Leser in Dantes Göttlicher Komödie." *Deutsches Dante-Jahrbuch* 29–30 (1951): 130–140.

Gossett, Thomas. *Uncle Tom's Cabin and American Culture.* Dallas: Southern Methodist UP, 1985.

Gossman, Lionel. "History and Literature: Reproduction or Signification." *The Writing of History: Literary Form and Historical Understanding.* Eds. Robert H. Canary and Henry Kozicki. Madison: U of Wisconsin P, 1978. 3–39.

Graham, Kenneth. *English Criticism of the Novel, 1865–1900.* Oxford: Clarendon, 1965.

Green, Robert. "*Hard Times:* The Style of a Sermon." *Texas Studies in Literature and Language* 11 (1970): 1375–1396.

Gribble, James. *Literary Education: A Revaluation.* Cambridge: Cambridge UP, 1983.

Haight, Gordon S. *George Eliot: A Biography.* New York: Oxford UP, 1968.

———, ed. *The George Eliot Letters.* 5 vols. New Haven: Yale UP, 1954.

Haley, Bruce. *The Healthy Body and Victorian Culture.* Cambridge: Harvard UP, 1978.

Hardy, Barbara. *Forms of Feeling in Victorian Fiction.* Athens: Ohio UP, 1985.

———. "Mrs. Gaskell and George Eliot." *The Victorians.* Ed. Arthur Pollard. London: Barrie, 1970. 169–195.

———. *The Novels of George Eliot: A Study in Form.* London: Athlone, 1959.

Hartley, Allan John. *The Novels of Charles Kingsley: A Christian Social Interpretation.* Folkestone, England: Hour-Glass, 1977. 43–61.

Harvey, W. J. *The Art of George Eliot.* London: Chatto, 1961.

———. *Character and the Novel.* Ithaca: Cornell UP, 1965.

Hayles, N. Katherine. "Anger in Different Voices: Carol Gilligan and *The Mill on the Floss.*" *Signs* 12 (1986): 23–40.

Henberg, M. C. "George Eliot's Moral Realism." *Philosophy and Literature* 3 (1979): 20–38.

Henley, Nancy, and Barrie Thorne. *She said/he said: An Annotated Bibliography of Sex Difference in Language, Speech, and Non-Verbal Communication.* Pittsburgh: Know, 1975.

Hewitt, Nancy A. *Women's Activism and Social Change: Rochester, New York, 1822–1872.* Ithaca: Cornell UP, 1984.

Hiatt, Mary. *The Way Women Write.* New York: Teachers College Press, 1977.

Hirsch, Stephen A. "Uncle Tomitudes: The Popular Reaction to *Uncle Tom's Cabin.*" *Studies in the American Renaissance.* Ed. Joel Myerson. Boston: Twayne, 1978. 303–330.

Holland, Norman N. *The Dynamics of Literary Response.* New York: Oxford UP, 1968.

————. *5 Readers Reading*. New Haven: Yale UP, 1975.

Hornback, Bert G. "The Other Portion of *Bleak House*." *The Changing World of Charles Dickens*. Ed. Robert Giddings. London: Barnes, 1983. 180–195.

Horton, Susan. *The Reader in the Dickens World*. London: Macmillan, 1981.

Hough, Graham. "Language and Reality in *Bleak House*." *Realism in European Literature* Eds. Nicholas Boyle and Martin Swales. Cambridge: Cambridge UP, 1986. 50–67.

Hovet, T. R. "The Church Diseased: Harriet Beecher Stowe's Attack on the Presbyterian Church." *Journal of Presbyterian History* 52 (1974): 167–187.

Hunter, Lynette. *Rhetorical Stance in Modern Literature*. New York: St. Martin's, 1984.

Huxley, Elspeth, comp. *The Kingsleys: A Biographical Anthology*. London: Allen, 1973.

Iser, Wolfgang. *The Implied Reader: Patterns of Communication in Prose Fiction from Bunyan to Beckett*. Baltimore: Johns Hopkins UP, 1974.

Jakobson, Roman. *Word and Language*. Vol. 2 of *Selected Writings*. The Hague: Mouton, 1971.

James, Henry. *Partial Portraits*. London: Macmillan, 1888.

Jardine, Alice. *Gynesis: Configurations of Woman and Modernity*. Ithaca: Cornell UP, 1985.

Jarrard, Mary E. W., and Phyllis Randall. *Women Speaking: An Annotated Bibliography of Verbal and Nonverbal Communication. 1970–1980*. New York: Garland, 1982.

Johnson, Barbara. "Apostrophe, Animation, and Abortion." *Diacritics* 16 (1986): 29–39.

Johnson, Edgar. *Charles Dickens: His Tragedy and Triumph*. 1952. Rev. ed. Harmondsworth: Penguin, 1977.

Johnson, Samuel. "Preface to Shakespeare." *A Johnson Reader*. Eds. E. L. McAdam, Jr., and George Milne. New York: Random House, 1964. 315–359.

Jones, M. G. *Hannah More*. Cambridge: Cambridge UP, 1952.

Jordan, Elaine. "Spectres and Scorpions: Allusion and Confusion in *Mary Barton*." *Literature and History* 7 (1981): 48–61.

Joswick, Thomas P. "'The Crown Without the Conflict'": Religious Values and Moral Reasoning in *Uncle Tom's Cabin*. *Nineteenth Century Fiction* 39 (1984): 253–274.

Kamuf, Peggy. "Writing Like a Woman." *Women and Language in Literature and Society*. Eds. Sally McConnell-Ginet, Ruth Borker, and Nelly Furman. New York: Praeger, 1980. 284–299.

Kanner, Barbara. *Women in English Social History, 1800–1914: An Essay and Guide to Research in Thirteen Categories of Inquiry*. New York: Garland, 1987.

Kearns, Michael S. "But I Cried Very Much: Esther Summerson as Narrator." *Dickens Quarterly* 1 (1984): 121–129.

Keller, Evelyn Fox. *Reflections on Gender and Science*. New Haven: Yale UP, 1985.

Kelley, Mary. *Private Woman, Public Stage: Literary Domesticity in Nineteenth-Century America*. New York: Oxford UP, 1984.

Kendrick, Walter M. *The Novel-Machine: The Theory and Fiction of Anthony Trollope*. Baltimore: Johns Hopkins UP, 1980.

Kennedy, Valerie. "*Bleak House:* More Trouble with Esther." *Journal of Women's Studies in Literature* 1 (1979): 330–347.

Kestner, Joseph. *Protest and Reform: The British Social Narrative by Women, 1827–1867*. London: Methuen, 1985.

Kingsley, Charles. *Sermons for the Times*. 1863. London: Macmillan, 1898.

———. *Yeast: A Problem*. London: Parker, 1851.

Kirkham, E. Bruce. "Harriet Beecher Stowe's Western Tour." *The Old Northwest* 1 (1975): 35–49.

Knoepflmacher, U. C. *George Eliot's Early Novels: The Limits of Realism*. Berkeley: U of California P, 1968.

———. "George Eliot." *Victorian Fiction: A Second Guide to Research*. Ed. George Ford. New York: MLA, 1978. 234–273.

Kolodny, Annette. "Dancing through the Minefield: Some Observations of the Theory, Practice, and Politics of a Feminist Literary Criticism." *Feminist Studies* 6 (1980): 1–25.

———. "Some Notes on Defining a 'Feminist Literary Criticism.'" *Critical Inquiry* (1975): 75–92.

Kruger, Barbara. "Remote Control." *Artforum* 24 (1985): 7.

Lansbury, Coral. *Elizabeth Gaskell: The Novel of Social Crisis*. London: Elek, 1975.

Lanser, Susan Sniader. *The Narrative Act: Point of View in Prose Fiction*. Princeton: Princeton UP, 1981.

———. "Toward a Feminist Narratology." *Style* 20 (1986): 341–363.

Laski, Marghanita. *George Eliot and Her World*. London: Thames & Hudson, 1973.

Leavis, F. R., and Q. D. Leavis. *Dickens the Novelist*. London: Chatto, 1970.

Lee, A. Robert. "*The Mill on the Floss:* 'Memory' and the Reading Experience." *Reading the Victorian Novel: Detail into Form*. Ed. Ian Gregor. Totowa: Barnes, 1980. 72–91.

Lerner, Gerda. *The Grimké Sisters from South Carolina*. Boston: Houghton, 1967.

Lerner, Laurence. "George Eliot's Struggle with Realism." *Daniel Deronda: A Centenary Symposium*. Ed. Alice Shalvi. Jerusalem: Jerusalem Academic, 1976. 89–112.

Levin, David. "American Fiction as Historical Evidence: Reflections on *Uncle Tom's Cabin*." *Negro American Literature Forum* 5 (1971): 132–136, 154.

Levine, George. "Realism, or, in Praise of Lying: Some Nineteenth-Century Novels." *College English* 31 (1970): 355–365.

———. *The Realistic Imagination: English Fiction from* Frankenstein *to* Lady Chatterley. Chicago: U of Chicago P, 1981.

Lucas, John. "Mrs. Gaskell and Brotherhood." *Tradition and Tolerance in Nineteenth-Century Fiction.* Eds. David Howard, John Lucas, and John Goode. London: Routledge, 1966.

Mann, Karen B. *The Language that Makes George Eliot's Fiction.* Baltimore: Johns Hopkins UP, 1983.

Mansell, Darrel, Jr. "Ruskin and George Eliot's 'Realism.'" *Criticism* 7 (1965): 203–216.

Mauskopf, Charles. "Thackeray's Concept of the Novel: A Study of Conflict." *Philological Quarterly* 50 (1971): 239–252.

McConnell-Ginet, Sally, Ruth Borker, and Nelly Furman, eds. *Women and Language in Literature and Society.* New York: Praeger, 1980.

McGowan, John P. "The Turn of George Eliot's Realism." *Nineteenth Century Fiction* 35 (1980): 171–92.

McMaster, Juliet. *Trollope's Palliser Novels: Theme and Pattern.* New York: Oxford UP, 1978.

Meese, Elizabeth A. *Crossing the Double-Cross: The Practice of Feminist Criticism.* Chapel Hill: U of North Carolina P, 1986.

Miller, Nancy. *The Heroine's Text: Readings in the French and English Novel, 1722–1782.* New York: Columbia UP, 1980.

——, ed. *The Poetics of Gender.* New York: Columbia UP, 1986.

Miller, Perry. "The Rhetoric of Sensation." *Errand into the Wilderness.* Cambridge: Harvard UP, 1964. 167–183.

Moers, Ellen. *Harriet Beecher Stowe and American Literature.* Hartford: Stowe-Day Foundation, 1978.

——. *Literary Women: The Great Writers.* 1976. New York: Oxford UP, 1985.

Moglen, Helene. "Literary Form and the Ideology of Gender." Boston Area Colloquium on Feminist Theory. Northeastern University Center for the Humanities. 6 Nov. 1986.

Monod, Sylvère. "Charlotte Brontë and the Thirty 'Readers' of *Jane Eyre.*" *Jane Eyre.* By Charlotte Brontë. Ed. Richard J. Dunn. New York: Norton, 1971. 496–507.

——. "Esther Summerson, Charles Dickens, and the Reader of *Bleak House.*" *Dickens Studies* 5 (1969): 11–25.

Morrissette, Bruce. *Novel and Film: Essays in Two Genres.* Chicago: U of Chicago P, 1985.

Moseley, Merritt. "The Ontology of Esther's Narrative in *Bleak House.*" *South Atlantic Review* 50.2 (1985): 35–46.

Müller, Wolfgang G. "Die Anrede an ein unbestimmtes Du in der englischen und amerikanischen Erzälkunst von E. A. Poe bis zu J. D. Salinger." *Literatur in Wissenschaft und Unterricht* 17 (1984): 118–134.

Nestor, Pauline. *Female Friendships and Communities: Charlotte Brontë, George Eliot, Elizabeth Gaskell.* Oxford: Clarendon, 1985.

Newman, S. J. *Dickens at Play*. New York: St. Martin's, 1981.

Newton, Judith Lowder. *Women, Power, and Subversion: Social Strategies in British Fiction, 1778–1860*. Athens: U of Georgia P, 1981.

Ohmann, Richard. "Literature as Act." *Approaches to Poetics: Selected Papers from the English Institute*. Ed. Seymour Chatman. New York: Columbia UP, 1973. 81–107.

Oldfield, Derek, and Sybil Oldfield. "*Scenes of Clerical Life:* The Diagram and the Picture." *Critical Essays on George Eliot*. Ed. Barbara Hardy. London: Routledge, 1970. 1–18.

Olmsted, John Charles. *Thackeray and His Twentieth-Century Critics: An Annotated Bibliography, 1900–1975*. New York, Garland, 1977.

Ong, Walter J., S.J. "The Writer's Audience Is Always a Fiction." *PMLA* 90 (1975): 9–21.

Parker, Gail. "Mary Baker Eddy and Sentimental Womanhood." *New England Quarterly* 43 (1970): 3–18.

Pearsall, Ronald. *The Worm in the Bud: The World of Victorian Sexuality*. 1969. Harmondsworth: Penguin, 1983.

Peterson, Carla L. *The Determined Reader: Gender and Culture in the Novel from Napoleon to Victoria*. New Brunswick: Rutgers UP, 1986.

Petrey, Sandy. "Castration, Speech Acts, and the Realist Difference: *SZ* versus *Sarrasine*." *PMLA* 102 (1987): 153–165.

Piwowarczyk, Mary Ann. "The Narratee and the Situation of Enunciation: A Reconsideration of Prince's Theory." *Genre* 9 (1976): 161–177.

Polhemus, Robert M. *Comic Faith*. Chicago: U of Chicago P, 1980.

Poovey, Mary. *The Proper Lady and the Woman Writer: Ideology as Style in the Works of Mary Wollstonecraft, Mary Shelley, and Jane Austen*. Chicago: U of Chicago P, 1984.

Pratt, Mary Louise. *Towards a Speech-Act Theory of Literary Discourse*. Bloomington: Indiana UP, 1977.

Praz, Mario. "Thackeray as Preacher." *Thackeray: A Collection of Critical Essays*. Ed. Alexander Welsh. Englewood Cliffs: Prentice, 1968.

Preston, John. *The Created Self: The Reader's Role in Eighteenth-Century Fiction*. New York: Barnes, 1970.

Prince, Gerald. "Introduction to the Study of the Narratee." Trans. Francis Mariner. *Reader-Response Criticism*. Ed. Jane P. Tompkins. Baltimore: Johns Hopkins UP, 1980. 7–25.

———. "The Narratee Revisited." *Style* 19 (1985): 299–303.

———. "Narrative Pragmatics, Message, and Point." *Poetics* 12 (1983): 527–536.

———. *Narratology: The Form and Function of Narrative*. The Hague: Mouton, 1983.

Punch III (1842): 192.

Rabinowitz, Peter J. "Truth in Fiction: A Re-examination of Audiences." *Critical Inquiry* 4 (1977): 121–141.

Rawlins, Jack P. *Thackeray's Novels: A Fiction that Is True.* Berkeley: U of California P, 1974.

Ricchio, Thomas E. "The Problem of Form in Mrs. Gaskell's *Mary Barton:* A Study of Mythic Patterning in Realistic Fiction." *Studies in English Literature* (Tokyo) (1984): 19–34.

Riffaterre, Michael. *Text Production.* Trans. Terese Lyons. New York: Columbia UP, 1983.

Rimmon-Kenan, Shlomith. *Narrative Fiction: Contemporary Poetics.* London: Methuen, 1983.

Rogers, Robert. "Amazing Reader in the Labyrinth of Literature." *Poetics Today* 3 (1982): 31–46.

Rose, Phyllis. *Parallel Lives: Five Victorian Marriages.* New York: Vintage, 1983.

Rosenberg, Bruce A. "The Formulaic Quality of Spontaneous Sermons." *Journal of American Folklore.* 83.327–330 (1970): 2–20.

Rosenblatt, Louise M. *The Reader the Text the Poem: The Transactional Theory of the Literary Work.* Carbondale: Southern Illinois UP, 1978.

Russ, Joanna. *How to Suppress Women's Writing.* Austin: U of Texas P, 1983.

Ryan, Mary. "The Power of Women's Networks: A Case Study of Female Moral Reform in Antebellum America." *Feminist Studies* 5 (1979): 83–145.

Schlicke, Paul. *Dickens and Popular Entertainment.* London: Allen, 1985.

Searle, John R. "The Logical Status of Fictional Discourse." *New Literary History* 6 (1975–1976): 319–332.

Sedgwick, Eve Kosofsky. *Between Men: English Literature and Male Homosocial Desire.* New York: Columbia UP, 1985.

Segel, Elizabeth Towne. "Thackeray's Journalism: Apprenticeship for Writer and Reader." *Victorian Newsletter* 57 (1980): 23–26.

———. "Truth and Authenticity in Thackeray." *The Journal of Narrative Technique* 2.1 (1972): 46–59.

Senf, Carol A. "*Bleak House:* Dickens, Esther, and the Androgynous Mind." *Victorian Newsletter* 64 (1983): 21–27.

Sheets, Robin Ann. "Art and Artistry in *Vanity Fair.*" *ELH* 42 (1975): 420–432.

Showalter, Elaine. "A Criticism of Our Own: Autonomy and Assimilation in Afro-American and Feminist Literary Theory," ts. Presented at School of Criticism and Theory, Dartmouth College, Hanover, NH, June 1986.

———. *A Literature of Their Own: British Women Novelists from Brontë to Lessing.* Princeton: Princeton UP, 1977.

———. "Towards a Feminist Poetics." *Women's Writing and Writing about Women.* Ed. Mary Jacobus. London: Croom, 1979. 22–41.

Sinha, Susanta Kumar. "Authorial Voice in Thackeray: A Reconsideration." *English Studies* 64 (1983): 233–246.

Sklar, Kathryn Kish. *Catharine Beecher: A Study in American Domesticity.* New Haven: Yale UP, 1975.

Smith, Barbara Hernstein. *On the Margins of Discourse: The Relation of Literature to Language.* Chicago: U of Chicago P, 1978.

Smith, David. "*Mary Barton* and *Hard Times:* Their Social Insights." *Mosaic* 5.2 (1971–1972): 97–112.

Smith-Rosenberg, Carroll. *Disorderly Conduct: Visions of Gender in Victorian America.* New York: Oxford UP, 1985.

Spitzer, Leo. "The Addresses to the Reader in the *Commedia.*" *Romanische Literaturstudien.* Tübingen: Niemeyer, 1959. 574–595.

Spivak, Gayatri Chakravorty. "Finding Feminist Readings: Dante—Yeats." *Social Text* 3 (1980): 73–87.

Stang, Richard. *The Theory of the Novel in England, 1850–1870.* New York: Columbia UP, 1959.

Stevens, Joan. "A Note on Thackeray's 'Manager of the Performance.'" *Nineteenth-Century Fiction* 22 (1967): 391–397.

Stowe, Harriet Beecher. *A Key to Uncle Tom's Cabin: Presenting the Original Facts and Documents upon which the Story Is Founded. Together with Corroborative Statements Verifying the Truth of the Work.* 1853. St. Clair Shores, MI: Scholarly, 1970.

———. *Sunny Memories of Foreign Lands.* London: Routledge, 1854.

———. *Uncle Tom's Cabin.* 1852. Ed. Ann Douglas. Harmondsworth: Penguin, 1981.

Suleiman, Susan Rubin. *Authoritarian Fictions: The Ideological Novel as a Literary Genre.* New York: Columbia UP, 1983.

———. "Of Readers and Narratees: The Experience of *Pamela.*" *L'Esprit créateur* 21 (1981): 89–97.

———, and Inge Crosman. Introduction. *The Reader in the Text.* Ed. Suleiman and Crosman. Princeton: Princeton UP, 1980. 3–45.

Sundell, Michael. "Thackeray Criticism: Its Fortunes and Misfortunes." *Studies in the Novel* 4 (1972): 513–523.

Sundquist, Eric J., ed. *New Essays on* Uncle Tom's Cabin. Cambridge: Cambridge UP, 1986.

Swanson, Roger M. "*Vanity Fair:* The Double Standard." *The English Novel in the Nineteenth Century: The Literary Mediation of Human Values.* Ed. George Goodin. Urbana: U of Illinois P, 1972. 126–144.

Sweet, Leonard I. *The Minister's Wife: Her Role in Nineteenth-Century American Evangelicalism.* Philadelphia: Temple UP, 1983.

Taylor, Barbara. *Eve and the New Jerusalem: Socialism and Feminism in the Nineteenth Century.* New York: Pantheon, 1983.

Thackeray, William Makepeace. *Vanity Fair.* 1847. Ed. J. I. M. Stewart. Harmondsworth: Penguin, 1978.

Thorne, Barrie, and Nancy Henley, eds. *Language and Sex: Difference and Dominance.* Rowley, MA: Newbury, 1975.

Tillotson, Kathleen. *Novels of the Eighteen Forties.* 1956. London: Oxford UP, 1961.

Tompkins, Jane P., ed. *Reader-Response Criticism: From Formalism to Post-Structuralism.* Baltimore: Johns Hopkins UP, 1980.

———. *Sensational Designs: The Cultural Work of American Fiction, 1790–1860.* New York: Oxford UP, 1985.

Trautmann, Fredrick. "Harriet Beecher Stowe's Public Readings in New England." *The New England Quarterly* 47 (1974): 279–289.

———. "Harriet Beecher Stowe's Public Readings in the Central States." *Central States Speech Journal* 25 (1973): 22–28.

Trollope, Anthony. *An Autobiography.* 1883. Oxford: Oxford UP, 1980.

———. *Can You Forgive Her?* 1864–1865. Ed. Stephen Wall. Harmondsworth: Penguin, 1972.

Uffelman, Larry K. *Charles Kingsley.* Boston: Twayne, 1979.

Vance, Norman. *The Sinews of the Spirit: The Ideal of Christian Manliness in Victorian Literature and Religious Thought.* New York: Cambridge UP, 1985.

Van Ghent, Dorothy. *The English Novel: Form and Function.* New York: Rinehart, 1953.

Vicinus, Martha. "'To Live Free or Die': The Relationship between Strategy and Style in Chartist Speeches: 1838–1839." *Style* 10 (1976): 481–503.

Watson, Kathleen. "Dinah Morris and Mrs. Evans: A Comparative Study of Methodist Diction." *Review of English Studies* 22 (1971): 282–294.

Welter, Barbara. "The Cult of True Womanhood: 1820–1860." *American Quarterly* 18 (1966): 151–174.

Wheeler, Michael. *The Art of Allusion in Victorian Fiction.* London: Macmillan, 1979.

Wijesinha, Rajiva. *The Androgynous Trollope.* Washington, D.C.: University Press of America, 1982.

Wilkenfeld, Roger B. "'Before the Curtain' and *Vanity Fair.*" *Nineteenth Century Fiction* 26 (1971): 307–318.

Wilkinson, Ann Y. "The Tomeavsian Way of Knowing the World: Technique and Meaning in *Vanity Fair.*" *ELH* 32 (1965): 370–387.

Wilson, Forrest. *Crusader in Crinoline: The Life of Harriet Beecher Stowe.* Philadelphia: Lippincott, 1941.

Wilson, W. Daniel. "Readers in Texts." *PMLA* 96 (1981): 848–863.

Wittig-Davis, G. A. "Ruskin's *Modern Painters* and George Eliot's Concept of Realism." *English Language Notes* 18 (1981): 194–201.

Woolf, Virginia. *A Room of One's Own.* New York: Harcourt, 1929.

Worth, George J. *Dickensian Melodrama: A Reading of the Novels.* Lawrence: U of Kansas P, 1978.

Wright, Edgar. *Mrs. Gaskell: The Basis for Reassessment.* London: Oxford UP, 1965.

Zeman, Anthea. *Presumptuous Girls: Women and Their World in Serious Women's Novels.* London: Weidenfeld, 1977.

Index